IS THERE MUCH MORE OF THIS?

Dedication

This book is for the family who put up with me disappearing around the globe. My wife Caroline, my daughters Helen, Lydia, Emma and Verity, step-daughter Sophia and step-son Edmund. And, of course, remembering those no longer with us – my late wife Beth and Mum and Dad.

First published August 2022

ISBN 978-1-7391249-0-8

Author Andrew Marriott
Designer Sarah Scrimshaw

Front cover Cartoon by Neil Collins
Rear cover Leyland Vehicles and Marriott Archive

Printed by The Manson Group Ltd, Hertfordshire AL3 6PZ

Publisher Performance Publishing Ltd
Unit 3 Site 4 Alma Park Road,
Alma Park Industrial Estate,
Grantham, Lincolnshire NG31 9SE, Great Britain

Acknowledgements

THANK YOUS

There are so many people who have helped me along the way. I have to start with my inspirational English teacher in Derby, Walter Hughes. Then the people who believed I could do the job – Wesley Tee, owner of *Motor Sport* and *Motoring News*, my business parter at CSS Barrie Gill, John Mills of Formula1 Films who gave me my first TV commentary work, John Bromley ITV's Head of Sport, Greg Oldham and Frank Wilson of the Speed Channel/ Fox Sports, Alan More who got my TV career back on track, Frank Nicklin, the Sports Editor of *The Sun*, Ken Lawrence Sports Editor of the *Daily Express* and many others. As far as my sports marketing life is concerned thanks to John Webb and John Symes at Brands Hatch, Jimmy Brown at Silverstone and Dave Lucas at the Birmingham Superprix. Then there were clients like Peter Dyke of Imperial Tobacco, Garth Coles at BAT and Mike Jacklin and John Hogan at Philip Morris. Max Mosley and Robin Herd let me handle the March PR and briefly persuaded me into team management. Of course many of the above are no longer with us but their memories live on.

Thank you to all the great motorsport competitors and team personnel who I have interviewed or commentated on over the years. They must stretch to many thousands but I am proud to have worked with so many World Champions and I have to single out Sir Jackie Stewart, Mario Andretti, James Hunt, and Barry Sheene for special mention.

Thanks also to two other great racers and winners, Scots both, Dario Franchitti and Allan McNish, for their words at the front of the book. Colin Vandervell got me into the co-driver's seat first but it was Andy Dawson who drove me to some great results in iconic cars like the Lancia Stratos and remains a great friend and keeps my classic Turner on the road. In my chapter Bedding Down I mention the many people I shared flats with – people like Mike Doodson, Tony Chapman and Duncan Rabagliati who are still great friends.

It is so difficult to mention all the individuals but thanks for the friendship and inspiration of people like Johnny Mowlem, whose racing career I documented on film and David Hobbs whose career I documented in his book. Thanks to my many fellow commentators but particular the gang in America, Leigh Diffey, Calvin Fish, Justin Bell and everyone who wore a Speed shirt. Later in my career it has been a great experience working with Gabriel Clarke and John McKenna at Noah Films.

Thanks to all the photographers whose photos illustrate these pages and not to forget the artists and their art works. The book does not cover my work curating motoring art exhibitions for the Royal Automobile Club and others but working with all the artists who have exhibited with me has been a great pleasure. Also a big thank you to all the tech guys, cameramen, sounds recordists, VT operators and editors who all helped me look good.

Finally thanks to Adam Wilkins of Performance Publishing who agreed to publish this book and his designer Sarah Scrimshaw for their great efforts to get all this between these covers.

Contents

Porsche 917. *Tim Layzell Art*

DARIO FRANCHITTI

MBE
Indy 500 winner 2007, 2010, 2012
Indycar Champion 2007, 2009, 2010, 2011

I have been telling Andrew he should write down all his stories for years and it seems that the coronavirus lockdown finally prompted him to do so. I have heard quite a few of his tales but until I started to read the book I had no idea of some of the stuff he has got up to over the years.

Ever since I started racing karts and Formula Vauxhall Junior as a wee kid, he has been there. I probably first heard him commentating on Sky TV but later when I started watching YouTube, there he was when I was just a toddler commentating for ITV on epic races like the Swedish Grand Prix where the Brabham fan car won or that fateful South African Grand Prix where Tom Pryce was killed. Or having fun poked at him by Barry Sheene in the pit lane after a motorbike race.

Later, of course, I was at the receiving end of his questioning, usually in the States when he was working for Speed TV at somewhere like Daytona. When I won my three Indy 500s, viewers back in the UK watched those races on Sky with Andrew in the control room producing the programmes. Unlike today there were custom-made programmes and features that made sure all the British drivers were fully featured.

We both have our favourite driver in common – the late great Jim Clark. Andrew has one up on me here because he got to know Jim while reporting Formula 2 races for *Motoring News* and was there that fateful day at Hockenheim when Jim perished in the forest.

His career may have stretched over six decades but he can still be found enjoying every moment of it. I am sure you will enjoy reading the book and marvel at the stories and how much the world of motor racing has changed.

ALLAN MCNISH

Winner Le Mans 24 Hours 1998, 2008, 2013
American Le Mans Series Champion 2000, 2003, 2006
FIA World Endurance Champion 2013

I know that Andrew likes to be something of a pioneer as you will read in these pages, but who else would persuade two Scotsmen to write forewords for his book without paying them? But as you leaf through the chapters you will see that his long and varied career has covered everything from winning International car rallies to promoting the first ever British truck race.

But we know him best, of course, for his voice and his commentary and pitlane reports. He was there to interview me after my three Le Mans wins and many of my American sports car successes. But he reminds me that I am one of the very people to deny him an interview – in the very stressful closing stages of a Petit Le Mans race many years ago. Apparently I am in good company and Rowan Atkinson has blown him out twice. Of course, I was more than happy to speak to ARM a few minutes later after I had calmed down.

As Dario has said, he always seems to have be around either in the commentary box or the pitlane ready to get that interview. He knows his racing and thus he always asks probing questions that get the heart of the issue.

This isn't really an autobiography because he swerves off in various directions, humorously writing about everything from Peru and India to nicknames and pseudonyms. But this book also illustrates how much motor racing and indeed technology has changed.

Introduction

I am often asked "Who is the greatest racing driver of all time?" Until recently I always said Jim Clark although now I have to admit Lewis Hamilton runs him close. This marvellous study of Jim was photographed by Les Thacker at the 1965 Oulton Park Spring Trophy Formula 2 race. Bending into the cockpit are team boss Ron Harris and team mate Mike Spence. Jim actually retired from the race but I chose this photo because it perfectly captures a different age. ***Saul Photography***

A NOTE FROM THE AUTHOR

"Is there much more of this?" asked the copytaker at *The Sun* newspaper as I dictated a Formula 1 report back in the 1970s. Maybe I was banging on a bit about the performance of James Hunt. But the words are still apt. I have been working in motorsport as a TV producer, reporter, commentator and print journalist for everything from *Motoring News* to the red top nationals, as a PR man, media director, motoring art exhibition curator, event promoter and even rally co-driver for some 60 years. So I have to wonder, is there much more of this? Despite Covid-19 intervening, I am still patrolling the pitlanes of Silverstone, Daytona and Le Mans – some 60 years after I first started writing a motorsport column for a local paper.

Over the years I have seen huge changes in motorsport, both good and bad, worked closely with hundreds of racers including a dozen or so World Champions, endured more tragedy than I want to remember but enjoyed some great times, too. I have stories to tell about brilliantly talented people, a few very stupid folk, some beautiful places and some dodgy ones.

With this kind of background, it is not surprising that people started to ask "When are you writing your autobiography?" Well, this is not quite an autobiography – but close. Instead, it is more a collection of essays.

I am proud to be part of the British Racing Drivers' Club, albeit as an Associate member, so unlike the Full driver members I don't actually own a tiny bit of Silverstone. I suppose I was elected because, many years ago, I was involved in finding considerable sponsorship for the track and promoted everything from truck racing events to motorcycle grass tracking at the circuit. Maybe it was like buying a peerage. Or maybe it was just a long service award.

Whatever the reason, payback came quickly. "Could you write a regular column for the BRDC *Bulletin*?" I was asked. The Bulletin is a beautifully produced quarterly magazine for the 800 or so members of the hallowed club. "No problem," said I, quickly followed by "Where do I send the invoice?" The response came that I wouldn't have to bother with that side of things because you wrote for the *Bulletin* as an honour, not a concept with which I was particularly familiar.

The very first article, thirteen years ago, was about my 1968 trip to the Argentine F2 Temporada series. I haven't missed an edition since. So the chapters of this book are loosely based

on those articles, in all cases updated, revised, chopped and changed. I have also tried to put them in some kind of chronological order.

I have covered the various aspects of my working life and my travels to far flung lands, race tracks, TV compounds and media centres. But throughout the many years of writing these articles – and now re-writing them – my primary aim has been to put a smile onto the faces of the readers. Motorsport is a serious business but a lot of funny things have happened along the way. I am a big fan of the author Bill Bryson and I make no apology for taking a few cues from his brilliant writing style. I hope you enjoy this six-decade wander down memory lane.

"Is there much more of this?" Not a lot, I suspect, but I hope it isn't quite over yet.

Andrew Marriott
July 2022

Chapter 1

ON MY SOAPBOX

At an early age, I discover the wheel and turn four of them over.

As I wrote in the previous pages this isn't really an autobiography, so no photos of me in a pedal car aged two and three-quarters mainly because, as Britain came out of World War Two, I didn't actually have a down-sized Austin A30.

But when I was about fourteen, together with a long forgotten friend we built a soap box cart which was actually a discarded wood packing case mounted on its side and vaguely attached to a trolley with wheels at each corner. You actually clambered in the back and sat inside it. A plank had been removed so you could see out of the front and there were holes for the ropes which controlled the steering. If Adrian Newey had been around he would have told us that it was inherently unstable.

My first wheels. ***Marriott Archive***

On a gentle sloping lane leading to the A6 trunk road in Duffield, Derbyshire, I was nominated to give the device its first test run. Within fifteen seconds it had not only toppled over, but the packing case had come off the base, I had rolled out and in the process gashed my knee down to the knee cap. I still have the scar but sadly there were no photos of the incredible cratemobile. It was probably then that I decided I should be a motorsport journalist rather than a driver or designer.

This decision was re-enforced when I managed to get an 'average' report on my test drive by the MRS racing school at Finmere Airfield in Northamptonshire, having failed to show talent in an aging Formula Junior Cooper. These days racing schools give you framed photos as part of your 'experience' but, again, no snaps exist.

I found out only recently that March founder and former FIA President Max Mosley, no less, took the same course a week or so before me and drove the same ragged old leaf-spring Cooper. But he apparently showed promise.

However I did manage to reprise the soapbox accident, this time in my mother's Mini. At the time I was giving my limited technical experience and car building expertise to a chap called Nigel Bennett who was constructing a 750 Formula car. The very same man went on to design Indy 500 winning Penskes, as you see I was already mixing with future stars!

After my shift, handing him spanners and hacksaws, I climbed aboard the Mini and headed down his road towards the A6 – a couple of miles away from the previous incident. It was raining, I mis-judged the braking, the Mini veered sharp left through a hawthorn hedge, dug into the ploughed field, came back through the hedge and finished upside down in a ditch against a large oak tree. There were no safety belts back then.

Completely uninjured I scrambled out of the shattered rear window just as a mate came along. Do you know what? He had a camera with him and took a picture – as you can see.

By the way Mother was not impressed but the car was not badly damaged and was quickly back on the road.

This is not a conventional autobiography but I should record that both my parents Robert and Vera Marriott lived much of their early lives in Wolverhampton although Mum was born in Preston. My father was a pattern maker in the foundry at the Sunbeam Motor Company and worked on castings used in the company's record breakers. There was a story that he once raced at the Isle of Man TT as a passenger in the factory Sunbeam sidecar team. The story continues that the sidecar came detached from the bike itself and he was injured. But I am not sure if this tale is actually true. What is true is that he was a brilliant golfer, played for Staffordshire and the Midlands Counties and wanted to turn professional but his parents stopped him. Being a professional sportsman was not considered a proper career choice in the 1930s.

My 5ft mother was a stunner in her day and she modelled for the

The first track I visited and reported from was Mallory Park in Leicestershire where I photographed this group of Lotus 18s. ***Andrew Marriott***

Birmingham based BSA company, draping herself (fully clothed in those days, of course) across their various cars and bikes for brochures and promotional material. For years I had a photo of her sprawled across a BSA Scout, but sadly it got lost in a move. She too was a fine golfer and the pair won several trophies playing mixed foursomes – which is rather different to a threesome!

My father was a keen motor racing fan but the golf took precedence, however one of my earliest memories is being taken to an early post-war Shelsley Walsh hillclimb meeting and later to Mallory Park.

The smell, the sound and the spectacle grabbed me. I started to buy *Motor Sport*, sitting at the back of the class reading it at undistinguished schools in Surrey, Wolverhampton and Derby. By then my father was climbing the corporate ladder with the largest steel foundry business in Europe called FH Lloyd in the heart of the so-called Black Country.

Sporting wise I loved cricket, was pretty rubbish at rugby, boxing (I still have the gloves) and fencing but not bad at table tennis. My father's corporate climb meant we now had an executive house in a place called Allestree just north of Derby where he was running a Lloyd Foundry. This architect designed pile even had own table tennis room. The trouble was that I usually practised daily with a bloke called Howard Middleton and he was just a stroke or two better than me. So when it came to the semi-finals of the Derbyshire Youth Championship, who did I meet but Howard and – you guessed it – he beat me and went on to win the title

We also played at a local youth club which led to my first interest in the opposite sex, a girl called Penny Fudge – sweet girl.

Our house by the way was called Fallows End as it was built on a virgin plot of land but Dad, a bit of a joker, called it 'Duck's Bottom' as there was a lake at the bottom of the garden with plenty of wild fowl.

It was outside Duck's Bottom that I had two further shunts. The first was with a pram which I managed to put on its side scattering the contents down

My first sport was cricket, I supported Surrey. ***Marriott Archive***

the road. Fortunately the contents weren't human but a load of Sunday newspapers, as I was earning a bit of cash with a paper round. There were so many papers on a Sunday that I was presented with them in the pram. Anyway they all got mixed up and No 23 were probably a bit confused to get a copy "News of the Screws" rather than their regular *Sunday Express*.

I crashed again at almost the same spot a few months later. Aged 16 I had acquired a French scooter called a Terrot – no Vespa or Lambretta for me – and I chose it because like an ERA racing car it had a pre-selector gearbox. You twisted the left handlebar and the number of the selected gear came up in a little window in the middle of an aluminium casing at the top of the forks. You then pushed down a pedal on the floor and it changed gear – no clutch.

Anyway I tried to tune this thing to go faster but my dexterity with the spanners was limited and on my subsequent test ride I turned into my road, the throttle stuck wide open and I careered through the fence belonging to the corner house opposite Duck's Bottom. I am not sure what their house was named but it probably should have been 'Squeaky Bottom' because that's what I had when I was scattering their palings.

I try Louis Jacobz' Anglo-Swiss Racing Team Cooper FJ for size at Mallory Park and dream of being World Champion. ***Marriott Archive***

The following year I was signed up to the British School of Motoring and learned to drive in a Triumph Herald with additional time in my father's corporate Vauxhall Cresta which had replaced a much more interesting Jowett Javelin. In this Cresta during one particular practice run before my test, I turned into our drive, misjudged the terminal understeer and knocked down a wooden gate post. Father was not impressed as I don't think the car was insured for a 17-year-old to learn drive in. I suppose it was of little surprise I failed my first test for 'going too fast'. Fortunately I nailed it the second time.

I ran out of talent in Mum's Mini and put it on its roof. I climbed out of the shattered back window uninjured. ***Marriott Archive***

Tragically my father died of cancer the following year by which time I was about to embark on an engineering apprenticeship with a company called International Combustion Ltd that made everything from the insides of power stations to hospital incinerators – more of that later. It just so happens that one of the directors was a mate of my Dad's and the father of race car designer Nigel Bennett. It was like that in those days.

I could write an essay or two about my times at International Combustion – molten metal sparking and running down my boot, huge pieces of machinery dropping from cranes, blokes losing fingers, blokes with no teeth, blokes sending me to the stores for a sky hook and glass hammer – but I won't.

What I will tell you is that I was on what was called a sandwich course and it wasn't to teach you how to put a piece of spam between two pieces of bread and butter in the works canteen. No, it was three days in the industrial grime of the factory based in the prosaically named Sinfin Lane and two days a week at the Derby and District College of Technology with the aim of obtaining an Ordinary National Certificate in Engineering specialising in Metallurgy. This seat of learning is now, of course, called the University of Derby – but I can't honestly say I went to Uni.

But my metallurgy studies are the reason I can be found throwing things at the TV when I hear commentators going on about steel brake discs because they just don't understand that steel contains 0.3 percent carbon and the discs are actually made of cast iron which contains 4 percent carbon. Not many people know that. More brittle, but harder, cheaper and dissipates heat better, you see.

Anyway at Derby Tech one of the modules was English, the word module hadn't been invented then we just called it subjects. The teacher was a brilliantly inspirational guy called Walter Hughes and he liked me and my writing. By now I was going racing on an almost weekly basis as a helper for the local Derby-based Team Turner and their little fibreglass bodied sports cars. With

One of the first Formula 1 drivers I spoke to was Jack Fairman. Here he is at Mallory Park with the Fred Tuck Cooper. ***Andrew Marriott***

the arrogance of youth I told Walter that a lot of the journalists writing about the races I had been to were scribbling poorly researched rubbish and that I could do better.

Walter told me that as well as lecturing us engineering students, he was also the Angling correspondent of the weekly *Derbyshire Advertiser* based in a town called Belper no less. Walter's advice was worth listening to as he gave me the editor's name and told me to write a trial motor racing column and send it in. By then I knew all the local racers and bashed a story out on my Mum's typewriter.

A few days passed and no word from the esteemed organ that was the *Derbyshire Advertiser*, I thought my motoring journalism career was over before it had started. Then one of the racers I had written about phoned and said he liked the mention I had given him in the paper.

So I called the paper and asked for the Editor. "Oh yes, I was going to ring you, we want you to write a column every week, it pays fifteen shillings." But strangely I never met the man who gave me my first break, I wrote the column for a couple of years or so, got an ONC in Metallurgy, and had my first article printed in *Motoring News*, 200 words on a Mallory Park Sprint. Two years later I was reporting races up and down the country for *MN* in between designing a few incinerators for International Combustion and, when the call came to join Teesdale Publishing, I wheel spun my way to London.

My father was proud of his Jowett Javelin. ***Marriott archive***

Chapter 2

FROM UNDER-FEED STOKERS TO THE LIGHTS OF LONDON

How I shoehorned my way to full-time journalism.

Picture the scene in the mid-60s. Derby Midland Station and a fresh-faced boy (me) with a small suitcase and a head full of motor racing minutiae climbs on to a train heading for the bright lights of London and his dream job at *Motoring News*, one of the country's major motor sporting publications.

I had been at the same station a few months earlier with what used to be called a rail warrant in my hand – the destination: Newcastle-upon-Tyne. Having just completed my engineering apprenticeship, I was supposed to be heading northwards to assist with the installation of an under-feed stoker and fan system in the Adamsez sanitary ware manufacturing facility (you couldn't make it up), a far cry from the racing action I had been reporting as a freelancer for *MN*.

But, instead, I headed south to London for an interview not with *Motoring News*, *Autosport*, *Motor Sport*, *The Autocar*, or *The Motor*, but a magazine which rejoiced in the title of the *Boot & Shoe Monthly*, one of a number of mesmerising trade titles produced by publishers Morgan Grampian.

I was 21 and had a burning desire to be a motor racing journalist and if I couldn't do that, any old journalist, even on a magazine dedicated to the footwear trade would be a start. No jobs were available on the motor sport magazines but I thought writing about soles and uppers might take me a step closer. Three months of helping to commission under-feed stokers and, most gruesomely, incinerators at hospitals (I will spare you the details) had soured my relationship with International Combustion Ltd of Sinfin Lane, Derby.

I'd passed the first round of interviews for the shoe mag position and was down to the final three. Maybe I didn't show quite enough passion for brothel creepers and bovver boots because I didn't get the job. Hey-ho, I carried on reporting the Mallory Park clubbies for *MN* Editor Mike Twite and the team at City Road.

Two months later Mike, aka Jim, was on the phone. I thought he wanted me to report from Rufforth, Elvington or even the long forgotten Ouston track. "Andrew," he said in his somewhat downbeat way, "thought you might be interested in a full-time job, the pay is terrible but there is a Cortina GT waiting for you. Start in two weeks, OK?" By now I had moved up in the world. I was actually designing the incinerators that burned unspeakable hospital waste and thanks to the marvels of my strategically-based baffles, they did so smokelessly too. Should I throw all this up for a life rushing around the world reporting initially on the stars of the future with the possibility of covering Formula 2 the following year and rubbing shoulders with the likes of Jim Clark and Graham Hill?

There are some choices in life over which you lose sleep at night but this wasn't one of them. So there I was back at Derby Midland station with a small suitcase contemplating that the next time I headed back to Derby it would be in *MN*'s Cortina GT.

From Euston I headed straight to the amazingly seedy offices of Teesdale Publishing Ltd, 15 City Road, London EC4. Back then we didn't have full postcodes and only big cities had any codes at all. Anyway, the office was full of yellowing back copies, curled up photographs and coffee mugs growing penicillin in their discarded dregs, plus a great team of journalists led by Mike/Jim, who was subsequently to perish in a vintage aircraft flying accident.

I drove past the old offices the other day. The ground floor is a Costa Coffee so no festering penicillin in the bottom of their cups, and the rest of the now shining steel and glass building shelters a hedge fund.

My racing career was short-lived. I raced fellow scribe Jeremy Walton's Escort Mexico at Castle Combe and then here at Thruxton and attempted not to be lapped. I am not really sure while I was trailing so much smoke. ***Ford Motor Company***

Having been installed at a desk with a sit-up-and-beg typewriter, I bashed out a few news stories and then pulled off my first scoop. I arranged for Editor Twite to road test a Bizzarini Grifo, all rivets and tuned 5.7-litre Chevrolet motor complete with crossover manifold and four vast Weber carburettors. It was owned by a slightly dodgy scrap dealer I knew from drinking in a pub in the Derbyshire Peak District. He was happy to lend it for the test because he thought the publicity might sell the beast of which he had tired.

I didn't tell him that Twite, despite being an excellent driver, had recently pranged (is that a 1960s word?) another Italian exotic at a recent Guild of Motoring Writers test day at Silverstone.

Anyway, my first day at *MN* was coming to a close and I suddenly realised I had no idea where I would be sleeping that night. I mentioned it in passing to the man at the next desk – who wrote under the initials ELW – but known to us as Ted Wilkinson. By the way, Ted subsequently became not only a publisher of a very successful give-away newspaper in North London but also the author of widely syndicated road tests and his reports on the latest marvel of motoring could, until recently, be found in everything from the *Exeter Chronicle* to the *Warrington Guardian*.

As an aside, let me just mention why Motoring News only put initials rather than names to indicate the authors of the various works of journalistic brilliance. I was Andrew Robert Marriott so became ARM. In fact James Hunt only ever addressed me as Arm. My journalistic handle quickly led me to write a weekly column called ARMChair Comment. This style had been adopted from the senior publication in the Teesdale empire, *Motor Sport*, and of course the most famous initials in the history of motor sports journalism, WB and DSJ – William Boddy and Denis Jenkinson.

The reason for this by-line quirk was that our publisher and amateur operatic star, the wildly eccentric and occasionally entertaining Mr Wesley Tee was a little paranoid. The said proprietor was worried that other publishers would wish to poach us and offer us more money to ply our trade at their rival publications. He thought they would not be unable to do so if the readers did not know our names! Of course this was a hopeless ploy because in a business as small as motoring journalism everyone knew everyone else.

Mr Tee also took this subterfuge so far that *Motoring News* did not allow

Standard House days. Getting an update from Roy Pike and Piers Courage, a re-union of Motoring News and Motor Sport old boys and girls and pounding out a Motoring News scoop on the portable typewriter. ***Marriott Archive***

us to have what in most publications is affectionately known as the 'flannel panel'. That is the bit at the front that lists who is the Publisher, Executive Editor, Assistant Executive Editor, Assistant Publisher, the Publisher's Assistant, the Editor, the Assistant Editor, Chief Sub-Editor, Deputy Chief Sub-Editor and finally the person who makes the tea.

Occasionally on *Motoring News* – yes I know it is called *Motorsport News* these days – we had to make up initials because people were doing what at my old engineering company was called 'a foreigner'. A foreigner back at International Combustion was producing something unofficially for yourself or a mate, typically a car part but, bizarrely, on occasion when I worked in the foundry, a fire grate or two. However, in the more genteel world of motoring journalism a foreigner was producing a piece of work for a magazine other than the one that paid you at the end of the month. A bit of freelance on the side, if you will.

Of course at *MN* it was easy to make up some random initials for someone who was contributing under the radar. But if it was the other way round and you were moonlighting for a rival, it was a bit more of an obstacle. I seem to remember writing a race report of a non-championship Formula 1 race at Jarama under the by-line of a certain Max Mosley. Various moonlighters were grouped under the pseudonym of Rob de la Salle with its Continental connotations. One of the several Robs was my old pal Mike Doodson, who appeared as MGD in *Motoring News*.

But on one occasion when he was still attempting to be an accountant and freelancing as our Oulton Park correspondent I was so angry with him that I changed his initials. He was commissioned to report on a another non-Championship Formula 1 race, this time at the Cheshire track.

In those days if you were somewhere 'Up North' you would bash out your report on a typewriter with a piece of carbon paper between the sheets so you had a copy. Once the work of motoring reportage was complete, usually at 3.30am on a Monday, you would head off to the local railway station and find the Parcels Office which was always round the back of the shunting yard.

If the bloke in charge wasn't asleep, then he would look up from his early morning edition of the *Daily Mirror*. You would request that the envelope in your hand be delivered to London on the grandly named Red Star service, for the very good reason that they stuck a big red star on the envelope. In the then nationalised rail service this was a code for urgent. "Won't make the 5.53, I'm afraid mate," was the usual response, although it was only 4.48. "Have to go on the 6.39 and that takes half an hour longer." There was never any use in questioning this executive decision.

But on the morning after the Oulton Park F1 race the package from MGD was not on the pre-arranged train and Mike could not be reached on

I even wrote some road tests for Motoring News, most famously in 1970 of this Bond Bug seen navigating around a city gent in London's Finsbury Square. Moments later I tipped it on its side leaving shards of orange fibreglass down Bonhill Street. ***John Dunbar/LAT***

One of my first colour photographs. I was at Monaco to report on the 1966 Formula 3 race so had the chance to photograph the Formula 1 action. Lorenzo Bandini in the number 16 Ferrari leads Jochen Rindt in the number 10 Cooper. Bandini finished second behind Jackie Stewart. ***Andrew Marriott***

the phone. Time was running out. I called him again: maybe the package was on a later train. No reply. I only discovered recently that Mike – who is still a wonderful friend – had actually had writer's block, brought on by the enormity of writing (or actually not writing) his first Formula 1 report or possibly by a surprise BRM win. At the time all I knew was that both Michael and his report had gone missing.

In the end I cobbled together 1500 words thanks to the help of a young man, fresh off the boat from Australia, who had been at the race and was hoping to make a career out of motoring journalism. He certainly succeeded: his name – Peter Windsor. Together with his help and that of a few others I finished the report minutes before the deadline. I was certainly not going to sign off the report under the initials MGD. As I had my report of another race meeting on an adjacent page (even ARM couldn't be in two places at once) I had to think of something. So the report was written by a new correspondent AWOL. No it wasn't Anthony Walter Oliver Lawrence – it was Away Without Leave!

Back to that late afternoon of my first day at *Motoring News*. Ted Wilkinson said he thought he could find me a space at his flat in Enfield. I didn't really know where Enfield was but apparently it was on the northern outskirts of London and also it was really handy for the station. This seemed irrelevant as I had in my hand the keys of my shiny white Cortina GT and I reckoned that my train trip from Derby was going to be my last on a "rattler" for some time.

In the event we headed in convoy to Enfield, round the back of the railway station and into a cul de sac where there was a Ginetta G4 parked minus its front bodywork, next to a somewhat faceless block of flats. Showing me to a small box room Ted said I could use the floor until I found somewhere else.

Promising was the well-worn but unstained mattress, not so promising was the shredded bonnet of the G4 which rested upon it. Additionally the room was occupied by a de-constructed vintage Rudge motorcycle. This didn't leave much room for ARM. This miscellany of the British motor industry was owned by a bloke called Reg, who was Ted's flat mate.

Ted proved an excellent host and had been one of the very last people to do National Service which had filled him with a sense of military discipline and some curious Army expressions. This he passed on each morning by appearing at my door with a steaming cup of coffee and the endearing words: "Off cocks. On socks," which I took to be an order to rise and shine.

After a month or so Ted found me a proper flat at the other side of Enfield sharing with a chap who worked for Lotus. From there I moved south to a succession of motoring habitations some of them at prestigious addresses such as 73 Baker Street, where a young South African called Jody Scheckter was a guest. Indeed the events from those heady days have filled Chapter 22.

Chapter 3

TEMPORADA TALES

A magnificent month in Argentina left indelible memories.

In my early years at *Motoring News* there was a regular ritual, which centred around waiting outside the oak door behind which was a big corner office with a large desk and behind that desk the imposing figure of the proprietor of the said publication. Proprietor too of magazines as diverse as *Guns Review*, *Motorcycle Sport* and, of course, the flagship *Motor Sport.*

After what seemed hours of standing more in hope than anticipation and rehearsing your words came the call "Come in, boy". Wesley J Tee would give you a verdict on whether you can actually make a long distance phone call to somewhere like Lincolnshire to chase up a story on BRM. If you were lucky you received a signed chit which you then took to the switchboard.

On one famous occasion I had the temerity to request an audience in what I knew would be a vain attempt to elicit a pay rise. It was a funny deal, the company provided you with a super car, reasonable travel expenses but a peanut wage. Having said that, working at *MN* admittedly gave you a wonderful and privileged inside ticket to the world of international motor racing. My pay rise request, of course, fell on deaf ears and the rebuttal was accompanied by the wave of a sheaf of letters. "Look at these boy, they all want your job!" Protesting that the hours were really long and that we didn't get enough Luncheon Vouchers (remember those?) Mr Tee gave me some sage advice "Boy," he said, "Two men looked through prison bars, one saw mud, the other saw stars." It is a piece of advice I have never forgotten.

But this latest request was worth a try and my plea for a good hearing was well rehearsed. I wanted to travel to report a

The magnificent backdrop of the Andes dwarfs this group of Formula 2 cars at El Zonda Autodrome in San Juan near the Chilean border. Tino Brambilla leads Jean-Pierre Beltoise, Piers Courage, Henri Pescarolo, Alan Rees and Clay Regazzoni. ***Andrew Marriott/LAT***

The Ferraris of Tino Brambilla and Andrea de Adamich were the surprise of the 1968 Temporada series and there were suggestions from the British teams of over-sized V6 motors. Here at San Juan, Brambilla retired with engine failure. ***Andrew Marriott/LAT***

new end of season Formula 2 series in Argentina called the Temporada . There would be four races over four weekends with top drivers like Jochen Rindt, Piers Courage, two Ferraris, Jack Oliver, Clay Regazzoni, Pedro Rodriguez, Jo Siffert, Jean-Pierre Beltoise, Henri Pescarolo and Jonathan Williams.

"Come in boy. What do you want?" As Sports Editor I explained that there was little to fill the paper with in December, this was a great new series, I was proficient enough to also take the photographs, there was a new track with a flyover, er, er, er, cheap ticket on Aerolineas Argentina, Ferrari unexpectedly sending two cars, er, er...*Autosport* aren't going to send anyone so we will out scoop them etc. It was a strong pitch but I doubted it would succeed.

The great man held up his hand. "See Miss Roberts, get the travellers' cheques, book the flights. That's it boy."

I could hardly believe what I was hearing. Perhaps I should also explain to younger readers that in these pre-credit card days travellers' cheques were like international money. Usually issued by American Express, you could later exchange them for local currency. Miss Roberts – we didn't dare call her Kath – duly came up with a neat little book of them with an attached note in green ink suggesting that she expected me to return with some of them uncashed.

Indeed a cheap ticket on Argentina's favourite airline was booked, the organisers were arranging the hotels and we were all set. Most of the British contingent were on the same flight. As soon as the seat belt light pinged off, a swarthy chap who wasn't part of the racing party, stood up in the aisle of the aged 707 and gripped the parcel shelf above him (no closable luggage containers then). His knuckles were white, his expression pained. He was there for an hour and as we speculated on his problem. A terrible fear of flying perhaps? Finally we concluded it must have been a particularly painful bout of South American piles! When flying as a group we racing folk had quite a few silly rituals – like when the flight attendant/stewardess/trolley dolly (ring your preferred description) showed how to do up a safety belt. As she/he clicked the belt, fifty racers clicked at the same time. When the emergency exit was indicated, fifty other arms pointed. That sort of childish stuff.

On one famous occasion that I witnessed but, of course, was not involved with, a massive pillow fight broke out between, I think, the Lotus and Brabham mechanics. The pillows split and, back then, they were filled with feathers which covered the cabin and got sucked into the air conditioning system. I later heard the plane had to be taken out of service to have the aircon de-feathered.

Anyway on this trip we touched down safely at Ezeiza Airport Buenos Aires. At the time President Juan Peron was leading the opposition party although there were pictures of his late wife Eva everywhere on the walls throughout the city. We were bussed to our hotel full of excitement.

Race one was scheduled for a 3.4km version of Buenos Aires Autodrome, known as circuit number 8 – a venue memorable not only for both the track restaurant, which served some of the best steaks in the world, but also some of the foulest smells from the vast and nearby municipal rubbish tip.

Frank Williams was running Piers Courage and a clutch of Argentine hopefuls whose cars arrived in the Autodrome garages as kits of parts were still in the process of assembly as practice commenced. Another entrant of note was Ron Harris who, having parted ways with Colin Chapman, was running a pair of stubby Tecnos for two other local hot-shoes, both called Carlos. One was Carlos Alberto Reutemann, another for a man who had neither the skill nor the looks of his team mate. He was called Carloss Marincovich, who we quickly nicknamed 'Revver' due to his inability to change gear on the screaming FVA engine until the valves were bouncing off the top of the pistons.

Matra had two beautiful MS5s, all French blue and riveted monocoques for Jean-Pierre Beltoise and Henri Pescarolo, the works Tecnos were being driver by Jo Siffert and Pedro Rodriguez and there was another for Clay Regazzoni. Jackie Oliver was in a lone Lotus 48 entered by the Irishman Gerry Kinnane and Ferrari, off the back of winning the final round of the European season, brought two of the glorious V6 Ferrari 166 Dino F2 cars for Andrea de Adamich and Ernesto 'Tino' Brambilla, older brother of Vittorio.

But the team to beat would surely be the Winkelmann Racing Brabham BT23Cs of Jochen Rindt, already an established Grand Prix star with Alan Rees doing double duty as both as team mate and team manager.

But they got quite a shock that first weekend because Ferrari romped home to a magnificent one-two, showing speed that hadn't been apparent earlier in the year. Tino headed Andrea with Jackie Oliver making up the podium in third, ahead of Clay Regazzoni. Half the field failed to finish in the torrid conditions.

A week later and race two was held 700km away at the Autodromo Oscar Cabalen, near Cordoba, a 3.2km-long track of which my main memory is a bizarre episode about 30 minutes before the start of the race. With drivers starting to pull on their helmets, white-coated waiters with matching gloves appeared carrying silver salvers of sandwiches – complete with the crusts neatly removed – and passed them around to the drivers and race personnel.

This time there was no Ferrari one-two as Tino Brambilla's motor faltered with ignition failure but Andrea raced to victory ahead of Jochen, Clay and JPB.

On race evening I made a decision which I was to regret for many years. After an excellent dinner I joined Jochen, Piers and their wives Nina and Sally for a game of charades, which proved highly amusing. At the end of the evening Piers told me that he and Jochen had borrowed a car and were going to drive 600km or so across the pampas to the third track on the schedule, the El Zonda Autodrome at San Juan in the far west of the country near the border with Chile. Foolishly, I declined. I had a *Motoring News* deadline to meet and needed to bash out the copy. What an idiot: I missed what would surely have been the trip of a lifetime.

Instead, I installed myself in the hotel, pounded the typewriter for a few hours, found the telegraph office in the town and despatched my Armchair Comment column via the telex ticker tape to the UK. Returning to the hotel, I happened upon Jackie Oliver at the poolside and he promptly pushed me in fully clothed. My watch never worked again and I

Jochen Rindt, his Winkelman Brabham BT23C sporting front and rear wings, missed the first day of practice at San Juan after a road trip into the Andes. His subsequent practice run in a sandstorm was both brave and inspired. He finished third in the race. ***Andrew Marriott/LAT***

suspect he didn't get much of a mention in the race report. But the main talk was of the Ferrari engines – were they really only 1.6 litres? Perhaps they might be using something a little larger.

Jochen and Piers arrived a day later with tales of a great road trip. The track was only a year old and in a narrow valley with huge mountains rising behind it and a flyover at one end. Jochen decided it wouldn't take much learning so he opted out of Friday practice to head off on another road trip, this time into the Andes.

Imagine if Lewis Hamilton decided he was going to visit the Barossa Valley and miss practice for the Australian GP! Team manager and number two driver Alan Rees was not impressed, particularly when Jochen turned up for final practice which coincided with a massive sandstorm swirling around this circuit tucked in a narrow valley. The rest of the field opted out but with the grit and dust whirling round, Rindt gave us a display of his magic and qualified well up the field. It was one of the most impressive drives I have ever witnessed.

The race itself provided Andrea de Adamich with a fine victory, Jean-Pierre Beltoise finishing second and Jochen a fighting third in the green and silver Brabham ahead of 'Seppi' Siffert and Jack Oliver.

Finally, with Christmas only a few days off, it was back to the Buenos Aires Autodrome for the fourth and final race, this time on the longer 4.2km, Number 6 circuit which fortunately coincided with the wind blowing that municipal dump stench away for the circuit.

The Ferrari over-sized engine accusations were out in the open now and the atmosphere in the paddock was febrile. Carlos Reutemann had been transferred into one of Frank's Brabhams, due to the unreliability of the Ron Harris Tecno, his natural talent already noted in high places.

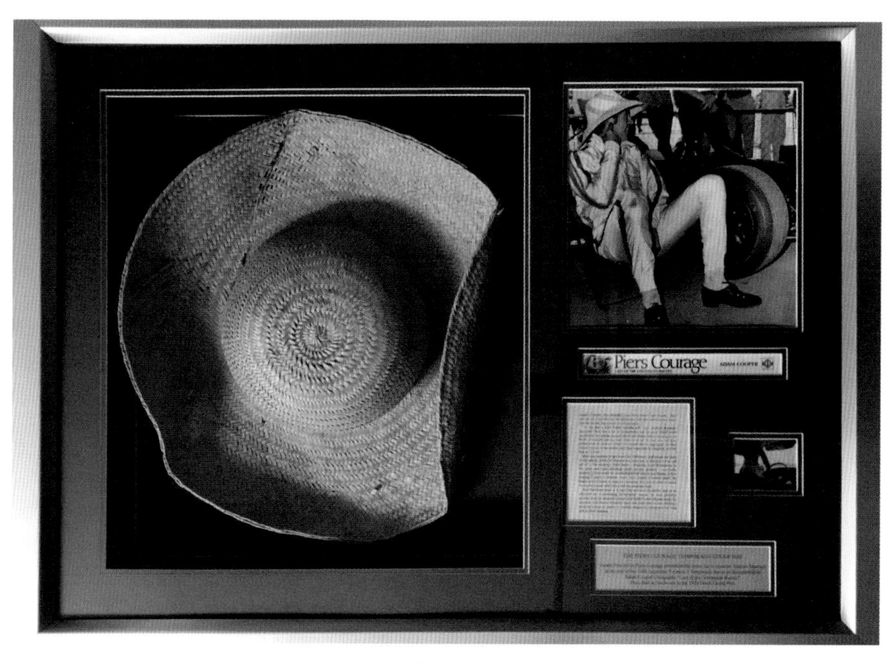

Piers Courage bought this straw hat at the start of the Temporada series and gave it to me at the airport when we were flying home. I have had it framed together with photos and an extract from Adam Cooper's brilliant Courage autobiography. ***Andrew Marriott***

Again we witnessed another bizarre incident, this time at the start of the race. The bespectacled Andrea de Adamich, whom I always found a most pleasant man, got his Ferrari sideways at the start – possibly all that extra power. There was, of course, no Armco between the race track and pit lane and a hapless bystander was felled by the Prancing Horse.

In a model of efficiency, a low-slung ambulance, based on some '60s Yank Tank, was on the scene in seconds, the injured man placed on a stretcher and inserted into the ambulance.

Making a better start than Andrea, the clutch was dropped, the ambulance doors flew open and the stretcher – which was on wheels – screamed out of the back of the blood wagon and on to the unrelenting pit road. Among the yellow flags and general chaos it was suggested, perhaps unkindly, that the man's broken leg was caused by the second incident not the first.

When the chequered flag fell, we were able to celebrate a great victory for Frank Williams Racing Cars and Piers Courage with Jochen Rindt second, Jo Siffert third and Jackie Oliver again driving to an outstanding fourth place in the lone Lotus 48. Andrea recovered from his early dramas to finish fifth and take the Temporada title, as team-mate Tino Brambilla again hit mechanical problems.

There was one final post-script. The Argentine partners who had done the deal with Ron Harris were less than happy with the performance of the Tecnos and invited Mr Harris to a meeting close to the Buenos Aires docks. Mr Harris distributed films when he wasn't running a racing team and they tended to have titles such as *Diary of a Half Virgin* so he was a man who had his eyes open. But it didn't stop him getting a ducking in the somewhat putrid waters of BA's harbour – allegedly.

Finally the journey ended back in the UK on a crisp Christmas Eve with me wearing a hat Piers Courage had given me and plenty of stories to tell as the turkey was served.

Chapter 4

WHITE VAN MAN TO MONZA

My journey from journalist to entrepreneur – including an exciting trip to Italy.

The South African Airways 707 blasted its way noisily out of Johannesburg's Jan Smuts Airport and I settled back into my seat with a lot on my mind. I'd written my *Motoring News* report of the 1973 South Africa Grand Prix and the copy was in my briefcase, the joys of a Saturday race. Jackie Stewart had won for Tyrrell with Peter Revson second for McLaren, Emerson Fittipaldi third in the JPS Lotus and, amazingly, cowboy-hatted Arturo Merzario had taken a surprise fourth place for Ferrari, for a second race in a row.

But that was history. During the weekend at Kyalami I had spoken with a man called Mike Jacklin, head of sports promotion for Lucky Strike cigarettes in South Africa. In fact, in the past I had done some PR work for him in Europe when the late Dave Charlton competed in a few Grands Prix.

He told me he had a big new job, moving to Switzerland to work for Marlboro and the so-called World Championship team which embraced the BRM and Iso Marlboro (Williams) cars and the Ferrari drivers. He wanted promotional ideas and, naturally, I said he had come to the right place. I would get back to him as soon as I settled back to work in the UK.

The 707 levelled out and I took a slug of Scotch – and the idea came to me. A give-away sports newspaper to be inserted into *Motoring News* which would cover all the Marlboro stories. Extra copies could be printed to be distributed at Grands Prix.

Three slugs of the Famous Grouse later and the name was there: The Marlboro Sports Special. But then came a realisation. Remember these were the days when the wild-driving, Gilbert & Sullivan-loving, penny-pinching Wesley Tee was, as previously discussed, proprietor of *Motoring News* and *Motor Sport*. Mr Tee would like the idea, but he would expect me to write it all for no extra pay and probably give me a load of grief along the way.

By the time we had touched down at Heathrow I had decided I had to leave the hallowed, if grubby, offices at Standard House and take the idea forward elsewhere. Fortunately I was already doing some freelance PR work for an outfit called Planners International and working closely with their consultant, Wheelbase TV presenter/commentator and former Ford Marketing Manager Barrie Gill.

Things moved quickly. Two weeks later Barrie and I were in Lausanne in Switzerland presenting the idea to my South African friend along with Marlboro sponsorship boss, the late John Hogan. Both he and some colleagues loved the concept and on a paper tablecloth at a nearby restaurant we drew out a page plan. Then "Hogie" dropped a bombshell. "We'll do it, but only if you can produce English and Spanish versions and deliver them to Barcelona before the start of practice." The race was in three weeks' time.

We did exactly that and somehow in the middle of it all I left my job as Assistant Editor of *Motor Sport* – well, the contract said one week's notice – but Mr Tee got the job to print it. A win, win as they say.

But it didn't go completely smoothly. There were a lot of late nights, great work by our brilliant editor Anna O'Brien and plenty of headaches getting the Spanish translation done.

The proverbial brown stuff hit the fan on the Thursday morning of the Spanish GP. Driver Pedro (actually I haven't got a clue what his name was but that sounds about right) turned up in the Montjuic paddock with a van full of the first ever Marlboro Sports Specials direct from the airport. We unloaded the English version but there was no sign of the all-important Spanish edition. After a series of phone calls it was discovered they were still in customs – there was a problem. Maybe someone needed a brown envelope of pesetas.

It was worse than that. The paper had been seized by some kind of censor. We were mystified. Had we in some way offended Spain's autocratic dictator Franco? But then we found out it was something to do with the main headline on the front page.

In English it read: 'Ickx – Second Twice. Will it be third time lucky?' What could possibly be wrong with that?

The Lotus mechanics fuel Jim Crawford's car in the Monza pits at the 1975 Italian Grand Prix. In an epic journey we brought the engine back to Cosworth in the back of an Avis Transit van. ***LAT***

However, there is often an however in these stories, our Spanish translating friends had decided to change the second line to, 'Will it be his year?' and then translate that. Our printers had handily decided to leave off the funny on-its-side-twiddly-thing above the letter N. So it actually read, 'Ickx – Will he be on his arse?'.

Apparently *el señor censori Español* had taken major offence and thought the moral turpitude of the Barcelona race-going public would be offended. Meanwhile I was ready with a black pen to start adding 20,000 funny S-on-their-side-twiddly-bits over each headline. At least I was saved that!

For all I know the copies of the first ever *Marlboro Sports Specials* – Spanish edition – are still impounded in Barcelona Airport and by now they will have turned a shade of decaying yellow.

Despite this disaster, Hogan and Jacklin forgave us, and the paper was very well accepted, became a big promotional success and was actually the foundation of a business which became one of Europe's largest sports marketing companies.

There were no more disasters until the following year's Italian Grand Prix. By now the Sports Special was in colour, Marlboro was sponsoring the McLaren team and we were on the crest of a wave. For some reason that I have long since forgotten, the printing ran late and there was no way we could air freight the copies to Italy in time for distribution as scheduled on Friday morning.

Enter a mate called Tony Chapman. Dead ringer for Richard Branson, and briefly, before they made the big time, the drummer with the Rolling Stones, motor racing fan and, at the time, self-styled executive van driver. In fact Tony worked for a trendy London art gallery and transported works of art around in a well-travelled Transit van.

Along the way he did manage to get stopped in the Mall on one occasion in the faithful Transit. "No commercial vehicles allowed in the Mall, sir," said the man in uniform. "But I am delivering a painting to Buckingham Palace," responded our hero. The story was somewhat flawed as the van was empty at the time.

Anyway, I had a crisis on my hands and I called Tony. Yes, he reckoned we could just about get the Marlboro Sports Specials to Monza in time, but his own van probably wouldn't make it. In stepped Mr Avis and the very next day we were heading the 800-odd miles to Monza, with a load of fag-sponsored promotional material known as the *Marlboro Sports Special*.

The journey was a blur until we got to Monza. I had my International Racing Press Association red leather media armband (so much classier than the hard cards FIA distributes these days) at the ready. But we hadn't had time to arrange a pass for Tony and we didn't have anything for the van either. Remember we were tired and had driven virtually non-stop from London.

We started off friendly-like, proudly waving the red armband around. But the Milanese gatemen didn't speak English and weren't impressed by the gold emblazoned item. As far as they were concerned we weren't going any further. Tony inched forward. Another guy joined in and I turned from being reasonable to starting to raise my voice. Tony inched forward some more, the van was now touching the front of the big metal gates, which were actually slightly ajar. You can probably guess the next bit.

The guys then decided we should be removed from the cab as the shouting got louder and the gatemen waved their arms around even more furiously as only Italians can. They came round the side of the Transit at which point TC dropped the clutch, the metal gates

My executive van driver Tony Chapman was the drummer for the Preachers (above) along with Peter Frampton in the 1960s. He was in an very early line-up of the Rolling Stones and later played for the Herd. ***Chapman Archive***

swung majestically open and the Transit accelerated down the hill towards the paddock. One guy started to run after us but it was too late. We managed to hide the van in the corner of a car park near the paddock fully expecting the Carabinieri to come and arrest us. But in fact there were no repercussions at all and papers were safety delivered.

The story of our escapade got around the paddock. In those days, of course, there were a lot less people involved in Formula 1 and it caused a certain amount of hilarity. But come Sunday afternoon with the race over Peter Warr, the JPS team manager came over. "I heard the story about the van," he said. "Are you going home empty?

"Well, chap, I need to get one of

Flamboyant art gallery owner Nicholas Treadwell's van wasn't up to a trip to Monza – so we had to hire one from Avis. ***Treadwell Gallery***

my DFVs back to Cosworth really quickly and it sounds as if you will beat the transporter home, can you take it for me?" We, of course, agreed although it was a little ironic that Marlboro was effectively paying for the van and now we were transporting a John Player engine.

Anyway the fact that Peter wanted to get his engine back before everyone else was totally in character. He was famous for being the first at the hire car counter. In fact there were certain Team Lotus mechanics who reckoned it was more important to him than winning a race. It didn't matter where the airport was, he knew exactly where to stand on the transit bus to get off first, was brilliant

The fabulous Cosworth DFV V8, the most successful Formula 1 engine in history. We took the Team Lotus engine back to Cosworth but I notice the engine in the photo below was tuned by Nicholson McLaren. ***CSS Archive***

Sports Special

MILLION DOLLAR FINALE DOWN IN THE GLEN

Super Stratos scor
a marathon win

Our give-away racing newspaper included excellent cartoons by Don Grant, the son of Autosport magazine founder Gregor Grant. Where have all the motoring cartoonists gone? ***Andrew Marriott***

at spotting the quickest passport line and, of course, had someone else pluck his bag off the baggage carousel. By the time anyone else made it to the rental car counter, he not only had signed the paperwork and got the keys, he was already half way to the track.

In fact if I do well in this respect on my travels I mentally present myself with: "The Peter Warr Memorial Rapid Exit Award".

But back to our story. The DFV was strapped on to the back of the Transit and off we set, Tony was at the wheel and in full roadie mode. As we drove out of the gates we did keep our heads down a little, and sustained by the odd pharmaceutical product, we were soon through Italy and barrelling through France.

We went round the Peripherique and headed on towards Calais with me gently dozing in the passenger seat. But opposite the then-almost-new Charles de Gaulle Airport we ran into a massive flash thunderstorm. Suddenly the Transit was aquaplaning. I woke up a milli-second before we hit the Armco, did a complete 360-degree spin and finished up still pointing in the direction of Calais. We stopped, looked around, were staggered by the relatively minor damage but were worried by the triangular shaped imprint in the van's side a DFV drive belt housing made. We'd also forgotten to tell Avis that the van was going out of the country.

From then on it was autoroute, ferry, motorway, St James Mill Road Northampton, motorway, Avis. We didn't point out to them that the humble Ford V6 engine had very nearly been joined by 470bhp of Cosworth V8. But we never heard another thing and we never told Peter Warr either.

At the end of the year at CSS Promotions we had a big offer from John Player to switch our promotional skills in their direction and that was the end of the Marlboro Sports Special. But I did have a wry smile 35 years later when Red Bull launched its *Red Bulletin* amid fanfares of being a ground-breaking idea.

There's also a final twist to the story. My mate Tony Chapman took his art transportation skills to a company called Martinspeed. He later went on to own the company, build it up into one of the world's top fine art shipping businesses

Marlboro Sports Special

1-2-3! DENNY LEADS THE MARLBORO MEN TO VICTORY

The Marlboro Sports Special was distributed to the crowds at various Grands Prix, often in the local language. Based on this promotion the CSS sports marketing agency was founded. Editions here from two different years – note Marlboro switched teams. ***Andrew Marriott***

and subsequently sell it for a sizeable but – of course – undisclosed sum. These days he spends his time whacking a small ball around the golf courses of Palm Springs, California or Portugal. But I think if I ever had a similar crisis, he'd be up for a mercy dash in a Transit van to Monza.

Chapter 5

THE GENTLEMAN OF THE PRESS

Back in the glory days of Fleet Street, the reporters had large followings and big expense accounts.

There is a common cry that the current crop of Formula 1 drivers are, by and large, a load of robots devoid of character. These multi-millionaire youngsters only speak sponsor-babble and, because they started their racing career barely out of nappies, know nothing of the world. Actually, that's not quite true as anyone who has dealt with Sebastian Vettel, Daniel Ricciardo or even young Lando Norris will tell you.

But what about the current crop of people who write and broadcast about them? They certainly don't have the colour or drinking capacity of the men who used to report the Grand Prix races of the '50s, '60s and even the early '70s. These were men, and it was a male-dominated world, brought up on the excesses and expenses of the old and now virtually lost 'Street of Shame' as *Private Eye* magazine called it: Fleet Street.

As I related earlier, I had made the transition to fully-fledged motorsport writer and was travelling around Europe covering International races and rubbing shoulders with the big names. But I was also bonding with some of the older journalists, including some famous scribes who, a couple of years earlier, I had read over the morning cornflakes back at home in Derby. I quickly discovered there were some brilliant and well-informed writers like Alan Brinton and John Blunsden, but quite a few others who hunted as a pack and picked up most of their copy across the bar.

Another belter by Braxton

Sunsport special inquiry into death on the tracks

STOP THIS RACE TO DISASTER!

DIDIER PIRONI has almost become just another statistic in motor racing's craziest and most dangerous year.

Time to put the brakes on—before it's too late

By Andrew Marriott

Point deluge spares Britain's blushes

Lowe's new rate of Notts

SITUATIONS VACANT

OVERSEAS WORK

OVER 400,000 PEOPLE PER YEAR GET THEIR SUNTANS FROM US!

JOBS AT SEA

PIRONI PROGRESS

NEW Topol smoker's tooth polish removes ugly yellow tobacco stains.

RACING EXTRA: LINE-UP AND TIPS FOR WINDSOR

TEN CLIENTS

RANGERS POOLS AGENT

MOVING UP IN THE WORLD!

THEY'RE WORRIED IN SPEEDWAY, TOO

CLOCK SHOULD GET THE CHOP

Eric's recipe for safety

GET YOUR BETTER JOB, BETTER PAY

The Sun gives V.F.M.

I was the motor sport correspondent for The Sun and later the Daily Express in the days when most of the national papers were in Fleet Street. This cutting covers Didier Pironi's 1982 Hockenheim accident. I wasn't at the race for family reasons although The Sun never knew and gave me this double page spread.

These were the days before we had cult TV motoring personalities like Jeremy Clarkson, Chris Harris and Mike Brewer, not to mention The Stig. So with the real power of television yet to be a full HD experience, the motoring writers were big names and had huge readerships unheard of today.

Back in the 1960s, the *Daily Express* was a more powerful paper than it is now and it had a dedicated motoring desk headed up by Basil Cardew, commonly known as Basil Mildew, David Benson and two-wheel man Leslie Nichol. The *Express* was a major sponsor of Silverstone events and the famous International Trophy meetings.

Basil's role not only included road testing the latest Austin Westminster or Sunbeam Talbot but also covering Grand Prix racing. His road tests were full of purple prose availing us on how he barrelled effortlessly over the South Downs or the Hog's Back, the swallows soaring overhead and the smell of newly-mown grass up his nostrils. There was only one catch. Several press fleet garage personnel revealed that quite often they delivered a car to Basil, picked it up a week later to find he had done 11 miles. Presumably the nearest pub was five and a half miles away.

It was Basil's opposite number on the *Sunday Express* (who wrote under the pseudonym Robert Glenton) who

The Express building in Fleet Street, the sports desk was run by a brilliant journalist – Ken Lawrence. ***Marriott Archive***

coined the phrase for the panel about a car's technical specification with the classic 'Will it Fit Your Garage?'. This rather assumed you knew the size of your garage, if indeed you had one at all.

But back to Basil. He had cottoned on to the fact I was more interested in finding out the latest chassis number than heading to the nearest drinking establishment, so saw me as a source of information on the latest Formula 1 happenings. On one classic occasion at the Dutch GP, Jacky Ickx, trying a little too hard in a Brabham, disappeared into the sand dunes where a dreaded Center Parcs now sits. After finding out that Jacky's car was a little worse for wear and he was dusting the dunes off his overalls (we didn't call them race suits back then), I made my way back to the press tribune.

It was after lunch so Basil had enjoyed a bevy or two and had copy time approaching. He beckoned me over. "You've got news of the Belgian boy," he enquired. "Is he dead?" "No," I replied, "he's perfectly OK." Basil looked a little crestfallen and must have

The Goodwood Revival meeting is always a brilliant event. One year it gave me the opportunity to dress as a 1960s motoring scribe although the modern Sky Sports microphone let the side down a bit. ***Desire Wilson***

detected my look of disdain. In an attempt to redeem himself, he slurred, "Can the panel beaters straighten it?" Now Ickx was in a rear-engined Brabham BT26, with fibreglass bodywork. They actually needed a man with a pot of resin.

Over on the *Daily Mirror* was another hard-drinking motoring correspondent. Pat Mennen who was florid of face – in fact, if he stood close to a Ferrari, it was a pretty good match. Pat was always immaculately dressed complete with a bow tie and he was another one who enjoyed a glass of the vin rouge or 20. Indeed, on occasion he would appear to be completely plastered and unable to walk, yet somehow the following morning immaculate copy would appear on the back page of the *Mirror*.

One of the last great hard drinking Fleet Street reporters was Ted Macauley, although he was based in Manchester. Note the obligatory glass of red wine. I bailed him out on a few occasions when he was otherwise engaged. ***Daily Mirror***

Over at the *Daily Mail* there was Mike Kemp, commonly known as 'Scratcher', and not because he scratched around for a scoop. At *The Sun*, in its pre-Murdoch days, there was my old colleague Barrie Gill.

Gill burst on to the Fleet Street scene from the *Bury Times*, keen to make his mark. His chance came quickly. The incumbent motoring writer had, I believe, lost his licence due to spending too long in the famous El Vinos Fleet Street watering hole before climbing into the latest road test machine. The Geneva Show, or some such, was only days away and the editor had a problem. Then he had a brain wave. He called for the new and razor-keen lad from 'up north'.

"Gill," he said, "last week you did a good job on that big motorway death crash, you're our new motoring editor!" From such opportunities are careers built. Gill later vaulted out of Fleet Street to the Ford Motor Company where he launched such cars as the Cortina and did the classic sponsorship deal with the boxer Joe Bugner, insisting that the Ford logos were imprinted not only on his shorts but also on the soles of the sometimes hapless boxer's boots just in case he ended up on the canvas after a KO-inducing upper cut.

Perhaps the last of the old-school journalists was Ted Macauley of the *Daily Mirror* who somehow combined a role as a show business reporter with covering motorcycle sport and, particularly, the Isle of Man TT. He became best mates with Mike Hailwood, who provided him with plenty of good stories. Tall and with a silvery tongue, Ted was never short of female company. Every race was another opportunity to make a new conquest, which unfortunately left little time to actually visit the race track from which he was reporting. How he managed to cobble together a story between his other activities I was never quite sure.

The International press gave me this award for running the British GP press office with my CSS team. ***Andrew Marriott***

Journalists wait for a Ferrari Formula 1 press conference to begin. No chance of a scoop here. ***Andrew Marriott***

My hero, Denis Jenkinson – DSJ – was a big inspiration and took me under his wing. ***Motor Sport***

Top US journalist and former racing mechanic Marshall Pruett likes to make himself at home in his special corner at Daytona Speedway Media Center – complete with glitter ball! ***Andrew Marriott.***

But on occasions (this was before the internet and mobile phones), I'd get a call from someone in the press office. "Englishman on phone for you". At the other end was a somewhat breathless Ted, wanting an update on what was happening at the track. Ted was such an engaging character that one could hardly refuse. It is rumoured that his expenses were also a work of art.

Back in the 1960s, there were few television and radio reporters. The magnificent Raymond Baxter was the man on the end of the BBC television microphone. For a couple of years, I sat next to him keeping the lap chart – remember, in those days there were no computer screens, no sector times. Raymond was a superb professional and it was a privilege to have worked with him.

On the radio side was Robin Richards, another man rich of tone and with a wonderful command of the English language. Robin seemed to be permanently covered in cigarette ash. He had a magnificent party piece which involved reciting the Lord's Prayer but with many of the words substituted by the names of London Underground stations: Harrow be thy name, for example. He was another great character and recently I was able to buy his autobiography in a junk shop.

Then, of course, there was John Bolster, not only the Technical Editor of *Autosport* but also the BBC's man in the pits. Known for his staccato delivery, perhaps prompted by falling out of his racing special 'Bloody Mary', and the deerstalker hat, Bolster was an inveterate storyteller with a turn of fruity language.

One of his best commentary lines was, "Leston is passing Uren on the Top Straight," accompanied by a cackle of laughter. But the swearing was his broadcasting downfall. Don't ask me why but the BBC was televising a sports car race from Aintree. "Let's go down to John Bolster in the pits..."

There was Bolster in his deer stalker hat. "Innes Ireland has just come into the pits in the Lotus 19," he intoned: "Ohhh, there is a problem. He has just stood up in the cockpit, he's kicked the fucking gear lever." Sadly we were never to see Bolster on the BBC again.

On another occasion, he returned to the then-single terminal Heathrow after a press trip to test the latest Renault Dauphine. Given the age profile of some of our readers, quite a few of you may remember that while there was no security, on re-entry you stood in front of a customs official who held up a card which you were requested to read and clearly asked: "Have you anything to declare?" You were then supposed to tell them you had 400 Senior Service or something similar.

There is no question that the Beaujolais had flowed on that press trip and Bolster had consumed sufficient that, when he looked at the card, he was seeing double if not triple. Bolster was already what we now call a national treasure and the man from customs knew who he was.

"Mr Bolster, surely you have something to declare," asked the man in uniform. "Yes," said Bolster and here I can't use the exact words "I have got something to declare. I am drunk and I've got a..." Then Bolster revealed the aroused state of his, well... you can work out what he said.

Yes, they were certainly fun times with some amazing characters in the press office in the days before they were called media centres. But with no timing screens, Twitter nor running press releases the journalists really did have to work for their scoops – between the trips to the bar, of course.

A selection of early press passes which came in lots of different shapes and sizes. These days you seem to get a boring hard card. ***Andrew Marriott.***

Chapter 6

'OGGERS' AND THE F3 GYPSIES

Fifty years ago drivers in the junior formulae could earn some starting money – among them some great characters like Terry Ogilvie-Hardy.

Trevor Carlin and his fellow Formula 3 team owners will probably laugh so hard that they will disturb the inner-workings of their race simulators, but when I was a kid you didn't need to have the budget of a dodgy African country to go Formula 3 racing. On the contrary, there was a band of racing gypsies who plied their trade across Europe and actually earned start money to compete in races with names like Autobahnspinne-Rennen and the Grand Prix Adriatique.

What a band of characters they were. From the aristocratic Earl of Denbigh, known to his mates as 'Rollo', to gritty hardened professionals from bush towns in Australia like Barry Collerson or wide-eyed Californians like Randy Lewis and Cliff Haworth. Indeed, the man who narrated much of the award-winning Senna film, John Bisignano, was one of those warriors. Just a handful made it to Formula 1 like tough Aussie Dave Walker, who went on to race for Team Lotus, while another, Frank Williams, became a leading F1 team owner, of course.

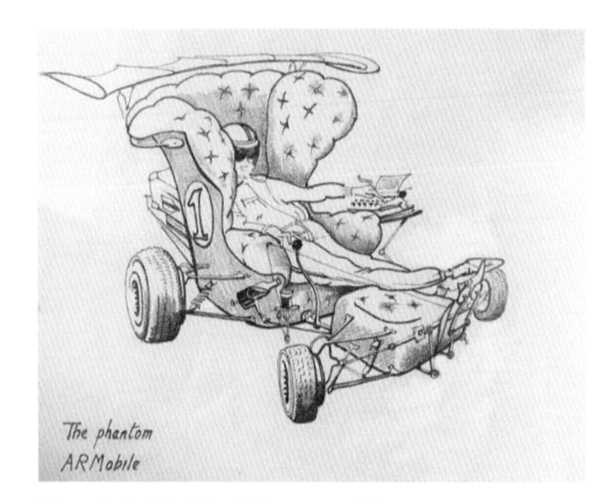

One of Ogilvie-Hardy's great skills was as a cartoonist. He presented me with this drawing for my MN column Armchair Comment.

The modus operandi was to purchase one Formula 3 car and a Volkswagen pick-up truck. The car was usually a Brabham, although the Merlyn was cheaper (unless you were Italian and thus bought something like a BWA or De Sanctis). Then you'd persuade a mate with a set of spanners to come along for a promised good life on the racing road. If you had a half-decent inheritance you probably even ran to a spare engine, which fitted under the flat bed of the Vee-Dub pick-up along with the tools, the tins of Heinz beans, the sleeping bags and other essentials. As the VW cab fitted three across its bench seat, some drivers even brought along their girlfriends/wives, although this was rarely a good recipe for a long relationship!

Now to that starting money. Fortunately, most summer weekends there were two or even three rival Formula 3 races somewhere in Europe, so the organisers at far-off tracks attempted to attract the best field they could by offering appearance money. Led by the redoubtable Paul Watson of Motor Racing Consultants, and other sundry managers including myself, start fees were negotiated via crackly phone calls and telegrams. The general idea was to play one organiser off against the other and insist that your man would not only be a front-runner but also attract an extra 3000 fans to some highly dangerous race track, probably around an Italian lake or an East European market.

Ian Ashley (left) and Mike Walker were Formula 3 works drivers earning a living racing around Europe. Both have aged well, perhaps because they still both race in their 70s. ***Andrew Marriott***

On occasion, the organisers weren't always quite as good as their telegram. Former Ferrari driver, the late Jonathan Williams, told of the day he caught the organiser of the Monza Lotteria escaping out of the window of his office with a bag full of lire, while most of the competitors dutifully queued outside that office waiting for their just rewards. Apparently the crowd hadn't been up to scratch and the fellow was in for a financial drubbing. But he hadn't counted on the wily Williams who, anticipating the move, had stationed himself under the chap's window.

There were humorous incidents aplenty. One story I heard, and it is so

Eccentric racer Terry Ogilvie-Hardy in the Monoposto Championship winning Project X. Note the Ferrari-style shark nose. ***Duncan Rabagliati Collection***

silly that it has to be true, concerns the Zolder track in its early days. A chap in a Merlyn who I think was called Alan Stubbs managed to run off the track and, in a fine display of quick thinking, decided it was best to swerve through the hedge rather than hit the marshals' post. This was such a successful move that he finished up fair and square on the perimeter road on the outside of the track, narrowly missing a late-arriving spectator. Unfortunately, those Belgian bushes had sprung back into place and our hero could not spin the car round and re-emerge from whence he came.

But with the presence of mind of a true professional he decided to drive his car along this road back to where it went under the track and back into paddock. However, when he got to the tunnel there was a burly Belgian ticket collector who refused to let our hero proceed – as he didn't have a pass on him! He's probably the same chap who, 20 years later, was collected on Rene Arnoux's bonnet and deposited half way to Hasselt.

Talking of lucky escapes, the previously mentioned fellow F3 warrior Barry Collerson lost control of his F3 car on the notorious Avus banking. Over the edge sailed the blonde Aussie, probably thinking he was going to finish up like the hapless Jean Behra who died when he plunged off this same banking. But luck was on Barry's side. His flying machine landed on an ice cream stand complete with a useful awning which progressively collapsed breaking his fall. Barry had a damaged nosecone but a free cornet!

But of all the characters competing around Europe in the late '60s few match up in terms of eccentricity and character than former Alexis works driver Terry Ogilvie-Hardy. When he wasn't racing on the Continent, 'Oggers' was the sales manager for a kitchen utensil manufacturer. He had one of those Birmingham accents which he tried to make posh. His hair was quaffed to the sides with flowing and slightly greying locks. Whether he was truly double-barrelled, I have my doubts. I travelled all the way to Jarama in Spain with him once in his VW transporter and got a look at his passport. It said clearly James Hardy. His response to my questioning was that the Passport Office mixed up his document with that of his brother – which still didn't answer where the Ogilvie dash bit came from.

At his funeral 30 years later, there was no sign of any brother either.

'Oggers' had managed to win the 750 Motor Club's Monoposto Championship with a front-engined Alexis which he had modified by virtue of a pair of tin snips and a sheet of aluminium from which he crafted a Ferrari shark nose. Thus equipped, the car was re-named Project X. Buoyed by this success, he decided in 1966 to put aside his job selling the finest saucepans and head to Europe, striking a deal with Alex Francis to race their Alexis Mk5 on the Continent as a works car.

I was tasked with sorting out his entries which was actually quite easy because the organisers liked to have several different makes of car, so the rare Alexis added to this car count. Plus the fact that he was Britain's Monoposto Champion handily translated to Britain's single-seater champ. For a while, we even decided to follow the Italian idea of using a pseudonym. Not for us something like 'Geki', 'Pal Joe' or 'Tiger', but none other than Mr X, the Mystery Businessman. I kid you not and I promise you we were successful in raising our start money demands with this ploy.

Part of the deal was that Terry would provide a report from far-off Formula 3 events for *Motoring News* where I worked at the time, when I wasn't managing him and a few others. The general idea was that he would ring me the following morning after the Grand Prix des Frontières at Chimay or some dodgy place behind the Iron Curtain, tell me what happened and I would then write a few paragraphs. This was good because *Autosport* often didn't have anyone at these races – and we loved to scoop them.

This was all very well in theory, but the phone calls usually had more to do with Terry's sexual conquests than what happened in the race. Terry wasn't a bad pedaller but when it came to sex he appeared to be a true champion. While the intricacies of the love-making were detailed, his knowledge of the results was limited to say the least. He usually knew who had won and that he had come 13th but he wasn't really sure who was fourth. It was frustrating in more ways than one. One memorable report came from Chimay, the murderous Belgian road circuit on the border with France and also famous for its beer. "What happened Terry?" I asked on the crackly phone line. "Bloody marvellous," was a pretty standard response, but this time followed by, "I don't have the results because I had to get out of town quick."

"Why?" I quizzed. "Well you see, I 'charvered' this girl across the bonnet of an E-type. I knew she was only 15 but I didn't know she was the police chief's daughter. When we finished you could see the shape of the louvres of my E-type's bonnet on her bottom. Absolutely bloody marvellous," he concluded triumphantly. These days he would quite rightly be locked up and on the sex offenders' register but somehow he got away with it.

On another occasion at Karlskoga in Sweden, I was party to him stringing along two different girls who appeared, asking for him at the foyer of a local hotel. While he performed with one, I was detailed to keep the other in conversation and then when gorgeous blonde Swedish girl one came down the stairs a little flushed, I despatched gorgeous blonde Swedish girl number two up to room eight or whatever. I think they even passed on the stairs.

Another phone call I received from him came from Schleizer-Dreieck – the German speakers among you will realise the track was basically triangular. "Bloody marvellous," said Terry and I anticipated another story of love-making this time with some East German peasant girl with large downdraft carburettors. Not so. "I got a special award at the prize-giving, a basket of local sausages."

Now this was a good prize because the F3 prize money was pretty limited and sometimes the budgets didn't stretch to much more than the tin of

Terry kept the shark-nose theme for his Alexis-based Project XR which he raced all over Europe. This photo must have been taken before his rear upright "snapped like chalk". ***Duncan Rabagliati Collection***

These two atmospheric 1960s paddock shots taken somewhere in Eastern Europe both feature Terry, in race overalls and dark glasses. It was something of a hand to mouth existence racing in Formula 3. *Duncan Rabagliati Collection*

beans. But it wasn't for setting the fastest lap or something like that. Apparently our hero had sustained a mechanical failure ("My upright snapped like chalk") and narrowly and, apparently with great skill, just missed plunging into a grandstand full of top communist party officials.

One of Terry's best results was at the fiendish road circuit of Opatija in what is now Croatia but was then a town in Yugoslavia. The results of the 1967 race show Terry finished a strong seventh, ahead of him three Merlyns led by the man who went on to race for Team Lotus, tough Aussie Dave Walker. But as Terry explained in another phone call interspersed with yet another conquest, "That makes it sixteen different nationalities this year". He had driven brilliantly. However I later found out that only the Merlyns (and the Alexis) could actually get round the fiendishly tight hairpin at one bite. The guys with Brabhams had to either chuck it in rally style or find reverse.

As I said, actually earning enough money to live and keep racing took some doing. One of the biggest costs was that of fuel for the transporter and here our man Ogilvie-Hardy was ahead of the game. As he didn't have many spares or cans of beans, he had fitted into the under belly of the VW pick-up an auxiliary fuel tank. This was big enough to take a day's production from a small Gulf State. Actually that sounds a bit too Jeremy Clarkson – the bald truth is it held 80 imperial gallons. Terry had somehow wangled a contract with BP to supply him with what was vaguely referred to as "fuel and lubricants for racing".

I was with him when he pulled into a BP fuel station just outside Montlhéry, and basically said to the pump attendant – who had a Gitanes hanging from his lower lip – "Fill her up my good man." Twenty minutes latter, Jean-Pierre was somewhat surprised to see Terry waving said contract and keeping his wallet firmly closed.

But I think my favourite story of all concerned Terry's mechanic, a former rock and roll roadie for some heavy metal band from Wolverhampton. Said former roadie rejoiced in the name of either CD Werton, or Seedy Werton. I never did find out which. Being of the time, CD or Seedy, whichever you prefer, had rather long hair of which he was inordinately proud, although I see no reason why, as it was lubricated by BP's free oil and baked bean juice.

In any event Terry, had moved on from the Alexis to a machine called Project XR, although in reality I think it was the same Alexis with the Mk2 iteration of his shark nose fitted. Come Monza and, unfortunately on the warm-up lap, he was having gear selection problems with his well-worn Hewland gearbox. Let Terry tell the rest of this story.

"I told Seedy the problem and he went to work on the grid. He was like greased lightning with the spanners, had the gear cluster out in seconds, sorted a selector arm and as the two-minute board went up he tightened up the last bolt. There was only one problem: most of his hair was still in the gearbox. There was nothing else we could do, we had to get a pair of scissors!" Being that it was already well-lubricated as described the hair proved no problem to the drivetrain and the flowing locks soon grew back on Seedy's head.

Subsequently, Terry went on to found the Griffin crash helmet company and later designed a revolutionary new sled for the Cresta Run. He was one of the many great characters that graced the Formula 3 races of the 1960s. "Absolutely bloody marvellous!"

Chapter 7

A VIEW FROM THE PRAT PERCH

My attempt at team management wasn't a complete success, and neither was my return to road testing.

In US racing circles, the mechanics sometimes have a special name for the large, sometimes two-storey pitlane constructions bristling with padded seats and television screens from where the team managers, engineers and other luminaries monitor a race. They call them the 'Prat Perch'. Well, I was there 40 years ago as the team manager of an allegedly crack works Formula 3 team. Except back then we simply leaned against the Armco and the only pit equipment we had was a stopwatch and a clipboard.

Meanwhile the chief mechanic, which probably means he was the most senior of the three motley guys looking after three cars, had a bunch of spanners in his back pocket, a screwdriver down his sock and a hammer in his belt. There were no multi-tray, £2000 tool cabinets in those days. But we were high-tech at Petonyer Team March – we had the latest super lightweight Les Leston plastic pit signalling board complete with a box full of numbers, and '+' and '-' signs. No blackboard and chalks for us.

The latest 'prat perches' tend to have two or even three levels. Here is the BMW stand at Sebring in 2021. ***Andrew Marriott***

We were, after all, the factory F3 team for Britain's newest Grand Prix outfit.

But let's rewind a little. There I was at the start of 1970 as the Sports Editor and Grand Prix reporter for *Motoring News* – I still find it hard to call our favourite newspaper *Motorsport News*. I had already embarked on another year of travelling around the world watching and reporting on a classic era of Formula 1, and getting paid for it too. I was also enhancing my meagre salary with a spot of moonlighting which had included writing all the press material for the newly-formed March Engineering. I was there as the PR man at Cadwell Park in the autumn of 1969 when Ronnie Peterson drove the delightfully canary yellow March 693 to its debut F3 outing. Recently a friend sent me a short film of the event although I failed to make a cameo appearance.

In early 1970, I went on to launch the incredible story that was the March Formula 1 team complete with Jackie Stewart, Mario Andretti, Chris Amon and Jo Siffert all on hand at our media event at Silverstone. The directors, Max, Robin, Alan and Graham had made it clear that, as well as building Grand Prix cars, they would produce chassis for virtually every other single-seater category including, very importantly, Formula 3. The car would be a development of the spaceframe 693 raced at the end of 1969. Quite why it became so much uglier over

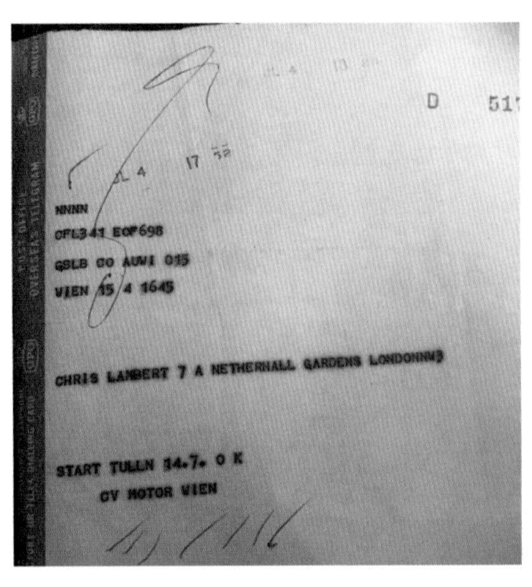
D 51
NNNN
CFL341 EOF698
GBLB CO AUWI 015
VIEN 15/4 1645

CHRIS LAMBERT 7 A NETHERHALL GARDENS LONDONNW3

START TULLN 14.7. O K
GV MOTOR VIEN

Communications with foreign event organisers was often by telegram. ***Andrew Marriott***

the winter only Robin knew. The 703 was not a pretty or competitive car having been rushed off the drawing board. It did go on to win races – but not until almost fifty years later in Historic F3 racing.

Indeed, a few orders were taken including one for the Formula 1200 champion, a Baltic Exchange shipbroker call Geoff Bremner. Geoff knew some high-flying guys in the City who ran a Lloyds underwriters called PCW, the initials of a city slicker called Peter Cameron-Webb. I may have the chronology wrong here but they had also agreed to sponsor a Lotus 59 driven by an up-and-coming Scottish F3 driver – and potato merchant by day – called Tom Walkinshaw.

With some smooth talking from Max, and probably Robin too, a deal was hatched where PCW would become the

Colin Vandervell was a revelation when he joined the team. Here he is at Brands Hatch, note the extra aero lip on the front nose. ***Simon Armer***

sponsor and financiers of the factory March F3 team. March would donate one car and pay the lead driver, the hard-charging but crash-prone Ian Ashley, Walkinshaw would switch from the Lotus to a March and Bremner would be incorporated into the squad as well – all in the matching red and white livery of Petonyer Team March with a full budget from the PCW-owned Petonyer Air Navigation outfit. Here comes the first catch. Petonyer, as you might guess, was an amalgam of Peter and Tony. I think there had been a Tony but he had been replaced by a second Peter, PCW sidekick Peter Dixon, another City type with slicked-back hair, a pin-stripe suit and an upper-crust accent.

The air navigation/taxi idea had long commuted itself into a more earth-bound black cab leasing business for cabbies who didn't want to buy their own cabs. That's how Petonyer Team March came to operate out of a less than salubrious Bethnal Green railway arch next door to the taxi garage and just round the corner from the notorious Blind Beggar pub, a haunt of arch criminals, the Kray Twins. Not that we had much time for a pint. But that's racing forward a bit.

Having set up this fine deal to challenge the best of Gold Leaf Team Lotus, the factory-supported Brabhams plus myriad other one 1.0-litre screamer F3 machinery, March decided a team manager was required. I got the call. I can't remember if it was Max or Robin but whichever it was, he was pretty persuasive.

I can't imagine what I was thinking but I agreed. I handed the keys of my fine BRM-tuned Lotus Cortina back to Mr Tee and swapped it for an Escort estate. I gave up the chance to dine with Jackie Stewart, Jochen Rindt and Graham Hill and instead munched bacon butties with Bev Bond and Tony Trimmer in the Snetterton café. But there was the little matter of my salary being doubled and promises of heaven knows what else.

That's where my troubles began. The season was already underway, March was struggling to fulfil orders and there was a lot of other problems. Luckily I found, as chief mechanic, a marvellous chap called Humphrey Corbett who, despite his public school accent, could wield the spanners with great dexterity. Humph went on to work in the sport for 40 years, later as a race engineer for Toyota and Red Bull and most recently as technical director of Fisichella Motor Sport. Looking at his CV on the web the other day, his first job in motorsport appeared to be as our chief mechanic! There were a couple of other guys but I can't remember who they were. We had an old Leyland truck as well into which we could squeeze all three cars.

Formula 3 was pretty hectic back then. In Britain there were three different championships running, and on certain occasions European drivers came across, swelling the field to over 70 cars. There were races every weekend, sometimes one on Saturday and another on Sunday. This was the final year of the 1.0-litre screamers with their sawn off downdraft Weber carburettors and megaphone exhausts. The Ford Anglia-based motors revved to 11,000 and they sounded brilliant! You either chose Lucas or Holbay as your tuner and if you were serious you put in a fresh 'mill' every meeting.

I think you tend to erase from the memory some of the bad things that happen, and I have to admit that my memory has deleted the day-to-day grind of running the team, the daily drives from London to Bicester, the crashes, the punctures, the blow-ups. Thanks to the internet, I've been able to trace our race results because I'd long forgotten them.

What I did remember, of course, was specific and now humorous incidents – mainly the crashes. There is no question that March's focus was on Grand Prix racing. The F3 car wasn't a match for Lotus or Brabham. This probably made the drivers try rather too hard. Funded largely by Firestone tyres, we did a great deal of testing often with Robin on hand in a bid to improve our lacklustre performance.

On one particular occasion I remember that Tom Walkinshaw had crashed at such a Snetterton test and bent the chassis. At the time I think our credit had run out at Arch Motors, who built the spaceframes. So the car was stripped back to the bare chassis and positioned alongside one of the grubby walls of the railway arch. Humphrey then slowly reversed the transporter into it, thereby straightening it. Bingo.

Ian Ashley was a delightful chap but was somewhat crash-prone. At one mid-summer Mallory Park he was pretty miffed because Robin had come up with a rear wing – aerodynamic devices were just coming in during 1970 for the lesser formulae. The management decision was to fit it to Tom's car. Ian was trying extra hard to prove he should have had it and crashed heavily at the Lake Esses, breaking his ankle.

With Ian out of action, I brought in a guy called 'Desperate' Dick Barker, who ha shown a lot of speed in an elderly Alexis. I think we also gave 'Cyd' Williams a race too. Mike Wilds' late wife Chrissie used to phone almost daily trying to get him in the car but to no avail. Fifty years later he is still racing – an amazing guy.

Ian was keeping me informed of his progress and advised that he would be fit again for the August Bank Holiday Oulton Park meeting. I saw him at the track sitting in his Austin-Healey Sprite and he said he was good to go. Running three cars with three mechanics was pretty busy and they were having trouble starting Ian's Holbay motor. Back then we didn't have any pre-practice management meetings so I had only seen our star driver in his road car and then sitting in the race car. Critically, I had not inspected his ankle.

Practice began and the Tom and Geoff were already circulating. Ian then drove down the pitlane giving me a cheery wave. The next thing I knew was that the yellow flags were waving as Bremner had crashed at Old Hall, the corner after the pits. As we were at the far end, I thought I better wander down there to survey the damage. I arrived just in time to see 'Crashley' arriving all locked, smoke pluming from the fronts and bang into his team mate's now abandoned car. As I stood on the other side of the track, he levered himself out of the wreckage and, lo and behold, he still had his left ankle in plaster.

After this incident we 'let him go' and replaced him with a bloke who was dominating the Formula Ford Championship at the time – Colin Vandervell. I have bored too many

Team Triplex . After racing for Petonyer Team March in 1970, Colin Vandervell moved up the ranks with various Triplex sponsored cars. I made sure he had promotional stickers. ***Andrew Marriott***

The March 693 re-union about 25 years ago. Howden Ganley sits in the car raced by James Hunt and Ronnie Peterson, Max Mosley and Robin Herd sit on the rear wheels. I handled the PR. ***Marriott Archive***

people with stories about Colin, but to me he is the most naturally gifted racing driver I ever worked with. I went on to manage him to Formula 3 and Formula Atlantic successes. But being a witness to Gerry Birrell's fatal accident and the death of rival Roger Williamson put him off racing. Ian went on to be very successful in Formula 5000, moved into a private Formula 1 Brabham and, after it took off, proceeded to drive through a TV scaffolding tower at Mosport Park in the 1977 Canadian GP. He, too, is still racing into his 70s. As for Tom Walkinshaw, he went on to greater success as a driver before his hugely successful, if controversial, career as a team owner.

I hadn't seen the March 703 at a race circuit in 50 years. But here is chassis two at the Goodwood Members' Meeting in 2022. Simon Armer has raced this car very successfully and won races, something we never achieved in period. ***Andrew Marriott***

People usually call me Andrew or Andy, but for some reason Tom always called me Drew. A few months before he died, we had some early discussions about me ghosting his autobiography – now that would have made a very interesting read. As for Geoff, he never gave up the day job and was still a ship broker when I last checked.

Meanwhile, our sponsors subsequently wrote some headlines without resorting to the dubious afterglow of sponsoring the March F3 team. A series of scandals came to light in 1982 and Cameron Webb and Dixon were expelled from Lloyds of London having appropriated £60m of other people's money. Subsequently PCW was arrested and, together with mate Dixon, skipped bail and disappeared to Hollywood, California, and died there in a nursing home a few years ago. To me, they were just a couple of toffs who came to races occasionally, were perfectly charming and – usually – paid the bills.

By now, I had worked out that I was probably a better journalist than I was team manager. So I was already starting to write for *Motoring News* again and this led to an incident which has been told many times before, but still worth repeating. Nobody at *Motoring News* wanted to road test a little device called the Bond Bug, a three-wheeled, fibreglass wedge-shaped machine which you entered by lifting the whole front bodywork. It was actually fiendishly clever, had a nice little aluminium engine and weighed next to nothing – so it was quite quick. I think someone at *Motoring News* had seen a few Petonyer Marchs with only three wheels, so I was the obvious chap to test it.

I remember I went to Snetterton in it and broke my record back to London. If you were brave you could even corner it on two wheels. I bragged about this when we came to do the photos in London's Finsbury Square, near the office (see photo on page 18). After that, ace snapper John Dunbar climbed back into the Bug with his heavy camera case. I didn't appreciate that this might change the weight distribution. He then offered the suggestion that I was bit of a plonker because I hadn't, as promised, cornered on two wheels. So I though that I'd show him and I cornered really hard into Bonhill Street, which also housed a Labour Exchange. Outside were about twenty people in the 'dole queue'.

They had a spectacular view when this orange thing that looked like a wedge of Double Gloucester cheese, screeched around the corner, tipping on its side and running along the kerb scattering shards of orange fibreglass everywhere. When it had come to rest with the two occupants not knowing whether to laugh or cry, we both in unison shifted our weight sideways and the Bug dropped back on its three wheels. I quickly motored into the *Motoring News* car park where the bloke who had come to collect it was waiting in reception.

I told him we had tipped it over earlier in the week and he said I wasn't the first. I actually knew this because I had attended the launch event at Woburn Abbey and the man from *The Times* had already performed that stunt.

A couple of months later, I returned to Standard House as Assistant Editor of *Motor Sport* magazine and turned my back on March, the railway arch in Bethnal Green and indeed the Escort estate. In its place a had a brand new car – it was orange and came from Tamworth. But it wasn't the Bug, it was brand new Reliant Scimitar GTE.

At least my period as a team manager had some positive results as our development programme paid off; the 1971 F3 car proved to be a race winner.

Chapter 8

NOT ALL SMOKE AND MIRRORS

We had some great days launching and promoting various Formula 1 teams.

Formula 1 stars Riccardo Patrese and Thierry Boutsen were in there somewhere as the drums rolled to launch the Williams FW13B, a top contender for the 1990 season. Television pictures were being beamed live across the Atlantic courtesy of the team's new high profile sponsor, the Canadian brewing giant Labatt's, but nothing was really very clear. Unfortunately the smoke machine coupled with the dry ice device had gone into overdrive and it took a full 30 seconds for the pair to emerge from the resultant smog.

And it was all my fault. The look on their faces was a picture except the media could not check out the choking grimaces because this man-made smokescreen had now drifted down into the audience in the temporary auditorium. Finally the smoke lifted and wafted away and we were able to continue with the proceedings. During my career in the Formula 1 sponsorship and PR business, I launched a couple of dozen Formula 1 cars including several Williams and Lotus machines which went on to be world-beaters. In a journalistic and broadcasting role, I have attended countless other Grand Prix launches and, even today, there is always the excitement of seeing a new Formula 1 car unveiled.

But back to 1990 and the Williams launch. The car was to be revealed in the museum area at Williams' Grove factory. At one end of this was a workshop where those cars heading for the museum were fettled for exhibition. It was behind a roll-up metal door. I decided we would turn this workshop into the launch area, the door would lift and Patrick Head's latest challenger would be revealed. To add a little drama, I'd arranged both a dry ice and a smoke machine. In rehearsal, the resultant effect was a little lame, so for the actual reveal I asked for the machines to be cranked up a few notches. Too many, as it happened. By the time the door came up, the workshop was completely filled with this fog of smoke and dried ice. Consequently Thierry and Riccardo's entrance was somewhat ghost-like.

There were rather more media in attendance that day than when I organised the launch of the 1978 Williams FW06, Patrick Head's first car for the team. This was after Frank had split from Walter Wolf and spent a season running a private March for Patrick Neve. The factory was in a former carpet warehouse on an industrial estate in Didcot and about 12 assorted press turned up – although they did include a cameraman and producer from the Visnews organisation and pictures of what turned out to be a very promising car went around the World.

There were no drivers at that launch and we were missing an important one, a certain K Rosberg, a few seasons later when we were called upon to launch Williams' new Canon sponsorship for the 1985 season. We had another problem, too – the car for the upcoming year wasn't ready so all we had to reveal was were the logos of a well known Japanese camera company on the side of the outgoing car. Not exactly headline-making news.

At CSS we transformed the Royal Albert Hall into a fine dining room for Essex Petroleum and produced countless press kits for sponsors such as John Player and Denim aftershave. I have no idea why a bikini-clad lady is shown with the JPS material – but in those days it was quite acceptable. ***Andrew Marriott***

As that Missing Finn was a former World Champion, the launch was going to lack a certain something, and there was considerable pressure on him to put in an appearance at the launch in a West End Theatre. But Keke decided that learning to fly a Lear jet in Florida was more important. He really did want to be a Flying Finn.

As it happened, we knew a man called Jeremy Barratt, the former PR chief of the BSM Driving School, who had a new venture he was promoting. It was actually a man-like robot which he controlled by a joystick and which had a loudspeaker buried somewhere in its robot face from which robot-style words came out.

It's difficult to believe, but I came up with the idea of dressing this robot in a custom made race suit, complete with the Canon logos. And I called it Keke Robot. Quite why the Japanese bought into this ridiculous idea I don't know. We revealed the car and introduced the two drivers: Nigel Mansell and Keke Robot. The robot, controlled by Jeremy behind a screen, waddled about the stage and the end result was prime-time TV coverage on both ITV and BBC and a happy new sponsor.

Without any question the most spectacular Formula 1 launches which we organised were run for the eccentric boss of Essex Petroleum, David Thieme.

The Zorro-hatted American had taken over primary sponsorship of Team Lotus back in 1980. Thieme was in the oil spot market business and was, for a while, spectacularly successful buying and selling tankers full of crude oil as they plied the high seas. In the process he was making huge profits.

He wanted to impress his 30 or so top customers by not only sponsoring Lotus but also putting on the biggest and most lavish launch ever. At CSS Promotions, we came up with the concept of using London's iconic Royal Albert Hall as the venue. In addition to the car

When the smoke finally cleared at the Labatt's Williams launch, there was Thierry Boutsen and Riccardo Patrese. Both were very professional and I enjoyed working with them. ***CSS Archive***

launch, we would put on an evening's entertainment on the stage which, since 1871 has witnessed everything from the Proms to Jimmy Hendrix. Thieme liked the idea but had one worry: he didn't want anyone to go hungry, and he wanted to feed them. The only problem back then – there were no kitchens at the Albert Hall.

But with big bucks, most problems can be solved and thus his guests, the media and a lot of hangers-on were treated to a lavish dinner cooked by legendary South of France Michelin starred chef Roger Verge and brought in by heated wagons from the kitchens of the Dorchester. When the meal was over, Shirley Bassey was the entertainment and would belt out *Diamonds are Forever*. It all worked very well, the client was happy and it certainly boosted the CSS Promotions bottom line.

A year later, Thieme wanted to repeat the exercise but in an even more spectacular way, and it was probably our finest hour. Through Mark Thatcher, we managed to persuade his mother to turn up and press the flesh with all Mr Thieme's key clients. Outside the Albert Hall, we'd done a deal, via an ex-MI6 character we knew simply as 'Mac'. Mac oiled the wheels so we could park Mr Thieme's double-decker hospitality bus in the bus lane opposite the Hall. Then we placed on top of the bus Mr Thieme's helicopter and it looked pretty spectacular, I can tell you. The helicopter, of course, didn't actually land on this forerunner to the current über-hospitality units, we craned it there. Nobody was quite sure if the roof of the bus was strong enough to take the weight of the chopper – there were a few anxious moments – but sure enough the bus did not become a single-decker.

This time the entertainment was no less than the legendary blind R&B star Ray Charles with the Scottish singer Barbara Dickson as the warm-up act. Verge again provided the food, and there was a free raffle too. The prize was a brand new Essex-liveried Lotus Esprit. I can't remember who won it, but he must have been a pretty happy chap – at least until the thing ground to a halt which Esprits of that time tended to do. The Albert Hall was swathed in mimosa and quite a lot of people got drunk on Dom Perignon champagne. The only problem was that before he had settled a fairly substantial part of our bill, Mr Thieme's star had fallen to such a degree that he was sought by certain authorities – never to be seen at a race track again. Or wave a pen over a cheque book.

Indeed, everyone who had quaffed the champagne had actually done so at the expense of CSS Promotions rather than Essex Petroleum – and most of them weren't even our friends. It almost brought our company to its knees but somehow we survived and I still have two bottles of the expensive champagne. I emptied both of them and sip for sip they have to be most expensive thing I have drunk.

Colin Chapman was very much part of these Essex launches, of course. But the F1 reveal involving the Lotus boss I remember the most was at The Royal Garden Hotel in 1971. It was the launch of the Lotus 56B turbine Formula 1 car. Chapman could hardly contain his excitement: he absolutely loved that project complete with its four-wheel drive and Pratt & Witney jet engine.

After the speeches and the reveal, he decided he had to start up the jet motor so everyone could see how quiet it was. He wanted everyone to experience the whoosh factor. There was one problem, the funnel exit from the jet engine was angled upwards and the basement Banqueting Suite of the Royal Garden had a low ceiling with an elaborate sprinkling system. I'll spoil a good story – there wasn't any jet fuel in the tanks, so everyone was spared a shower. Colin was crestfallen but soon recovered.

Race tracks can be ideal for Formula 1 launches; you can prove the car actually works and runs – Silverstone is always a good venue. As I related in another chapter, we chose Silverstone for the launch the first March Formula 1 car and later returned to unveil another company making its Grand Prix debut – the controversial Arrows.

Cigar-chomping Carl Haas moved into Formula 1 after snagging the Beatrice Corporation as a major sponsor. ***CSS Archive***

Colin Chapman, complete with his famous corduroy hat and with Essex Petroleum's David Thieme in his Zoro headgear plus his Racing Manager – ex-F1 driver Francois Mazet. ***CSS Archive***

The sleek Tony Southgate-designed car came after Tony, Jackie Oliver and Alan Rees had split from the employment of Don Nichols at Shadow. That car, of course, led to a court case, and the launch was just days before the new Arrows was due to make its debut in Brazil. Sadly, the launch shots were a little disappointing. That morning there was a heavy snow and the car was virgin white bar a small sponsorship decal for Varig, the Brazilian Airline, which was about all you could see in some of the photography.

Another new Formula 1 car which we at CSS Promotions launched was the Haas team. "Hold on a minute," I can hear you say, "surely the Haas team didn't make it's debut until 2015? You have finally lost the plot!"

But older readers will know that this is the second Haas Formula 1 team to grace Grand Prix grids. The first one was the brainchild of the late US racing entrepreneur Carl Haas, completely unrelated to Gene Haas, the machine tools magnate behind the current Gunther Steiner-led team.

The cigar-chomping Carl not only ran winning teams in Formula 5000 and Can-Am, but later went on to huge success in Champ and IndyCar racing together with backer Paul Newman and drivers like Mario Andretti and Nigel Mansell. Along the way he also sold countless Lola racing cars, Hewland gearboxes and other racing parts.

Back in 1984 Carl had the very good fortune to meet a man called Jim Dutt, the car-collecting, race-loving Chief Executive Officer of a huge corporation called Beatrice, which had started life as a small food processing company in Chicago in 1894. Jim was determined to aggressively expand the company. Already in the portfolio were such well-known brands as Tropicana orange juice, Butterball turkeys, Krispy Kreme doughnuts, and Danone yoghurt. Possibly less well known were such American delicacies as Becky Kay's cookies, Big Pete's specialty meats, Milk Duds (whatever they are), Ma Brown jams and jellies and the never-to-be-forgotten Binkers cat treats. Beatrice had also expanded out of the food arena and the empire included Avis Car Rental, Playtex bras, Samsonite luggage, the World Hand Dryer Corporation and countless others. I promise you, I have not made any of this up.

Imagine the conversation at a $500-a-plate dinner for some worthy Chicago charity when Carl has the good fortune to sit next to Mr Dutt. The conversation must have gone something like this: "Yeah, I've got all these great products to promote around the world, Carl." Quick as a flash, I imagine, came

One of our most audacious Formula 1 launch stunts was to position David Thieme's double decker hospitality bus outside the Royal Albert Hall and then crane his helicopter onto the top of it. ***CSS Archive***

the response. "Jim, I have this great idea. All the racers use rental cars, need luggage, have to wash and dry their hands, eat turkey, doughnuts, drink orange juice and a few even wear bras – you need a Formula 1 racing team!"

"Great idea, my new friend Carl, let's do it." So it came to pass and Carl was always good at budgets. He carved a deal – and this was in 1984 remember – for $30million to cover the F1 and IndyCar teams.

So he hired former McLaren grandees Teddy Mayer and Tyler Alexander to run the F1 team. To design the car he enlisted the established John Baldwin and Neil Oatley plus an aspiring up and coming race engineer called Ross Brawn. Later Adrian Newey was added to the line-up.

While the new Formula 1 outfit was officially known as Team Haas (USA) Ltd, the cars were built by FORCE, short for Formula One Race Car Engineering. But just to further confuse everyone the cars were to be called Lolas, to help promote the racing machinery Carl sold in the States. In fact, Eric Broadley was officially a consultant, but I don't think he made many trips to the factory Mayer had set up in Colnbrook, close to the original McLaren headquarters and just a few miles from Heathrow.

We are talking late 1984 here. The 1000bhp turbo era was upon us, and Haas also pulled off a major deal by signing a three-year exclusive for a new Cosworth-designed Ford four-cylinder motor to power the Oatley/Baldwin/Brawn chassis. It was going to have more horsepower than even BMW. Ultimately, Keith Duckworth and his team, after the huge success of the DFV, completely failed to get the motor to work and decided to switch to a V6 instead. This delayed everything and compromised the design of the car. Alan Jones, by then a World Champion of course, was tempted away from his dairy herd in Australia and out of retirement for a considerably large sum.

The plan was to race in the latter events of 1985 with just one car and, because of the Cosworth delays, the power would come from a Hart turbo engine, as already used by Toleman.

Although CSS Promotions was handling the sponsorship and PR affairs for Williams at the time, we were approached by Teddy to look after the Beatrice team and, after discussion with Frank Williams, it was agreed there was no conflict. Secretly I suspect Frank probably thought we could later persuade Mr Dutt to switch his sponsorship allegiance.

Anyway we weren't complaining and we set to work on the launch of the car with what you would describe as a 'decent budget'. The launch was planned for Brands Hatch and the idea was that the car would start round the back of the GP track, burst through a big paper sign as it entered Clearways and then stop in front of the amazed press and TV cameras on the grid, where Alan would climb out and wave to the crowd. Do you know what? That's what actually happened, but not before a couple of amusing incidents.

Firstly, Mr Dutt was worried from where he and his high-rolling executives were going to watch this extravaganza. At the time we already had a hospitality box at Brands Hatch and that was suggested. But it was decided that it wasn't up to the Beatrice standard and so we acquired the lease on another one – which was then stripped out completely and built to reflect an English pub. No expense was spared. The wine glasses were the finest crystal and the best bitter and expensive wines were on tap and so on. It would also be perfect to entertain at that year's late-season European Grand Prix. After that I don't believe Beatrice ever used it again, but I can assure you we put it to good use.

Meanwhile, Carl was worried about the condition of his best Cuban cigars, so we arranged for a humidor to be installed in the Brands garage the team would be using on launch day.

The Lotus 56B turbine car would have set off the Royal Garden Hotel's sprinkler system had Colin Chapman had his way. ***CSS Archive***

We were contracted to a number of Formula 1 outfits over the years but the most successful were Lotus and Williams. *CSS Archive*

Subsequently this was part of the pit equipment and went round to all the races, so Carl's favourite cigars were always in top condition. However, because of the fuel – and remember what that turbo jungle juice was like – he never smoked them at the race track, just sucked on them.

As the launch approached, I was summoned to Colnbrook to meet with Teddy Mayer to discuss the press kit, which I would be writing. Back in those days, of course, there were no electronic storage devices or downloads. Instead there would be a shiny folder, even shinier black and white photographs and reams of releases, profiles plus a car technical specification. It was here that Teddy, who wasn't always a laugh a minute, caught me by surprise with his wry sense of humour.

He had a general disdain for the majority of the journalists and explained that they never really read this stuff properly, just printed it verbatim. So he insisted that on the technical specification we included something completely outrageous – I think it was the wheelbase of the car and we quoted it at whatever was the length of a London bus. "They'll all print it," he said. And they did.

The team made its debut appearance at the Italian Grand Prix at Monza. AJ qualified 25th out of 27 and in the race retired when the engine failed after six laps. We'd invested in our own photocopier for the garage – imagine that – because I was keen that the first press release to hit the press room would be the Beatrice one. In those days, the smattering of PRs used to have the press room staff to print the releases. If you weren't on the ball, or friendly with the girl behind the counter, you might have to wait an hour or so. It wasn't exactly a problem winning the press release race that day with the car out so early. I only wish I still had a copy of it, because I suppose I put some outrageously positive spin on a disastrous debut.

The rest of the season wasn't really much better although in Australia, Alan had the honour of being the first to drive on to the then brand new Adelaide street circuit. He managed to qualify 19th, stalled on the grid and carved though the field up to sixth place but after 20 laps, it blew up again.

For the second season there was a new car but the promised Ford motor was still not ready. Alan Jones was joined by Patrick Tambay in the second car. I won't go through all the trials and tribulations, but suffice to say when it came the Ford engine proved a disappointment, both Mario and Michael Andretti almost drove for the team and Eddie Cheever did, and ultimately Alan scored four points and Patrick two. The team finished eighth in the Constructors' Championship. Funny the current Haas team seems to finish eighth as well – some things never change.

By the time the season was half through, Beatrice CEO Jim Dutt was gone, his extravagant spending both corporately and on the racing having caught up with him. He had taken Beatrice to a position where, for a short period, it was one of the biggest conglomerates in the world. In fact, he was ousted in a boardroom coup while he was entertaining some 600 employees at an IndyCar race at Road America. He went on to run a rather smaller company called Mailboxes Coast to Coast – which didn't sponsor anything. Beatrice was subsequently sold to the US private equity firm Kohlberg Kravis Roberts who broke it up and sold off the likes of Avis and even Big Pete's meats.

The new CEO was, you have guessed it, not a racing fan and Carl Haas found himself without a sponsor for the upcoming 1987 season. Unfortunately, a replacement backer could not be found, while Ford was disillusioned with the engine, so the team was wound up and FORCE was sold to Bernie Ecclestone. The stripped-down organisation went on to build the Alfa 164 Procar, which never raced, and I suspect the workshop is now a DHL depot.

But during the two years or so that Beatrice was in Formula 1 it certainly used the sponsorship to good effect and a number of the brands really embraced it. I seem to remember journalists had deals to get cheap bottled water and discounted turkeys and hams, although I don't remember any deals on Playtex underwear.

At the time I was issued an Avis Platinum card, which for some reason I still have and use regularly. When I first got it, I told people that Jim Dutt, Carl Haas, Alan Jones and myself were the only people had them. That was obviously an exaggeration but it was pretty exclusive and qualified me for a 30 percent discount and a double upgrade. When I plonked it down at Avis car centres around the world, it definitely got their attention. These days it doesn't have the same cachet but I still get the occasional great upgrades

In a sad end to the story, in November 2002 Jim Dutt, aged 77, committed suicide at his home. Just last year, Carl Haas joined the Victory Circle in the sky after a great motorsport career. Formula 1 was the only category in which he wasn't a winner.

For the absolute surprise factor, the prize has to go to the launch of the six-wheel Tyrrell P34. I was still a journalist when I attended this reveal. It was at Ford's then London Regent Street showroom. We all paraded in and here was a car with a dust-sheet over it. You could quite clearly see where the sheet covered only *four* wheels.

But unbeknown to the assembled press, the Tyrrell team had constructed a curved wood filler which fitted between each pair of front wheels to give the profile of a single wheel. As the sheet was pulled off to reveal the car, two other mechanics took away the wood fillers and for at least 10 seconds there was stunned silence, until everyone broke out in applause.

In more recent times, in the mid-'90s we had a period of spectacular show business style F1 launches. McLaren revealed its 1997 challenger the MP4/12 at Alexandra Palace with the Spice Girls in attendance – I seem to remember they mimed rather badly. I actually lived nearby and was able to obtain press passes for two of my daughters, who managed to wriggle their way right to the front of the stage. Dad earned a few 'brownie points' that day. Later that evening, I interviewed the drivers for Sky Sports and couldn't resist asking them "Who is your favourite Spice Girl?" I remember

We worked hard to generate stories away from races and associate a sponsor's different programmes together. We staged this drag race at the Holme Pierpoint Watersports Centre between Nigel Mansell's F1 car and Bob Spalding's JPS backed powerboat. ***CSS Archive***

that Mika Hakkinen played ball and eventually nominated 'Ginger'. Don't tell Christian Horner.

Eddie Jordan's team also organised several spectacular launches – one of them involved the Cirque du Soleil – and there were a few comments about him being something of a clown. Another year he had a top magician, someone like Derren Brown, who made the car disappear. Earlier in his career I suspect he would have liked the same chap to have made some of his creditors do likewise.

Although not a Formula 1 launch, another reveal we organised was also for Williams sponsor Labatt's which was heavily into promoting its Canadian beer through motorsport. We persuaded them to sponsor a pair of Sierra RS500s to be driven in the British Touring Car Championship by team owner Laurence Bristow of Bristow Helicopter fame, and the hard charging Tim Harvey.

This 1989 launch was held at Chelsea Harbour. After the initial welcomes and coffee, everyone was asked to file outside. The next thing they saw was a Bristow helicopter flying over a nearby railway bridge with a Labatt's liveried Sierra hanging under it on a sling. It then proceeded to fly to the helipad outside the hotel and lower the racer onto the deck. As launches go, it was pretty cool. But the strange thing was that we had to get permission from Railtrack (or whatever they were called back then) for the helicopter to fly over their railway line. Indeed, we had to pay for a man with a red flag as part of this deal. Exactly what he would have done if the 11.53 from Banstead was wanting to use the track, I have no idea.

Another memorable launch was for the Swiftair brand, which was an international postal signed-for service provided by the Royal Mail. We had somehow shown them that a great way to promote this service was through a sponsorship with the Ray Mallock/Ecurie Ecosse-run Spice World Sportscar C2 programme. This launch was held at what was then the nightclub called the Talk of the Town and children's book character Postman Pat was definitely in attendance, although I think he had left Jess the cat behind. I was subsequently his minder on the grid at Brands Hatch one afternoon and Pat was signing a lot of autographs – much to the chagrin of drivers.

More recently we seem to have moved into the era of virtual launches which only happen in cyberspace, or staid affairs with lots of corporate speak. Where has the fun gone?

Chapter 9

FIFTEEN MINUTES OF FAME

I star in the first ever It'll Be Alright On The Night programme, and that wasn't the only problem as the Brabham fan car raced to victory.

It still happens occasionally, those quizzical looks. Sometimes it might be at dinner party or perhaps in the paddock. Occasionally it dawns on them: "You were that bloke on that programme *It'll Be Alright on the Night*, trying to interview Mario Andretti and it was all a frightful cock-up."

Yes and no! Yes, I was the guy who appeared on the very first of Denis Norden's blooper shows *It'll Be Alright on the Night* on ITV. I was, or so it appeared, trying unsuccessfully to thrust a microphone in the direction of America's finest racing driver to the backdrop of people screaming backwards and forwards on a TV talk-back circuit between Anderstorp in Sweden and London's South Bank TV Centre.

I admit it was comical and obviously terribly frustrating when the time booked on the expensive satellite circuit ran out just as all the technical problems had been solved. After 30 minutes of frustration, I was finally going to ask Mario about the Brabham BT46B, aka the famous fan car.

One of Denis Norden's favourite words, upon which he hung with quizzical deliberation for comic effect, was 'however'. Now the truth can finally be told; there was a very big 'however' from my side. In the *Alright* clip, the screen switches to colour bars indicating the satellite feed has been broken at the moment my mouth starts to utter the opening question to the Team Lotus ace. Sorry folks, it never happened. The boys who had been screaming at each other on that production circuit, two seasoned ITV professionals called Mike Hack and Keith Neimayer, had actually arranged for an extension on 'the bird'. While this probably cost several thousand pounds, it wasn't exactly as Mr Norden suggested.

The rear of the Brabham fan car was supposed to be revealed on ITV's World of Sport with me pulling off the cover – actually a rubber dustbin lid – but Bernie Ecclestone had other ideas. ***LAT***

Indeed the interview went ahead, and Mario told us in no uncertain terms that the fan car should be banned. He really didn't like being sand blasted by Niki Lauda and John Watson in this product of Gordon Murray's fertile engineering brain. Indeed, the interview which, according to *It'll Be Alright on the Night* never happened, was used prominently at the top of ITV World of Sport to preview the Swedish Grand Prix live coverage coming a little later in the afternoon.

But there were a lot of other 'howevers' during one of my most memorable motor racing broadcasts. More of that later – but first let's fill in some of the background surrounding that 1978 Swedish Grand Prix.

If you remember we are in year two of the high downforce revolution, led by the phenomenal Lotus 78 of the previous year and refined into the 79 by Colin Chapman and his team for the 1978 season. Others, like Williams, had joined in with the FW07, but Brabham was saddled with the ultra-wide and thirsty flat-12 Alfa Romeo engine, which

Niki Lauda on his way to victory at Anderstorp in the 1978 Swedish Grand Prix in Gordon Murray's fabulous fan car but it was never to race again. ***LAT***

made a similar aerodynamic solution a big problem for Bernie Ecclestone's design chief Gordon Murray. He's the guy, remember, who Bernie claimed to have found under a dust sheet in the Brabham design office when he bought the team from Ron Tauranac!

Gordon's initial idea for the BT46 was not to use conventional radiators for the car but flat panel heat exchangers – a kind of the reverse solar panel. It didn't work, in fact it was hopeless. But Gordon quickly bounced back and, in huge secrecy, developed the fan car version of the BT46 in time for June's Swedish GP – a race strangely held on a Saturday and hence ITV's interest in broadcasting it.

But let's return to the *It'll Be Alright* incident. The plan was to record an interview mid-morning with Niki Lauda standing with the fan car and, at the end of the piece, I would pull off, with gusto, the rubber dustbin lid which neatly fitted over the rear orifice and thus reveal the fan to the amazed viewers back in the UK. The interview would effectively be live but recorded in the World of Sport technical area to be played out an hour later and introduced, of course, by Dickie Davies.

All was set up although we knew it wouldn't be easy because Swedish TV had, for some quirky Scandinavian reason, refused to televise the race. So Bernie, in one of his first forays into TV production, had brought in a French group, who pretty well to a man didn't speak English and certainly had less than a smorgasbord of Swedish.

The cameraman who would shoot our piece could only communicate with us in sign language. However, it didn't need even his Gallic gesticulations for us to realise that we were in the brown and smelly. The reason? He started to take the camera to pieces just minutes before we were supposed to transmit the interview to London. The fact that he scattered the various electronic pieces on the pit road simply didn't inspire confidence.

By then Herbie Blash, the Brabham team manager, had advised us that all interviews with his drivers or close up shots of the fan car were off limits, because of the rising furore over the speed of the fan car and its sand blasting capabilities. Plan B was to interview Mario.

Thus I stood, microphone in hand, face to face with Mario as our cameraman bolted the last part of the camera back together again – and I swear there was one piece still on the pit lane. Then followed a long wait

Gordon Murray has resurrected the fan car concept with his T60 supercar. ***Andrew Marriott***

while Anderstorp and London tried to communicate. I finally I got the thumbs up, just as the contents of the then Swedish Touring Car Championship took to the pit lane – and those Camaros were loud.

Finally, the interview went ahead and was beamed to London and everyone was happy. It was recorded back in London just 10 minutes before the piece was scheduled to go to air but we'd made it. I thought nothing more of it until some months later when a researcher from the then-unknown *It'll Be Alright on the Night* show called. She explained they had this piece and they'd like to use it and furthermore they would send a contract for £50.

I was somewhat bemused because as far as I knew I had waited around to get an interview while some technical issues were resolved – and it certainly wasn't the first time that had happened. I hadn't heard anything of the increasingly desperate and hilarious interchange between Sweden and the South Bank Studios, nor considered the kind of spin the Norden team could put on it.

What I did remember was the technical and logistical problems I had encountered with the actual race transmission. Now, Martin Brundle, David Croft et al listen to this. My commentary position was in the open air at the top of a concrete grandstand. It was a small section of that paddock grandstand simply roped off. There was just me, no co-commentator, pits reporter and one producer who was in the OB truck. Back then, there was one commentator and ten million viewers, now there seem to be ten commentators and one million viewers – I guess that's progress.

At the appointed time, I received the countdown to start commentating. "Three, two, one," at which point the monitor went completely blank. Now you may not know, unless you have been to the midge-infested race track that is

Pole sitter Mario Andretti, survived his interview with me and takes the lead at the start but the picture on my monitor was indecipherable. Niki Lauda alongside with John Watson in second fan car behind. ***LAT***

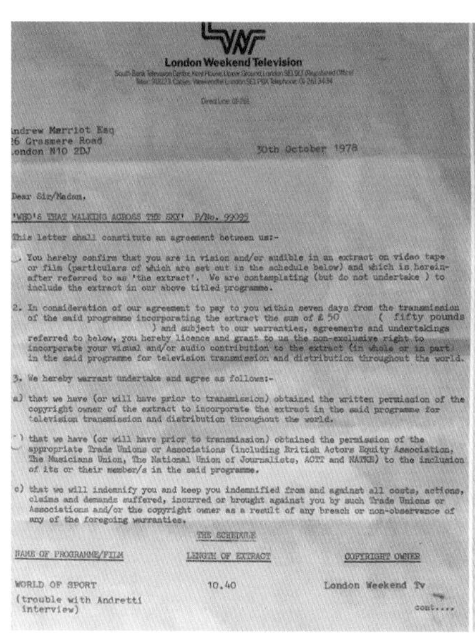

London Weekend Television

ndrew Merriot Esq
6 Grasmere Road
ondon N10 2DJ

30th October 1978

Dear Sir/Madam,

'WHO'S THAT WALKING ACROSS THE SKY' P/No. 99095

This letter shall constitute an agreement between us:-

. You hereby confirm that you are in vision and/or audible in an extract on video tape or film (particulars of which are set out in the schedule below) and which is hereinafter referred to as 'the extract'. We are contemplating (but do not undertake) to include the extract in our above titled programme.

2. In consideration of our agreement to pay to you within seven days from the transmission of the said programme incorporating the extract the sum of £ 50 (fifty pounds) and subject to our warranties, agreements and undertakings referred to below, you hereby licence and grant to us the non-exclusive right to incorporate your visual and/or audio contribution to the extract (in whole or in part) in the said programme for television transmission and distribution throughout the world.

3. We hereby warrant undertake and agree as follows:-

a) that we have (or will have prior to transmission) obtained the written permission of the copyright owner of the extract to incorporate the extract in the said programme for television transmission and distribution throughout the world.

) that we have (or will have prior to transmission) obtained the permission of the appropriate Trade Unions or Associations (including British Actors Equity Association, The Musicians Union, The National Union of Journalists, ACTT and NATKE) to the inclusion of its or their member/s in the said programme.

c) that we will indemnify you and keep you indemnified from and against all costs, actions, claims and demands suffered, incurred or brought against you by such Trade Unions or Associations and/or the copyright owner as a result of any breach or non-observance of any of the foregoing warranties.

THE SCHEDULE

NAME OF PROGRAMME/FILM	LENGTH OF EXTRACT	COPYRIGHT OWNER
WORLD OF SPORT (trouble with Andretti interview)	10.40	London Weekend Tv

cont....

My LWT contract – sadly no repeat fees, if only I had realised! ***Andrew Marriott***

Anderstorp, that the pits and paddock complex are about a mile from the start-finish line. All I could see was an empty corner in front of me, a blank monitor but I could hear the distant sound of race cars forming up on the grid. I welcomed the viewers, took them through the fan car controversy, read out the grid all to a blank screen. I could only assume they were seeing grid shots back in the UK.

However – that word again – as I heard the engine revs rise indicating the start of the race, the screen flickered into life but in a stroke of technical turmoil, the bottom half of the picture was superimposed over the top half. This made it somewhat difficult to decide who was leading. Fortunately a few seconds later they arrived in my sight and then, miracle of miracles, I suddenly had a wobbly but discernable picture.

It was about 10 laps later when a gust of wind blew all my crib cards away. They rose up, all those notes of research, and fluttered down behind the grandstand. Now it was just me, a flickering screen and my memory.

Then that superimposing deal happened again. Somehow I was able to pick out John Watson rotating the fan car, thus leaving his team-mate Niki Lauda to disappear into the distance to score the one and only win for the Brabham fan car. As you will probably recall, the team withdrew the car because of the general outcry among the rivals led by a highly agitated Colin Chapman. Bernie was once again almost certainly thinking three moves ahead.

It was great to catch up with Mario Andretti at Goodwood a couple of years ago. After this photo was taken I told him about our TV blooper appearance, he had no idea, so I sent him a copy. ***United Autosport***

Denis Norden's telling of the Anderstorp incident showed his immaculate timing. ***LWT***

Fortunately a full frame picture returned to my monitor for the closing stages and I was able to commentate in a half sensible manner over the historic victory.

I also 'starred' in another *It'll Be Alright* clip. Occasionally, I was asked to appear on some Saturday morning ITV kids' show. On one particular occasion they got children from the audience to make the introduction to the next item. So Matilda, or whatever she was called, looked at her card and read out "Coming up after the break, Andy Marriott will talk about grand pricks." The presenter jumped in and said that it was actually about Grand Prix racing but quick as a flash she replied "No, it says grand pricks here!" Maybe she wasn't far wrong.

Since then, of course, the *It'll Be Alright on the Night* clip has been played many times, including in the 'Best of', on video and now on the internet. Sadly, my contract had no repeat clause so I only got £50 and 15 minutes of fame out of it. But you all now know, it *was* alright on the night. Subsequently, when the programme was reprised in 2018 and presented by David Walliams, they used the footage again but cut it up in a different way which made me look even more incompetent. After a lawyer's letter they finally paid me again – more than £50 this time. If you want to have a laugh you can find it on YouTube, but make sure it is the original piece.

Chapter 10

MUG AT THE MIC

I have thrust microphones at thousands of racers and other personalities. Here I remember some of the humorous and occasionally painful interviews.

"One last question for Barry," were the words that crackled from the ITV scanner van into my headphones as I interviewed Barry Sheene following another win in the ITV World of Sport Superbike series at Donington Park. I had interviewed Bazza many times before but he was in a particularly playful mood that summer's day. As I asked for that final thought I felt something touching my groin area. Out of the corner of my eye I could just see his leathered arm reaching forward and he was starting to squeeze my you-know-whats. He gave them a little tweak, straight-faced gave his final answer and as I painfully threw back to Chris Carter in the commentary box, he dissolved into uncontrollable laughter. "Got you there, Moriarty," he giggled. Maybe it was payback for the pig incident I described elsewhere.

Nigel Mansell had a similar but slightly less painful trick but it was equally disconcerting. As you concentrated on getting his latest thoughts, he made a habit of grabbing hold of the cable connecting the microphone and, out of camera sight, start to steadily tug on it, so it felt that the microphone was going to fly out of your hand. He's pulled that trick on me several times. Having said that, Nigel is always a great interview and he really knows how to use a camera to get his point across.

Alain Prost interviewed for hospitality guests at Silverstone. I once door-stepped him outside a Monaco portaloo. ***CSS Archive***

It's been my pleasure over 40 years or so to interview hundreds of racers from young karting kids to World Champions and, most famously, the attempt to interview Mario Andretti which appeared on the very first *It'll be Alright On the Night*, as recounted in the previous chapter.

I'm often asked who are the best – and the worst – drivers I've interviewed over the years. Let's start with the worst, the least erudite, and uninformative. You only need one guess: Kimi Raikkonen. Kimi neither knows nor cares what the TV boys want. For him, it's all a great chore and I still haven't figured out how he can talk with his teeth seemingly clamped together. He even remained tight-lipped through his period in the WRC and rallying is a sport where there is a bit more time to talk once the stage is over. Finnish colleagues tell me he's no better in his native tongue.

Mika Hakkinen, in his early days, was little better than Kimi. I remember going to Hethel to interview him when he had just joined Team Lotus and he was close to monosyllabic. But over the years he's become close to garrulous.

You feel your age when you are interviewing the son of someone you interviewed regularly. I question Freddie Hunt and I have interviewed three generations of Andrettis. ***Creventic***

Mind you, he'll never come close to a fellow Finn and Lotus racer who is certainly the chattiest guy in the paddock, Heikki Kovalainen. Back in his F1 days with Renault before his move to Japanese GT, you could always find him in the famous Grand Prix interview 'bull pen'. After everyone else has headed off to their helicopter, there was Heikki still telling a reporter in minute detail about his race. We like that.

Talking of current Grand Prix drivers, Red Bull was certainly blessed with two of the best when it comes to tell telling it like it is – Sebastian Vettel and Daniel Ricciardo. Vettel's command of the English language and knowledge of English comedy is extraordinary while 'Smiler' often has strong views well put. Maybe a swig of the Red Bull helped them.

Someone else you couldn't stop talking when he got going was former motorcycle World Champion Freddie Spencer. I interviewed him on the grid before the start of the 1982 Daytona 200, Freddie was astride his Yamaha TZ750. The signal was given and the field swept away on the sighting lap,

Nigel Mansell could be playful, pulling the microphone cord. ***CSS Archive***

What a privilege to have interviewed the great Ronnie Peterson. This was live at the South African Grand Prix for South African Broadcasting. ***Ben van Rensburg***

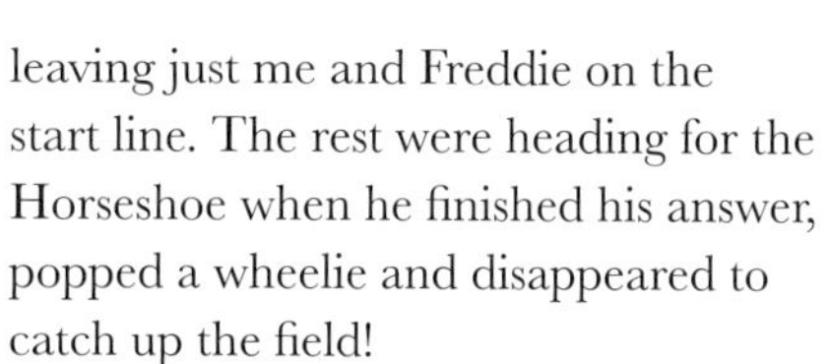

David Coulthard was superb at the mic, even in his early days. ***CSS Archive***

leaving just me and Freddie on the start line. The rest were heading for the Horseshoe when he finished his answer, popped a wheelie and disappeared to catch up the field!

Back with the difficult ones. I am afraid I have to single out an American, who sadly lost his life in a horrendous ChampCar accident, Jeff Krosnoff. A really lovely guy and as fluent as they come – until the microphone appeared. One year, he did the Le Mans 24 Hours for the Silk Cut Jaguar team and I interviewed him before qualifying. I think he stopped me at least six times saying, "Can I do that again? It didn't come out quite right."

I have worked the Le Mans 24 Hours on over 50 occasions, mainly for America's Speed Channel and NBC, and most recently for Radio Le Mans.

I always get a tremendous buzz out of reporting and interviewing from the pits. You are right in heart of the action, you can talk to the drivers within seconds of them finishing a mega-stint and can still see their eyes on stalks and the veins in their necks bulging.

But with the adrenalin pumping, words can sometimes come out that are unintended and it seems to be the French speaking in English who are the worst. A few years ago in the closing stages of a very wet race I asked former, albeit briefly, F1 driver Pascal Fabre about the conditions. "Fooking terrible," he replied. In the Speed Channel truck, corporate America went into overtime. Nobody had ever used that word on their network before. I was told on talkback to apologise on Pascal's behalf. I threw back to the booth and they apologised about six more times.

At least it stood them in good stead a couple of years later when Amanda Stretton checked in with Paul Belmondo about another driver's tactics. "He's a fucking cunt," replied the incensed Belmondo. He probably said some other stuff too, but by then the director had hit the kill button and the commentators were already apologising from the Speed booth in the grandstand! About 15 times! "Paul doesn't really understand the nuances of the English language," we were informed. I think he does.

The Americans can be a bit sensitive. At the Petit Le Mans a few years ago, I was reporting on a pit stop by Adrian Ferndandez's crew and commented they were rushing around in a most un-Mexican way. I threw back to Leigh Diffey who had already been instructed to say, "Andrew didn't mean to infer that the Mexican race is generally lazy."

But back to the good interviews. For some reason, the majority of the best interviewees seem to be American or Scottish. I once wrote an article for a website on "My Ten Best Formula 1 Interviewees" and I was surprised how many were Scottish. Jackie Stewart is always a great guy to talk to, he's a rent-a-quote but I don't mean that unkindly.

He can talk about any racing subject, and plenty more besides. He's incisive and interesting even if you don't agree with him. David Coulthard is another driver I have always felt gave terrific answers and really engaged with you. Perhaps that was how he got the current Channel 4 gig. Allan McNish is another Scot who sets just the right tone with great answers full of insight and equally good is Indy 500 winner Dario Franchitti – another superb driver who has found his way to the commentary box.

Think of the BTCC and no question John Cleland was always a good and a sometimes controversial interview, especially if he was talking about Frank Sytner. Among other national competitors, I would single out GT and historic racer Calum Lockie who always has a ready answer. All of them Scots. But the exception that proves he rule is Damon Hill. His vocabulary is superb and he always gives great answers to the questions. In fact, it is case of like father, like son. Although his dad once interviewed *me* after something I wrote about a certain race performance. Come to think of it, this was more an interrogation/bollocking. There are so many others who are erudite and I'd like to name them all, but Le Mans nine-time winner Tom Kristensen comes to mind.

There are basically three types of TV interviews. There is the very controlled sit down in a studio with scripted questions type, there is the stand-up and get the latest update interview and then there's the grab-them-while-they-are-legging-it-down-the-paddock-with-your-cameraman-walking-backwards-and-you-are-pushing-five-screaming-Italians-out-of-the-way type of interview.

For many years, a most enjoyable annual job was working as paddock reporter for Silverstone TV at the British Grand Prix. It was always a pretty challenging weekend. I often had to indulge in the third type of interview (cameraman walking backwards) usually with Max Mosley, Bernie Ecclestone, Tom Walkinshaw or even Kimi Raikkonen with frankly mixed results. Added to that we usually had to interview a plethora of VIP celebs, politicians and non-motor racing sports stars. Being the wrong side of 50, I have to admit I'm not exactly sure of the

I have interviewed plenty of rock stars, several who love historic racing and compete regularly. This is Neil Primrose of the Scottish band Travis. ***Robin Thompson***

minute career details of some of the soap stars/rappers and other assorted headliners who pitch up to mix with Lando, Lewis and the gang.

I did know who Guns N' Roses lead singer Axl Rose was although his answers to my questions weren't particularly coherent. Then there was Lewis's on-off squeeze Pussycat Doll Nicole. Before she was whisked into the McLaren citadel I asked her two questions and got two answers to two completely different questions. More embarrassingly, I asked an Arsenal striker what it felt like to save a goal – I'd somewhat mixed up his position on the field of play.

But I've had some good interviews amongst the VIPs. I was hugely impressed by yachtswoman Ellen MacArthur, likewise with former *Countdown* star Carol Vorderman who knew a remarkable amount about Formula 1, while weathergirl Sian Lloyd, the former Mrs Jonathan Ashman of FIA fame, was a delight, too.

Others have been less talkative, refusing to offer any pearls of wisdom into the Silverstone TV mic, including English cricket star Kevin Pietersen, Rowan Atkinson and unsuccessful English football manager Fabio Capello, and I tried really hard with him.

The politicians usually have plenty to say. Former Labour cabinet minister Peter Hain is, of course, a regular at the Grand Prix and a huge racing fan. I managed to interview John 'Two Jags' Prescott in a year when there were two Jaguars on the grid and he graciously laughed at my rather obvious barbed question. Kenneth, now Lord, Clarke, the jazz-loving former Conservative chancellor, was certainly the most engaging and interesting. In fact, he was chairman of British American Racing for a while.

Back with the big names of Formula 1, one of my favourite interviewees was Ayrton Senna. If you waited until around until three hours after qualifying, you usually got an excellent interview with Ayrton. He knew that you had been patient and if you asked the right questions you'd not only get good answers but sometime some very interesting asides. Mind you, at the end of one season in Adelaide we agreed to interview him the next day at his hotel for Sky Television to sum up the year. Unfortunately, he then got an offer to go up in an Australian Air Force F16 fighter jet and forgot to tell us or the McLaren PR staff. I think the interview took place five hours late – and all he wanted to talk about was the flight experience.

But perhaps my favourite interviewee was the American wrestling star Hulk Hogan. I caught up with him at the Daytona 500 one year, again for Sky. He was the grand marshal or something similar. The interview started quite normally but, by the time I got to the third question, he had me in a head-lock and I finished the interview with his golden tanned forearm locked against my cranium. He's obviously done it to reporters many times before, it was well practised and made a great shot. What was the question again?

The Le Mans interrogators. It was always fun working with Justin Bell for Fox Sports, even if he did tower above me. ***Fox Sports***

Others great interviewees have to include Mario Andretti, Alex Zanardi, Michael Schumacher and Scott Pruett – who always managed to throw in a "hello to my family back home". Roger Penske is still outstanding and there are plenty of other top team managers up and down the IMSA sportscar pit lane, but I have to single out Wayne Taylor. If there is any controversy in the air, Wayne will have a view.

Someone I remember as a superb interviewee was the great American Speedway World Champion from 1982 and 1983, Bruce Penhall. I was working for CBS at the time and, prior to the set interview, I was taken to be introduced to him in the baths at Wembley Stadium. He was stark naked at the time which was a little disconcerting, but fortunately he donned his leathers by the time of the interview.

Occasionally the boot is on the other foot and I have been the interviewee. Usually it is all friendly stuff, but at an Australian reporter really tried to skewer me a few days before the opening of the Sydney Motorsport Park, then known as Eastern Creek International Raceway. The track was funded by the NSW Government and there was some issue with the safety of the grandstand. This rottweiler reporter was definitely anti-racing and made me squirm.

It is always easier when your subject speaks good English. It never really works when you try to do it through a translator. Nearly all the top racing professionals have to learn English, although the little man in the Marlboro hat, Arturo Merzario, never mastered it, and neither did some of the Japanese. Some often learn from the mechanics they work with so you might pick up a hint of Brummie twang from a Brazilian.

But it is always a privilege to be able to thrust a microphone forward. Perhaps the biggest buzz is Le Mans where you can still grab drivers as they climb out of their cars. I don't see the touchline reporters ever getting an interviewer with a star football player at half time or with a top tennis star between sets. So working in motorsport is a special privilege.

Another interview with 'Our Nige', with 1972/1974 World Champion Emerson Fittipaldi and working alongside Murray Walker at the Race of Champions for Sky Sports. ***Marriott Archive***

Chapter 11

LIES, DAMN LIES AND STATISTICS

From insects in beards to over enthusiastic shaving, I heard the best racing driver excuses.

These days I keep a daily diary in a bid to help me remember what I've done, who I've met, who has died and what I had for breakfast. Had I kept some kind of journal 40 years ago, this whole book would have been easier to write. Nevertheless, I can still remember the first time I met Australian Tim Schenken outside one of those famous railway arches in Chiswick where Chas Beattie fettled and built what seemed to be half the grid of Formula 2 and 3 cars. As a prissy young *Motoring News* reporter from the provinces, I can recall to this day that Tim's language was particularly fruity and I was shocked. Tim's career has embraced dominating in the junior formulae, driving for the likes of Surtees and Brabham in Formula 1, racing sports cars for Ferrari and subsequently becoming Australia's top motor racing official and the race director for the Australian Grand Prix.

But when I first met him he was fresh off the boat from Sydney and he had certainly homed in on the right place to get advice for his racing. He was just six days younger than me and I immediately took to this brash newcomer despite the swearing. Over the next few seasons he gave me plenty to write about as he rocketed through Formula Ford, Formula 3 and Formula 2, amassing race win after race win. I was convinced he was World Champion material but once he made it to Formula 1 his career flat-lined, maybe as a result of making the wrong contract choices.

But the point of this chapter is about racing drivers' excuses and, believe me, I have heard a few. Back in the early 1970s, my journalist mates and I compiled what we referred to as the 'Tim Schenken Book of Excuses'. Now, it is at this point that I really need to reach for the diary that I never kept, because I can't recall if the famous book was named after Tim because he gave us a lot of excuses or that he came up with the idea, but I am pretty sure it was the latter.

Is an excuse a lie? Mark Twain said lies, damned lies and statistics. I'm sure a lot of drivers I have reported upon or interviewed dished out both lies and excuses. I love the quote of another Aussie racing pioneer to Europe, the late Frank Gardner's classic, "I had a box full of neutrals and no ideas," which wasn't probably wasn't really an excuse but a genuine fact. But we have heard countless excuses from the mundane stories of missed pit boards, bodged radio communications and broken gear levers to some more prosaic reasons for screwing up.

Researching for this chapter, I discovered that the famous Tim Schenken 'virtual book' has been rediscovered and there is now a chap on the internet called David who actually runs a Facebook site for racing drivers' excuses. But here I'm relying more on my own memories than those of others. Plus I don't always believe what I read on Facebook, although I do find it has several terrific groups who post excellent old photos and recollections.

One absolute classic excuse I heard, and I need that diary again because I can't remember the perpetrator, concerned a missed braking point at the original Österreichring. I visited the track quite recently for a DTM race and, while the setting is still marvellous, the track isn't what it was and the excuse can not be used any more.

You may remember the track is in the glorious Styrian Mountains in Austria, it is real *Sound of Music* country. Surrounding the track are picture-perfect chalets and lush fields. Before the track was shortened and became the Red Bull Ring, there was a fast straight leading to the daunting Dr Tiroch Kurve. Alongside the track was a field that contained a herd of cows complete with the mandatory cowbells. Our hero recounted how there was a particular cow close to the fence and, in the absence of brake-markers, he had ear-marked the bovine for his braking point.

Unfortunately, this hapless racer was not a country boy so he didn't realise that when a cow finishes munching a particular piece of Austrian grass, she moves! You've probably guessed the rest. But the story is not quite as good as it could be, the braking-marker beast found its next

Tim Schenken invented the 'book of excuses' ***CAMS***

Did Henri Pescarolo really have an insect in his beard which caused him to crash? ***CSS Archive***

patch of grass by walking *away* from the Tiroch Kurve! Thus our man braked early and about 14 rivals passed him.

Indeed, there are plenty of excuses where the blame is very firmly placed on the track itself. One guy complained, "They put the Armco in a really silly place." All kinds of substances on the surface have, apparently, caused problems. This ranges from oil, water, ice, snow, hail and various broken pieces of engine. But I think my favourite is probably, "I got caught out by the sap from the overhanging trees." That would be Cadwell Park, then. Maybe there should be a variation of the red and yellow flag for that.

Feet also seem to give drivers problems. I have heard, "I left my favourite red driving boots behind and had to buy a blue pair at the track." There have been countless excuses involving getting something stuck under the pedals – take your pick from drinks bottles, a Pepsi cola can, or even a cigarette packet. But in this category most of all I like the story of the guy who couldn't put in the lap times because, "My feet were cold." I'm not sure Christian Horner would be very impressed if Max Verstappen came up with that! Anyway, they probably have race boot warmers in the Red Bull Energy Centre.

Problems with tyres often feature large in the litany of excuses. I'm sure we've lost count of the number who have spun or even crashed because their tyres were too cold, too hot, generally rooted, the wrong compound, the wrong construction, slicks when they should have been wets, wets when they should have been intermediates, the wrong pressures, backs on the front, fronts on the back and had even left in the supplier's workshop too long. But my favourite is a chap who blamed his problem on someone stealing a valve cap and this unbalanced a wheel.

Then there was this American driver-turned-team owner, and I will spare his blushes so no names. But he was racing a Porsche in the Daytona 24 Hours. Occasionally, even in January, it can get pretty hot in a 911 and this guy's lap times were pretty good but towards the end of the session they started to drop off dramatically and he finally pulled into the pits a couple of laps early, his face wracked with pain.

Once he had extracted himself from the car he confided to one of his team-mates that the problem was with what is sometimes euphemistically known as 'down below'. Apparently, prior to the race, he had got a little enthusiastic with the razor and given himself something similar to what I understand is known in certain female circles as a 'Brazilian' – except this chap had left no hair untouched but, in the process, had also nicked himself. Wince now!

It seems that his race suit was unlike a grand hotel for it didn't have much 'ballroom'. He'd got very hot and sweaty and the perspiration had worked its way into the over clipped area. The pain was so bad he couldn't concentrate any more. Was it an excuse for slowing down? Actually, it sounds much more like a very good reason.

Indeed, shaving – or rather the lack of it – enters into one of my all-time favourite entries in Tim's book and it concerns the four-time Le Mans winner Henri Pescarolo. I know this one to be absolutely true because he told it directly to me. Le Grand Pesca had crashed at Leeukop Corner at Kyalami. I think it might have been in a Williams, which at the time rejoiced in the ridiculous name of a Politoys.

Why had the Frenchman lost control and hit the barrier? As best as I can remember he said: "Ze problem was ze insect. It had been in my beard for two or three laps." I presume the reason for this was that it was trying to hide from the fluorescent green colour that Henri sported on his crash helmet for his whole career. "Zen," said Henri, "as I came up to Leeukop, ze bug climbed out of my beard and into ze eye, I blinked and missed ze braking." Excuses don't come any better than that.

Chapter 12

DOG DAYS IN DALLAS

Changing technology confused many of us. There were plenty of frustrations for race reporters 40 years ago.

First there was a stream of expletives, then a chair was flung across the room and finally a journalist slumped to the floor of the windowless room in the Texas State Fairground administrative building, his head in his hands, gently weeping.

That man was one of the regular British press corps reporting the one and only Dallas Grand Prix. July 8 1984 had been a sweltering hot Texas day and there had been a huge amount to write about. The race was delayed due to the track breaking up, Keke Rosberg delivered Honda's first victory since 1967 as Williams scored the first of many victories for the Japanese company. Rosberg's use of a 'water-cooled' skull cap prompted the inevitable headlines of, 'Keke keeps a cool head' and, lest we forget, Nigel Mansell heroically attempted to push his Lotus across the line and collapsed in the 100deg F heat on the finish line.

Jeff Hutchinson was an all round good guy who had made the somewhat unusual journalistic jump from *Scooter Weekly* to *Autosport* and on to a successful freelance career which provided with him with a decent lifestyle in Switzerland, and a pilot's licence. He was later to fly Heinz-Harald Frentzen's executive jet and is now based in Australia, still piloting his own plane.

I can't remember for whom he was writing that fateful Dallas day, but it was one of those 2000-word, lap-by-lap, takes-three-hours-to-write-type reports. Now, in the very old days before computers, we used to write our race reports on a typewriter (remember them?) and we used something called carbon paper. You put a sort of sandwich in the typewriter, your top copy of pristine white A4, then behind it a piece of the blue carbon paper which always left a stain on your fingers, and then another piece of paper, which was sometimes a shade of yellow, green or even pink. Now if you were double-dipping and selling the same story to more than one source, you might even put in a second carbon and another piece of paper.

By a miracle of old fashioned science, when you typed out a story you got two more copies, although the second one could be a little feint. In fact, if you were triple-dipping, the bottom copy, was hardly readable unless you hit the keys really *hard*. Hey, who needs a photocopier! For you older readers, sorry to go through all this but our computer age kids have no idea how resourceful we were back in the 1980s. I always did two copies because there was always a chance one might get lost.

Your typed copy then went either to a sub-editor who improved/altered it or possibly straight to a typesetter. This person, for some reason usually a man, then sat in front of a huge machine called a linotype and basically typed your whole story again which came out until the '60s as metal slugs. Photo type setting followed until the world went all electronic and digital. History lesson over.

Of course, if you were in somewhere like Dallas and your publication was in Manchester what came out of your typewriter was useless. Thus you put the typewriter to one side and resorted to something called a telex machine. I woke up in the middle of the night a few weeks ago to do what men of my age do in the middle of night and tuned in to a BBC Radio 5 programme called *Up All Night*. The regular presenter is a fine fellow called Oludotun Adebayo MBE – who, amazingly, is fluent in English, Nigerian and Swedish – but he was having the night off and his stand-in was a bloke called Jim Davis. Jim must be quite new because he doesn't even have a Wikipedia entry, so I don't know if he speaks a mix of different languages. Anyway, he was in discussion with some insomniac phone-in caller who wanted to know what a telex machine was. Jim didn't know and invited anyone who did to phone in – I would have done so, but I had gone back to sleep by then.

I would have been able to tell Jim and his listeners that telex is short for Teleprinter Exchange, and the machines could be found in newspaper offices and, indeed, in Formula 1 press rooms. They were also known as tickertape machines. You would type your story on a normal keyboard and literally cut a long thin roll of ticker tape paper. When you struck a key, it punched a series of holes into the tape, which equated to letters. Usually at a Grand Prix, the local telecom company, say Western Union in the States, would provide several operators to assist and send messages. They could actually read what you had written by looking at the tape while, to me and everyone else in the

Keke Rosberg on his way to victory in the 1984 Dallas Grand Prix on a sweltering day. The tube to his helmet fed a cooled skull cap. *LAT*

press room, it was just a load of holes in a ribbon of paper. Of course, you could only send to another telex machine, which de-coded the dots and printed out the story. It was close to magic.

Once you had written your story, you had this long, maybe 20ft, snake of paper ribbon on the floor. To send the story you would place the start of the tape in the sender unit, have the operator dial the number of the recipient for you – and off it set ticking its way across the ether about 100 times quicker than you had typed it.

But there were pitfalls aplenty. If you weren't very careful it would get snagged up, stop, snap and quite possibly jam the machine. As the operator, who in somewhere like Brazil, probably didn't speak English, had about eight machines to watch, it paid for the journo to gaze mesmerised as the tape ticked its way through. There was a method whereby you wound the tape around the thumb and little finger of your hand in a figure eight configuration, which allowed the tape to majestically unfurl itself without damaging itself. Now, you are starting to think Mr Jeff Hutchinson hadn't mastered this technique and his tape had finished up like a half-eaten bowl of Barilla's finest spaghetti on the floor of the sweltering Dallas press room. Actually, it's much better than that. But hold on a second.

There were some brave souls who used to produce type-written copy, hand it to the operator, who would punch it in for them, but based on the fact they probably couldn't understand what they were re-typing, it never seemed like a very sound idea to me. Other slightly less bold characters with the taste of a cold beer in their head would wheelspin out of the press room the moment their tape started ticking its way back to their far-flung office. But they were taking a gamble the tape wouldn't grind to a halt.

I always used to wait until the whole thing had gone through: I'm good like that. I forgot to mention there was a sizeable tariff of charges for the telex provision and in certain countries – Brazil comes to mind again – and large service fee as well.

You could actually send a telex without cutting a tape by simply dialling a number and typing the message out but you could only go at the speed you could type and at the same time you were trying to finely craft a piece of journalism in a vain attempt to match the mastery of DSJ, Pete Lyons or Peter Windsor. Incidentally, I don't think Jenks ever used a telex, working for a monthly, he hand-wrote his copy – very neatly, it has to be said – and posted it to the *Motor Sport* offices. It still is a monthly magazine.

If you bashed out the story via telex, the costs spiralled very quickly as I almost found out on a famous occasion in Venezuela. I was reporting their World Championship 500cc Motorcycle Grand Prix for *The Sun* from a god-forsaken track called San Carlos. So much happened there that there's probably another chapter in it. To whet your appetite, I can tell you I saw a pig walking down the main street of the town minding its own business while the no-go photography areas were enforced by gun-slinging soldiers. I know because I had the barrel of a gun stuck right next to my Nikon.

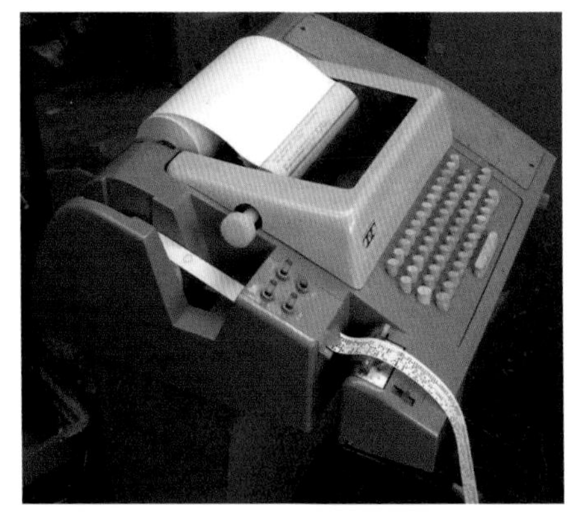

Old technology. We often sent our stories via telex machine complete with tickertape. ***Marriott Archive***

Anyway, Barry Sheene wheelied across the line on his Suzuki RG500 ahead of local hero Johnny Cecotto to take the victory, and I raced across the small press room to get on the sole telex first. A race win for Barry would make the lead *The Sun*'s back page if I got the story to them quickly. Normally, I would have phoned it through to a copy-taker, but I'd already proved in qualifying that waiting to get a line to England might take a couple of hours. The telex would be quicker.

Jeff Hutchinson fell foul of the Dallas press room telex operators. ***Marriott Archive***

I sat down at the machine and then, in rather the way you find a lavatory without the loo roll, I found the telex without the somewhat narrower strip of essential paper. The telex machine did not seem to come with an operator. The press centre boss was more interested in brewing up some mind-altering mixture and I didn't want to give up my position as there was a swarthy looking guy from the *Caracas Chronicle* making signs that he also wanted to use the equipment. There was nothing for it but to bash out the clichéd 500 words live onto the machine.

As I explained, this took quite a while. Fortunately, it went well but I reckoned the bill would be about three million Bolivars. I can't remember how many Bollis there were to the pound but we were staring at the best part of £1000. However, by now the man from the *Caracas Chronicle* had given up, the Press Officer had collapsed in a corner and there was nobody to pay!

Back to Dallas. In the mid-1980s, computers were coming in and the telex

A bank of copytakers took down your story. I understand I wasn't the only journalist to be asked "Is there much more of this?" ***Marriott Archive***

machine was in its final throes. Indeed, Western Union had produced a brand new machine, which was something of a mongrel, a cross between the old technology and the new. You no longer cut a tape, the data went on to a floppy disc. The actual message, however, was still transmitted in the same telex way. The problem was that, rather like some of the cars that had been racing, the testing had been minimal and, like Nigel Mansell, they were starting to collapse in the heat. Indeed, there had been some hiccups in practice where the machines had suffered the same fate as some of our older readers – memory loss.

Jeff had written his story and called over the operator to actually send it. Unfortunately, our all-Texan guy wasn't particularly familiar with the new machine either. He confidently pressed the button to send the beautifully written 2000 words flying across the world – and wiped out the lot. Not one syllable remained, except in Jeff's head. "Well, it worked at the Texas Cowboys game last weekend," our hapless operator offered somewhat unhelpfully. Jeff's face was getting redder and he looked as if he was about to explode in a similar fashion to a V16 BRM.

After about 20 minutes, all attempts at finding it in the memory of this new whizz bang machine had failed and Jeff – as they would say in modern parlance – finally lost it! Once he had calmed down, he had to start writing the whole story again and this time the operator had the instructions to hand.

But this was just one of many numerous press office incidents that kept us amused 35 years ago. One befell *The Guardian*'s Formula 1 reporter Maurice Hamilton at Monza. The big news agencies like the Press Association, Reuters and all the Fleet Street national papers had a group of people called copytakers. They sat at a rows of desk, headsets on – sometimes as many as thirty of them – each with an Underwood typewriter. As a reporter you phoned through to the paper and were connected to the next available person.

One minute they would be tapping out a story being dictated from some war torn country and next could be a sports story. Some of them were brilliant and knew all the spellings of difficult names and so on. At Monza you went to a desk filled in a little chit and they placed a call for you to your newspaper – you might then have to wait for half an hour for the call to come through. You then went to a phone booth.

"Senor Hamilton, booth number five please." Maurice went straight through to the copytakers and crisply dictated his 500 or so words for tomorrow's paper. After that you always asked to be put through to the sports desk to warn them the story was coming through and try to persuade the deputy sports editor to give it a prominent place on the sports pages. But when Maurice gave the name of the chap he wanted to speak to he was firmly told there was no one of that name at the paper.

A little confused he asked "That is *The Guardian*" . "No mate", came the reply "This is the Daily Mirror". The Monza telephone operator had mixed up the phone calls and poor Maurice had to start the whole process again. But we never found out if *The Guardian* had actually received the Mirror's story.

It was such a copytaker who, as I related in my introduction, who gave me the title for this book "Is there much more of this?" I was reading an article written by the media observer Roy Greenslade the other day and, apparently, I was far from the only journalist to be wearily asked this question.

Of course the digital age wiped out virtually all the Fleet Street copytakers at a stroke in the mid-'80s complete with people like despatch riders. Before photographs could be transmitted digitally in fractions of a second, newspaper had a fleet of motorcyclists. I remember when I was running the Press Office at the British GP, they would start arriving about ten minutes before the end of a race. The race over, the photographer would pull the film out of his camera and hand it to the guy who would then roar back to Fleet Street to get it developed.

Top US artist Lee Roy Nieman produced the art work for the Dallas Grand Prix poster and other races too. ***Andrew Marriott***

At *Motoring News*, when we were at some far off race like the Argentine Grand Prix, we would hand films to a driver or team boss who was catching a plane out that night and arrange for someone to meet him in arrivals at Heathrow. Sometimes no one was going so we actually went to the airport and looked for a friendly face in the London check-in queue and ask if they would take this package of films back for us. Unbelievably back in those pre-terrorist there was always someone to oblige.

But I still see anguished looks in media centres when computers have crashed – so nothing really changes.

Chapter 13

FORESTRY TALES

Crazy days as a co-driver and we won some silverware too.

It seems quite a few of my chapters start with "...and a bloke phoned me," and this particular tale of my days as a rally co-driver has at least three of them, without which we wouldn't really have a story.

It starts with a phone call from a mate way back in 1972. His name was Colin Vandervell, son of the industrialist and founder of Vanwall racing car Tony Vandervell. As I have recounted in a previous chapter he had huge but unfulfilled talent as a single-seater racer but despite managing his track efforts I had no idea he had done a bit of rallying as a university student.

"Andy," he said down the line, "you are going to co-drive for me in this year's Lombard RAC Rally." While I knew a bit about rallying and even shared a flat at the time with two of the top co-drivers in Britain, including one who had actually won the RAC Rally, I had never navigated/co-driven in my life. I was a racing man, I wasn't overly keen on being catapulted through the forests on a dark November night.

But with Colin it was hard to say no. He already had a plan. He would have top rally preparations guy Rod Cooper of Supersport convert his Escort Mexico racer into a rally car. This orange machine, sponsored by the somewhat unlikely Potterton Boilers, still bore the scars of a gruelling season trading paint with the likes of Jody Scheckter and Gerry Marshall among others. But I thought that if I did compete, it would make a good story for *Motor Sport*.

It turned out that Colin had briefly rallied a Volvo PV544 and he recounted how his co-driver had jumped out of the car at the end of one stage and run screaming into the forest, never to be seen again. Colin thought this was very funny! Anyway, he sold that car to Williams designer Patrick Head. With a little trepidation, I accepted.

My first ever rally, competing with Colin Vandervell in his ex-racing Escort Mexico in the 1972 RAC Rally. We retired when the gearbox broke but were leading our class. ***Marriott Archive***

In the hot seat complete with my full face Griffin helmet. ***Marriott Archive***

With the power of the press behind me back in those balmy days, the boys at Belgrave Square, where the Motor Sport Association was then based, decided I could have a licence – the fact I had never even sat in a rally car wasn't even a factor. Then it started to get serious. Flatmates Brown and Davenport gave me a real crammer course and I headed off and bought a load of OS maps.

Colin suggested we go and practice and, about a month before the event, we headed off to the blindingly fast complex of roads on the Epynt Army ranges in Powys, which we knew would be part of the route. This was when you competed on the RAC blind, without pace notes or a recce, but I don't think we realised practising it was actually illegal. I later learned that some dastardly co-drivers wrote their pace notes on rice paper and ate them as they crossed the finish line. Epynt was all narrow tarmac road and don't think we tried the car on any loose surface until the event started.

With no known rallying success, but as something of a publicity crew, we were seeded at number 132 out of the 200 cars entered. Back then, the event embraced over 70 special stages and

Disappointed, dejected and dishevelled. With Colin Vandervell after we retired from the 1972 RAC Rally in the Potterton Boilers Escort Mexico. We started at number 132 and were leading our class. ***Marriott Archive***

was spread over the best part of five days. We were entered in Group 1, class 2. The service crew consisted solely of my former March F3 chief mechanic Humphrey in a Mini van.

Off we set, and it soon became apparent that Vandervell was as much at home in the forests as he had been around the streets of Monaco. We almost caught a couple of cars on the shorter early stages but, when we got into the longer sections, we were overtaking people all over the place. On one stage in Wales, we passed no fewer than five competitors. By the end of the second day we were leading the class. This was all too much for the gearbox and it gave up on the famous Pickering stage in Yorkshire.

As I wrote in my article at the time, it had been terrifying but I had caught the bug. There is nothing like the smell of baked mud on the exhaust system! Colin said we would have another go next year but in a full Group 4 Escort.

A couple of days after the magazine report came out, this bloke phones me. He says his name is Andy Dawson and he liked the article, and asked if I wanted to co-drive for him in the coming year's Escort Mexico Championship. I couldn't do all the rounds due to F1 commitments, but I said I was game.

I quickly found out this Dawson was pretty serious about his rallying. At the first event the night before the rally, most of the rivals were in the bar downing pints but we were out in the hotel car park practising wheel changes in case we got a puncture on a stage.

We quickly became firm friends and, while I can't claim to be the world's greatest co-driver by a long chalk, I seemed to bring him luck. Plus I think I was able to use some psychology to get the best out of an ebullient character who was never happier than getting into a controversy or moaning about his rivals, officialdom and goodness know what else. As well as being one of rallying's fastest emerging talents, he was an outstanding engineer.

The records show we won two international events together and both were pretty unusual. The first was the 1976 Mintex International Rally. We were contracted to Datsun (now Nissan) but, for some reason, they didn't want to enter that event so we were able to pick up a ride in the fabulous wedge shaped Ferrari-engined Lancia Stratos run by Chiswick sports car dealer and race team The Chequered Flag.

It was a wild ride and we were in a huge battle at the front with the

Andrews Heat for Hire Escort crewed by Russell Brookes and my old flat mate John Brown. On one stage, we actually met one of the doctor's cars coming straight at us down the track but fortunately he dived into a ditch. Later, the rear bodywork of the Stratos came up and acted as an air brake.

Victory was all down to the final stage at the Oliver's Mount motorcycle race track outside Scarborough. I don't remember the exact details, but there was some talk of the stage being annulled, perhaps because of the fog. We had taken the lead on that very last section, so if it stayed in the event we won, if it was scrubbed we were second.

Back at the Grand Hotel in Harrogate, the stewards deliberated and eventually decided the stage would count – we had scored the first ever victory for a Stratos on gravel and, for the Chequered Flag, their first rally win. By now it was past midnight and the prizegiving was at the top of some grand staircase with the Lady Mayor officiating.

Remember, it has been a long night waiting for the results and the beer had flowed for some. As we started to walk up the stairs, a very drunk rally driver on a balcony about three floors above decided to urinate – the Lady Mayor's hat never smelled very good after that. Then, when we were a few steps from the top, two Norwegian competitors who had been sitting near the presentation table, simultaneously

This was a publicity shot prior to the 1976 RAC Rally. I had sourced sponsorship for our factory Datsun from Ralgex, a muscle rub cream which they still sell. Andy Dawson is on the right. Roger Clark won that year. ***Marriott Archive***

passed out and rolled down the stairs either side of us.

The following morning, The Chequered Flag boss Graham Warner decided he wanted to have photographs taken with us spraying champagne and holding the trophies. Once this photoshoot was over, we handed the cups over so they could be displayed in Chiswick. But then Graham also asked for the Flag rally jackets back so we had to peel them off, which I thought was I bit cheapskate.

Our next event in the Stratos was at the Granite City Rally near Aberdeen and we reckoned another win was on the cards as the car would have good traction in the snow. Stage one, corner one and Dawson hung the tail out a bit far and the rear hit a large rock hidden in the white stuff and snapped the rear upright. Game over.

Our other big win was in South Africa. This bloke by name of Arthur Abrahams called me out of the blue. He was the competitions boss of Castrol SA at the time and he had knew about Avon and Texaco Tour of Britain events which I had helped organise. He had joined forces with British Airways and was putting together a similar event embracing all the best race tracks from Kyalami to Killarney, plus some fantastic stages. He wondered if we would consider driving one of the factory Mazda entries for the Sigma Motor Corporation. One of our team mates would be Jody Scheckter. There

Success with Dawson. In the middle and at the end of the 1976 Mintex International Rally which we won in the Chequered Flag Lancia Stratos. On the right Andy on the track in the 1977 Tour of South Africa, in the Sigma Mazda – which we also won. ***Marriott Archive***

were entries from all the top South African rally drivers, including Sarel van der Merwe and Alfa Romeo driver Jan Hettema, who turned out to be our biggest rival. Also coming from the UK was Tony Pond.

Dawson was an excellent all-rounder and I think we led all the way. We started with a win at Kyalami, but the most memorable victory was at the old South Africa Grand Prix track at East London which was re-opened specially for the event. It was Jody's home town, but Andy managed to beat him; I don't think our team mate was too happy. A little later and he beat us on a stage – he was ecstatic. Another key section was a huge stage called Joubert Pass in the Eastern Cape. It started in the little town of Lady Grey, where the local Women's Institute had laid on a magnificent afternoon tea.

We were the first car over this mountain pass – the third highest in South Africa and we climbed up over 2000 metres and then down into the veldt and then up again to the finish in Barkly East some 40 fabulous kilometres. When we got to the end of the stage, amazingly there was a gaggle of spectators and an ice cream van. We leapt out of the car and I quickly bought two ice cream cornets and we sat on the bonnet of the Mazda licking the cones. We waited about four minutes and Hettema in the Alfa arrived – we had destroyed him on that stage. Call me big-headed, but it was a brilliant piece of psychology. When he saw us he knew it was all over.

Other memorable rally moments included a fifth place overall on the 1977 Lombard RAC in the Cariba at Woolworth Escort RS1600 – a sort of satellite Ford factory entry. But for an off in the Lake District, we were on for a possible podium finish but it was still a great result. But we were almost disqualified at the start beneath the old twin towers of Wembley Stadium.

I had pulled off a good sponsorship deal with Woolworths, then a major high street name, which was using it to promote its own-brand fruit crush – it was horrible stuff. In fact, it smelt pretty similar to Woolworths Sabre men's aftershave which we had promoted on the Avon Tour of Britain Capri. Woolworths was throwing a good deal at this sponsorship and had lined up some promotions girls to follow us around and distribute samples. One was Miss Great Britain. Ever the publicist, I suggested she and her promotion girl mate sit on the bonnet as we drove away from the start – a great photo opportunity. But then an official intervened and said we would be disqualified for "outside assistance." It makes you weep.

On the attack in the 1977 Lombard RAC Rally with Andy in the Cariba at Woolworth Escort RS1600, a works development car. We were as high as third and after a Lake District off we eventually finished fifth overall. ***Marriott Archive***

There is an engine in there somewhere. Phil Cooper and I check the electrics of the factory Morris Marina after it stopped in the Sutton Park Ford. ***Marriott Archive***

This was my last RAC Rally. As well as competing with Colin Vandervell and Andy, I also co-drove the event and as part of the British Leyland factory team in a Morris Marina with a brilliant bloke called Phil Cooper. For that event, I did a deal for the car to be backed by BBC Radio Sport – this was before Radio 5 Live. The general idea was that, at certain times during the day, I would jump out of the car, find a phone box and call into the rally report programme being hosted back at Broadcasting House by my work colleague Barrie Gill.

The whole deal almost collapsed on about the third stage when we hurtled through the famous ford in Birmingham's Sutton Park and ground to a halt with flooded electrics. Luckily, we finally got it fired up again and eventually finished fourth in class behind three Skodas. But more rewarding was winning a decent trophy for the best media promotion of the event.

I also won a trophy the following year for the highest place media person on the rally. This time Dealer Team Vauxhall asked me to co-drive for an important General Motors executive called Bob Walker, an American brought over to run its Ellesmere Port Vauxhall plant. He'd done a bit of club rallying and wanted to do the RAC – I think he only got an entry because he arranged for a stage around the factory.

Anyway, the DTV people reckoned he needed a 'professional' co-driver to help him.

Frankly, he wasn't up to the job. For a start, he didn't even have an intercom in his helmet. I managed to get him a free Griffin lid wired for sound. Unfortunately, he told me his wrong head size and the helmet was too small. So he bound his head with a bandage so he could squeeze in on and protect his ears and he hardly took the crash hat for the duration. He also attacked various gate posts and in Dalby Forest and refused to put the dreaded Chevette into top gear because "It was more controllable in third!"

We were running back at about number 176 and when we got to a major halt at Aviemore in deepest Scotland, snow thick on the ground. Bob said he just couldn't go on. It didn't help that both rear shock absorbers were broken. Anyway, I got the DTV boys to fix that and he still said he couldn't continue. But I knew all the other entries for the new media award had retired and I really wanted to add that to my trophy collection. There was only one thing for it: I started to punch him – and I am not a violent man. So we continued and I did indeed collect a decent cup!

Co-driving on the 1973 RAC Rally with American GM executive Bob Walker who really didn't get the hang of rallying. At least I was well paid and won the prize for the highest placed journalist. We started at number 169 and finished 76th with Prince Michael of Kent a few places in front of us. ***Marriott Archive***

My shortest ever co-drive was for James Hunt on the 1974 Avon Tour of Britain. James had won the previous year's inaugural event in Richard Lloyd's Chevrolet Camaro. We put together a deal for him to compete in a Vauxhall Magnum sharing a car with disc jockey Noel Edmonds – back then, his breakfast show was about the biggest thing on the radio. He was also a pretty handy saloon car racer, so he could share the driving if James got bored.

The event was to start from the Holiday Inn, Great Barr, on the outskirts of Birmingham at 8.30am and Noel would actually present his radio show from the hotel. There was only one problem: he didn't come off the air until 9am. The first competition section was a race at Silverstone at about 9.30am. There was talk about letting James drive to the track on his own, but the worry was that he would set off for London to find 'comfort' with one of his many conquests. So yours truly got the job of navigating him to the Northamptonshire track while Noel, after finishing his programme, jumped in a helicopter and was waiting there to meet us. From then, I continued my job as press officer which included spreading the news that the Magnum had hit a tree in Thetford Forest. I later heard that James had done this deliberately as the car wasn't very competitive and he had fallen out with Noel.

But back to Andy Dawson, he had the offer to compete in the World Championship for Datsun/Nissan in the 1978 season and asked if I would co-drive for him. But it was not something I could do as well as the sports marketing

At CSS we put a deal together for James Hunt and Noel Edmonds to compete together in the Tour of Britain. When the event started Noel was still doing his Radio 1 breakfast show. ***Marriott Archive***

On the attack in a factory Datsun Violet on the way third place in the 1976 Scottish International rally with Andy. We finished just behind Russell Brookes and Roger Clark in their Escorts after a big battle with Pentti Airikkala in another Escort. ***Marriott Archive***

business, which had really taken off. Looking at the long term, I decided to stay with CSS and hung up my helmet – but it was a tough decision.

I kept in touch with the sport, reporting and commentating as well as running PR campaigns and press offices for various organisations including for Network Q and the Texaco Tour of Britain. Then, in 1984, I got another of those unexpected phone calls. It was Mike Baker from British American Tobacco, who we worked with on the John Player Special account. "What do you know about rallying in China?" he asked. This turned out to be one of the biggest adventures of my life, as I'll recount in the next chapter.

Our two-car Fiesta team dominated the MPG Marathon in 2018. Paul Clifton won the best MPG category in the diesel car, we won the petrol section. ***Ford Motor Company***

All this rally experience later put proved valuable. We went on to produce a regular programme on Sky Sports called *Rally Fever*, with my producer Caroline Samuels doing most of the hard work and picking up the odd award too.

Even in the last ten years, that know-how has been put to very good use. I re-united with Andy Dawson for the annual two-day fuel economy event called the MPG Marathon. We ran the factory effort for Ford between 2011 and 2018, winning everything including best improvement over manufacturer's figures – believe it or not in a Ford Mustang to a best ever MPG award in a Ford Fiesta. We also able to assist one of the BBC's Transport Correspondents and a couple of up and coming formula racers to win the event.

In 2016 Dawson and I won the Best Improvement Over Manufacturer's Figures class in the factory Ford Mustang, seen here at Silverstone. We achieved 36.6 mpg, an improvement of 75 percent. ***Ford Motor Company***

Rallying has a secret club called Ecurie Cod Filet – founded of course by a fish merchant. There is no membership fee and no application form. They ask you to join and I am proud to be a member and attend the occasional gathering and bang on about the old days. Nothing can ever take the place of competing at the top level in something like the RAC Rally.

Chapter 14

INTO THE JUNGLE

A rallying adventure that started with stardom and finished in a mud hole.

"John Hogan's on the phone," someone shouted across the office, which was no surprise as our sports marketing business worked closely with Marlboro's rising marketing star on a number of Formula 1 campaigns, including the *Marlboro Sports Special* newspaper.

No-nonsense Australian 'Hogie', who tragically died from covid in 2021, went on to mastermind Marlboro's hugely successful grand prix campaigns and later worked for Jaguar F1 and Just Marketing with Zak Brown. He was someone who came as quickly to the point as his somewhat King George VI style delivery allowed him.

Apparently, Marlboro sponsored a rally in the land-locked South American country of Paraguay. Now this may not appear to be Marlboro's biggest market but the sales figures indicated that they actually imported enough of the cowboy's favourite smoke into that country for every Paraguayan, peasant or President, to be smoking three cigarettes simultaneously around the clock.

As well as being a health hazard in more ways than one, it was clearly impossible. So where were all the fags going? Brazil was the answer, smuggled across the border due to import restrictions. The Brazilians liked their Marlboros, possibly something to do with Hogie's campaigns with Emerson Fittipaldi.

John, of course, didn't tell me this at the time, just that Paraguay was strategically important to Philip Morris, the company behind the big US brand. This was the reason he had promised the Marlboro Paraguay boss Señor Supercig (not his real name) a world-class entry for his rally in the form of a gorgeous Lancia Fulvia HF to be driven by Sandro Munari no less. Except that Lancia boss Cesare Fiorio had just called to say there was a problem and he couldn't send the car after all. Hogan remembered I was rallying with a guy called Andy Dawson when I wasn't rushing around the F1 tracks of the then pre-Bernie world.

"I need you to get me out of the Paraguayan sh... sh... sh," said Hogan. Ultimately we did get him out of it, although we finished up in the South American brown and smelly ourselves, but that is racing forward. A quick call to my rallying mate Dawson followed. At the time, he was the reigning Kleber Tyres Rally Scholar of the Year, and I thought he might fancy an all cigarette-funded trip to a South American rally. Andy's scholarship back then in 1974 came with the loan of a works prepared Datsun Violet rally car. The car was for use in a British campaign so Andy needed to get permission from the Japanese company's competition manager Mr Wakabayashi to fly it to a South American dictatorship.

The only problem was that Wakasan didn't share our enthusiasm for this event, or maybe he knew that there was strong opposition in the form of a factory Toyota, which had dominated the event the previous year and was expected to do so again. Cut it any way you like, he said no.

What I should add at this point is that Mr Hogan's phone call to me came just over two weeks before the cars were due to be flagged away from the centre of Asunción. If you are a *University Challenge* fan, you will know that is the capital of Paraguay. Further, it had taken the Japanese three or four days to decline competing in this world-famous event, so time was pretty short.

The previous year, we had competed in the UK in an ex-works Hillman Avenger and Dawson still had quite a lot of spares for the model. To cut short a story which involved a lot of all-nighters and ducking and diving, a week later the two Andies – that's Dawson and me, not the South American mountain range settled into a pair of first class seats on an Iberia 747.

As the Pratt and Whitneys blasted us out of Madrid bound for Asunción, we were secure in the knowledge that in the cargo hold was a rally-prepared Hillman Avenger, although this Avenger had become a Dodge Polara. Remarkably, considering the short lead time, we had talked to the Paraguayan Chrysler importer who told us they sold the Avenger as a Dodge and would contribute to the budget and provide a

EL PODIO

UN SAFARI POR LA SELVA PARAGUAYA

Marlboro Trans-Chaco: El Rally mas pulverizante del siglo.

The gun-toting Juan Carlos Calvo. *Corsa*

Our Hillman Avenger cum Dodge Polara in action on the start order deciding Rallysprint. Andy was fastest so despite our Number 33 we started first. Unfortunately this crumpled photograph is the only shot I have from the whole event. ***Andrew Marriott***

service crew. In the Avenger's boot were a few spares and, importantly, my lucky leather rally boots. I'd also managed to arrange for my Brazilian girlfriend Eliza to join us and look after the interpreting and manage the catering.

But this incredible adventure was only just beginning. As we touched down at Asunción, we were greeted by the massed ranks of the Paraguayan media. They were getting a double bang for their buck, two allegedly famous European rally stars and a genuinely celebrated Paraguayan football star, fresh from a hat-trick for Real Madrid, on the same plane.

No more than 30 minutes later, we were all in a television studio as guests on a bizarre lunchtime programme which involved us eating a fat steak while being interviewed, interspersed with tunes from Paraguay's answer to The Beatles. My mother always told me not to speak with my mouth full but I couldn't help it. My O-level Spanish seemed to go down rather well and they didn't seem to mind we'd been on a plane all night.

Next stop was our hotel, which I thought was a Ramada. It was actually called the Itaenramada and had nothing to do with the US chain. Nevertheless, it was the luxury befitting world rally stars. I just checked on Trip Advisor, it's still there but has since sprouted a Casino. That night, we were whisked off to a major cabaret spot where the spotlights picked us out in the audience and the main act was the best plate-spinning routine I have even seen. Mind you, I haven't seen many.

The following morning we were brought back to reality with a bump. Our Marlboro minders had, apparently, bribed the wrong officials, so the car was still stuck in customs and we would miss the recce. This would be something of a set-back, as the Trans-Chaco was a tough three-day 2500km event through the South American jungle, not something you wanted to tackle without some prior knowledge.

The second part of the bad news didn't worry us so much. Apparently, President Alfredo Stroessner, the dictator who controlled Paraguay for 30-odd years, was delayed checking out his Swiss bank accounts and would not be waving us off at the start. But they'd found a substitute, a South American racing driver called Fangio.

I don't really remember the next couple of days apart from attending a fashion parade by the side of the pool, finally getting the Polara out of customs, and finding out that we needed to carry a survival kit of food and liquids in the car. We also learned that the starting order of the rally was based on the performance at a rallycross event. Mr Dawson had done a bit of rallycross in his time, but was worried the Polara would be no match for the factory Toyota Celica, to be driven by a previous winner of the Trans-Chaco or even the professional looking entries from Fiat Argentina.

We had discovered that Toyota's ace Juan Carlos Calvo was generally considered something of a big head and that the locals, far from cheering on their own, wanted us to whip his Paraguayan posterior. On then to the pre-event rallycross Andy, spurred on by sipping copious amounts of a curious brew called Yerba maté made from holly, set the fastest time of the day. Quite where they grow holly in South America we never did discover. At the end of his run – no co-drivers in the cars – Dawson was dragged from the car by enthusiastic fans. At first, we thought it was a lynch mob but in fact they carried him shoulder high to the podium. He has put one over the dreaded Calvo.

I have since realised that I should have been concentrating on that maté stuff. I could have imported it, put it in a can, called it Red Sheep or Bull or something, owned two Grand Prix

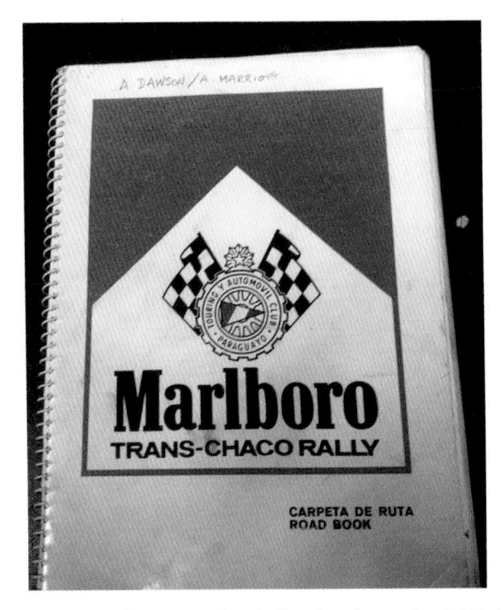

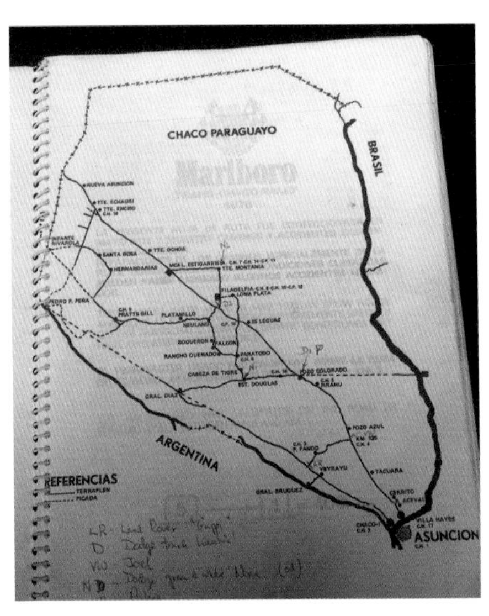

The Trans-Chaco roadbook showing the route of this incredibly tough event based on the capital Asunción.

Andrew Marriott

teams and been one of the richest men in the world!

We would start the rally number one on the road. The cars were taken to a parc fermé for an afternoon start the next day. Eliza prepared our survival pack with everything from apples to cheese sandwiches. We had lunch with Fangio (again the schoolboy Spanish helped) and then set off to pick up the car. I was wearing my lucky boots, hardly appropriate for the 40-degree temperatures. The drive from the parc fermé to the centre of Asunción was a few kilometres and enough to notice the Halda distance-measuring device was not working.

Dawson quickly figured out the drive cable must be broken and a swift inspection confirmed this to be the case – except that it had been done deliberately with a hack saw. The parc was not so fermé! It was the start of quite a few dirty tricks. We drove to the start to be mobbed by thousands of rally fans all wanting to get a sight of these gringos in the Polara. In a pre-start radio interview, we told our tale of woe and said we needed a Polara speedo cable to fix it. Ten minutes later we had eight of them!

Fangio flagged us away for the first 8km stage to a ferry crossing. I had no problems with the navigation: Dawson just drove between the walls of people! On the rickety ferry we fitted the speedo cable and SS2 had us heading north towards the Chaco through rolling pampas. At the end of the stage, we were definitely in the lead but had two rear shock absorbers poking through the wheelarches. Dawson attempted a fix, temporarily delayed when a venomous snake joined him under the car.

The next stage was into the Chaco jungle proper, a massive stage of over 200km. Some of our rivals were taking

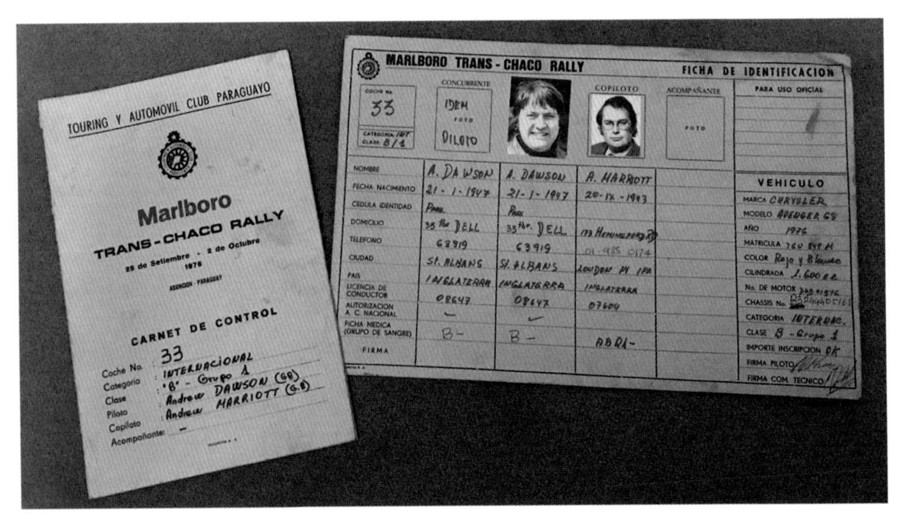
TOURING Y AUTOMOVIL CLUB PARAGUAYO

Marlboro
TRANS-CHACO RALLY
29 de Setiembre - 2 de Octubre
1976

CARNET DE CONTROL

Coche No. 33
Categoria INTERNACIONAL
Clase 'B' - Grupo 1
Piloto Andrew DAWSON (GB)
Copiloto Andrew MARRIOTT (GB)
Acompañante –

MARLBORO TRANS - CHACO RALLY — FICHA DE IDENTIFICACION

	CONCURRENTE	PILOTO	COPILOTO
NOMBRE	A. DAWSON	A. DAWSON	A. MARRIOTT
FECHA NACIMIENTO	21-1-1947	21-1-1947	20-IX-1943
DOMICILIO	35 St. DELL	35 St. DELL	
TELEFONO	63919	63919	
CIUDAD	ST. ALBANS	ST. ALBANS	LONDON
PAIS	INGLATERRA	INGLATERRA	INGLATERRA
GRUPO DE SANGRE	B-	B-	AB RH-

VEHICULO
MARCA CHRYSLER
MODELO DODGE
AÑO 1976
CATEGORIA INTERNAC.
CLASE B - Grupo 1

I still have the official Carnet de Control and Fica de Identification – just to prove I didn't make all this up.

Andrew Marriott

The Trans-Chaco is still a fixture on the South American rally schedule and these days the cars have bodywork protection – although the crowd control remains somewhat limited. The Chaco jungle is a vast area covering over 300,000 square miles. ***TCR***

shortcuts, locking gates and generally not behaving in a sporting way. After one of the toughest nights of rallying ever, we emerged on to the Chaco Highway in the lead but found our service crew had failed to make it and we were virtually out of fuel. But on this wide dirt road, we found a garage and filled up with some of the lowest octane fuel on the planet.

Within a few kilometres, the engine was telling us it didn't like the stuff, it probably would have preferred the maté, and a few minutes later we couldn't avoid driving into a huge mud hole. In our efforts to extract the car, it overheated and cooked the head gasket: game over.

While waiting for assistance, I suggested we might have one of Eliza's cheese sandwiches from our survival kit, which was in a big cool box packed with ice. What a sight! The ice had all melted, the sandwiches and the rest of the food had been pulped into an unsavoury porridge by the pounding of the Chaco, and we ceremoniously poured this contents into the putrid mud hole, whereupon an unmolested apple popped to the surface.

The jungle adventure was over and we were towed backed to Asunción. John Hogan's face had been saved: we'd given Marlboro plenty of exposure and had the trip of a lifetime.

Calvo won the rally for a second year running but at one stage he too got stuck in a mud hole just a few metres short of the time control. The marshal refused to book him in. Calvo returned to his Celica, took out a gun and shot the official in the leg. It got him a six-month suspension of his licence but he still won the rally. The Argentine motoring magazine Corsa even had a photo of him waving the gun.

The luxurious Itaenramada hotel is still one of Paraguay's best places to stay. ***Itaenramada***

I left my favourite rally boots in the car caked in the Chaco mud. When the Avenger finally returned to the UK, they were missing! Someone in the back streets of Asunción is probably still wearing them.

Chapter 15

CHINESE ADVENTURE

Sea slug, Stig and super stages, rallying comes to China.

I just knew we were going to crash – probably in the next ten minutes or so. I just hoped it wasn't going to hurt. We were in this Toyota minibus bumping along a dirt road somewhere in Hunan Province in the middle of China. As well as yours truly, there was my client Mike Baker from British American Tobacco, Wilfred Wan from their Hong Kong office, a film crew led by Alistair George Akers-Douglas, the 4th Viscount Chilston and actor turned producer Hal Hamilton. There were also and a couple of Chinese motoring journalists, although I rather doubt they had ever driven a car.

We were on a reconnaissance of the route for the forthcoming 1985 Hong Kong-Beijing Rally deciding on filming locations and checking out other logistics. We also had the two minibus drivers – one from Hong Kong and the other from Beijing. Unfortunately, Driver 1 only spoke Cantonese and Driver 2 was fluent in Mandarin and they seemed to communicate mainly by making marks on the palm of their hands.

But one thing they did not seem to communicate about was actually changing gear in this little 10-seater. You see, on the gearknob it had inscribed 1-2-3-4-O-R. The O was short for overdrive but it was actually fifth gear. The R was for reverse but, of course, our drivers did not know the Latin alphabet.

So we drove out of Hong Kong, through the border and somehow changing the side of the road as we went, and set off with our Hong Kong driver using only the first four gears. When we got on the open road, and dodging the occasional tractor, the Japanese motor was screaming its guts out. We shouted 'change gear' to no avail and we concluded the guy was probably afraid of trying either O or R in case he put it in reverse.

Later, our second driver took over and he had no problem at all cranking it into fifth gear but, for some reason, only used one side of the gate. So he went first, third and then to O, which worked rather better. But his driving was certainly erratic and there were dangers lurking around every corner – which ranged from massive pot holes to one bloke who had a dead pig on the back of his bike. Fortunately we gave that a wide birth.

This way to the Great Wall of China with the final control nearby. ***CSS Archive***

We rounded another corner to be confronted by a mini-tractor thing being overtaken by a truck coming head on at us. Our driver reacted quickly and swerved off the road and into a paddy field with quite a splash. The Toyota finished up on its side, everyone seemed to be alright, although some of the film crew's aluminium boxes had taken a pounding. Not being an expert in the production of rice, I wasn't sure how deep the water was, which was now seeping into the van.

I didn't explain that, as foreigners, we were considered deeply suspicious and, although the rally had the full backing of the Chinese government, we were being followed by a car of secret plain clothed police. Thirty seconds later, they were on the scene, did a lot of shouting at the drivers, and helped us clamber out of the passenger door.

By now, half the nearby village had stopped tending the paddy fields, slaughtering ducks or pigs or whatever they were doing and came to take a look at this curious sight. They too got shouted out by the secret police and, the next thing we knew, the rest of the village had not only arrived but tied a sturdy rope to the front of the vehicle. It was dragged back onto the track bumped back on its wheels and less than half an hour afterwards we were heading for a place called Li Ling. The minibus did smell a bit after that.

A little dazed, we finally arrived at our accommodation for the night, the Li Ling Porcelain Workers' Guest House No 5. The No 5 did not indicate the number of stars it might have got if

Our four Chinese rally trainees in a class room session. ***CSS Archive***

The route of the 555 Hong Kong Rally took the cars through this arch in the Grand Wall of China under the watchful eye of the military. ***CSS Archive***

Trip Advisor had existed back then, but maybe was an indication of the size of the cockroaches in reception. Waiting to fill in some paperwork, we did idly bet on which roach would make it up the wall first.

Finally, I checked in to the room I was sharing with Hal and was pleasantly surprised to find it was en suite. We were quite impressed with the shower pressure, but the shower head was perilously close to a flex with some bare wires. Was this actually some kind of Chinese torture chamber?

I don't think this establishment had received Western visitors before and they were very excited and had prepared a special dinner – it must have been their signature dish, a large duck which had been delicately carved into many portions and then re-assembled back into the shape of a duck which arrived on a large silver salver. Somehow they had re-attached the neck and head complete with a somewhat charred beak. Frankly, it was a work of art and looked pretty tasty and the texture, we hoped, better than the first course which was, apparently, of sea slug. This is a dish I would not recommend. As I said, it was a large duck and some was left over.

As we departed the following morning, we were handed a packed lunch and one was specifically presented to Alistair Chilston. Somehow, they must have cottoned on to the fact that he was a member of the British aristocracy, so the brown paper bag probably contained an extra helping of now day-old sea slug.

Off we set again taking in the amazing scenery and regularly avoiding several accidents until we reached a spot which was going to be the start of a special stage and a possible filming location. We settled down to our Chinese picnic. The 4th Viscount reached into his serving, and do you know what he pulled out? It was the duck's neck and head complete with that blackened beak. It was obviously a very special treat befitting his status.

That afternoon we headed towards Wuhan, which was already a large city but back then no Europeans had heard of it. Twice I thought we would die. The first was a horn blaring near miss with a truck but the second was a very close encounter with a bridge parapet. Amazingly, we made it to what was the only five-star western style hotel in Wuhan.

After a decent shower – no bare wires this time – we headed to the bar. Over a decent Scotch, I told my client Mike that, although BAT was a marvellous client and this was a great adventure, I was a father with a young family and there was no way I was getting back on that minibus. His response was immediate. "Thank god," he said, "we are going to find a plane and fly the rest of the way to Beijing." And we did.

At this point, I should probably add that climbing aboard a clapped out CAAC Iluyushin Il-18 Russian turbo-prop plane was only marginally safer than getting back on the minibus. I found out later that NATO reporting name for this type of plane was Coot. We did get a sandwich on the flight and the filling was duck – so maybe that was the reason.

Unsurprisingly, we made it to our Beijing hotel, this time a stark state-owned place, before the rest of the party arrived. Somehow they had survived but not before the mini van had been launched off a pile of gravel left in the road and finished up on its side again.

My last memory of the trip was checking out of the hotel. On the reception was a shiny new computer screen. The man behind it needed to add up my considerable phone bill – somehow we had got through to London a couple of times – and he promptly put his abacus on top of the computer, slid the beads around and presented me with the total.

Chapter 15

It was quite a trip, but how did this all start? Well, some months earlier I had received a call from BAT asking me what I knew about Chinese rallying. After I had responded to the effect that it didn't really exist, I got the response that maybe it could. Mike Baker and his boss Garth Coles called me to a meeting and explained that they had received a proposal from the Hong Kong AA that they sponsor a brand new first ever car rally from Hong Kong to Beijing. For both political and promotional reasons, it appealed to them and the BAT cigarette brand 555, popular in those parts, could benefit. Would I write a feasibility study?

Our Chinese crews competed in Mitsubishis prepared in Hong Kong and Lu Ning Jun gave a very good account of himself. ***CSS Archive***

We'd mostly worked with BAT on the John Player Special brand, including Formula 1. That same year, Ayrton Senna had been secretly delivered to our Covent Garden offices where he signed his contract with Peter Warr to join Lotus. So they were great clients and we were the trusted agency.

Pretty soon, I discovered that the Hong Kong AA's boss Phil Taylor was a very bright guy and had employed the enigmatic Jim Porter, best known as the co-driver to Roger Clark, to work out a route. They had both obviously done their homework and so I recommended that the event really could work. Hence a few month later I set out on that scary minibus journey.

I am pleased to say that Opel, Nissan and Toyota all agreed to enter factory cars with big-name drivers. Then I got another of those phone calls from Mr Baker. The gist of this was that Rothmans were sponsoring Opel and did I think they might win the event. Yes I did. So could we find another team who could beat them. Budget wasn't a problem, but there was a requirement that the only logo the cars could carry would be 555. No tyre manufactures decals, or anything. This ruled out the obvious candidates Audi – and they were sponsored by a rival tobacco brand.

So I got together with old rallying mate Andy Dawson who has recently parted company from running the Nissan factory team. To cut a long story short, we were able to purchase two of the previous year's World Championship winning Quattros and even hire for the number one car the reigning World Champion Hannu Mikkola.

Then came another phone call from Mike, this time enquiring about Chinese rally drivers. With no rallying, there weren't any, other than a few Hong Kong born chaps but they didn't fit the bill. Apparently a deal could be done for the Mitsubishi Hong Kong importer to run a pair of cars – if we could create the crews. To cut another long story short, a few months later we were at Heathrow with a minibus and this one wasn't going to crash into a paddy field.

We loaded onboard the very wide-eyed, first time outside of China, Lu Ning Jun, Liu Shi, Zhao Yanxiang and Zhao Wei Wei – and I don't think he was any relation to the famous artist. They all wore shiny suits and had not one word of English between them. Fortunately, we had hired a Mandarin speaker from the BBC World Service as a translator.

They had been selected because their day job was as driving instructors/ testers. But most of the training and testing was done in primitive lorries. One of the four was undoubtedly a member of the secret service and his job, apart from learning to be a rally driver, was to stop the other three leaving the hotel at the dead of night and disappearing into the kitchens of Northampton's Peking Palace eatery. But which one? We thought we knew.

Their driving skills left a something to be desired and this was going to be a mammoth task. Andy recruited a rally driver called Simon Everett (his brother is a rather famous actor) for the task. He didn't speak any Chinese, so the interpreter had to come along for the ride. Either Simon or later Andy would shout *BRRRAKE* which was then translated and then the guy would brake. It didn't really work but Andy was able to learn the Mandarin for things like 'opposite lock' and 'full throttle', which worked better. This was after they had been persuaded to exceed 30mph – which we found out was the Chinese speed limit in a truck. They were very law-abiding.

Liu and Lu were the better drivers, so they got that job while the two Zhaos became the co-drivers and were taught how to cope with a road book and tulip diagrams. In truth, the whole thing worked remarkably well. Meanwhile, Andy's team had set about giving the two Quattros a thorough rebuild. As a test session the pair of us re-united as a rally crew and took part in a single venue rally together which was a great thrill.

This fantastic episode in my life could fill a book on its own, but briefly it proved a great success. That first year Hannu Mikkola, co-driven by Arnie Hertz, dominated and finished ahead of the late Lars-Eric Torph in a factory Nissan with the Rothmans backed Opel of Erwin Weber third with Andy less than a minute behind after a few problems with the second Quattro.

On the final stage, the cars even roared through the Great Wall of China and we sprayed champagne at the finish in Tienamen Square. Even the champagne bottle had 555 branding on it. The event itself had overcome some challenges. Back then, there were no petrol stations in China, fuel had to be picked up at municipal fuel dumps. We had our own tanker carrying competition-grade fuel but basically they could not keep up with the rally and most of the stages after Wuhan had to be cancelled

Kicking up the Chinese dust. The DAD run ex-factory Audi Quattro with team boss Andy Dawson at the wheel in the 1985 Hong Kong-Beijing Rally. ***BAT***

For the next year, the plan was to run the same two Quattros and the two Chinese in Mitsubishis. But before the September event, our Chinese crews were flown to the UK to get some extra competition mileage under their belts and a pair of Peugeots 205s were hired. They were entered in the Scottish International but I was worried they wouldn't get much of a result. Thus I did a deal with the organisers for trophies (which we provided) to be awarded for the best finishers from outside Europe. As there weren't any other overseas competitors, all we needed was for one of the two pairs to actually finish. They both duly obliged in 47th and 50th places, out of the 50 finishers. I reckon the photo of them holding the trophies aloft made the front page of the *China Daily News*.

This time Hannu wasn't available but we had another World Champion in the car – Stig Blomqvist – and he totally dominated the event, winning by almost two hours over none other than our Chinese protégé Lu Ningjun in a Mitsubishi Starion. The Scottish experience had obviously helped. The event had proved really tough and only 17 of the 43 starters finished. There was one particular stage which was over 100km long, and the big concern was tyre wear. Andy set up a pre-arranged pit stop and Stig and co-driver Bruno Berglund were able to pull in have a quick drink of water and continue on fresh tyres. This is hardly a regular occurrence on a rally. Unfortunately, a possible 555 one-two-three didn't happen as Andy crashed his Quattro out of the event.

For the third and final year the decision was made to switch to a Sierra 4x4, this was before Cosworth came along with a decent engine. In retrospect, it probably wasn't the best car to pick and it needed a lot of development. Again, another World Champion was added to the driving strength with cars this time for both Stig and Ari Vatanen as Andy decided both driving and team managing was too much of a tall order.

Ari's car had a bad misfire and he soon retired, but Stig was heading for his second successive win when he ground to a halt with a mysterious electrical fault. Somehow, he got the car going again but finished third behind the works Toyota of Bjorn Waldegard and Fred Gallagher with the works Nissan of Mike Kirkland second. One more stage and Stig probably would have caught him.

The campaign also expanded into other Far East and Middle East vents with success in places like Indonesia with Dutch driver John Bosch and Australian Ross Dunkerton, who amazed us with his ability to shin up a coconut tree. But after three years BAT went in another direction – but it was certainly a challenging job well done.

Lu Ning Jun continued his rally career and went on to compete in the Paris Dakar Rally on seven occasions as the factory driver for Chery Automobile – and making it to the finish as recently as 2010. He has retired from the sport these days – but continues to exceed the 30mph speed limit.

Chapter 16

TV TIMES AND COMMENTARY COCK-UPS

Either in front or behind the camera, it was never dull.

A few years ago I did something I promised I'd never do and I am still traumatised. I Googled myself. The reason for this was that, a week or so earlier, mainly thanks to the driving skills of my old rallying partner Andy Dawson, I had won an event called the MPG Marathon, as I mentioned earlier.

It's an annual event organised by *Fleet World* magazine, policed by the RAC and one of the tracker companies, which involves driving about 480 miles over two days using as little diesel or petrol as possible, and maybe annoying and holding up the odd trucker along the way. By using some racing techniques such as drafting on the motorway sections like the NASCAR stars and some old rally know-how, we managed to achieve a record-breaking 108.9mpg in the very aerodynamic and miserly Eco-something-or-other 1.6 diesel Ford Fiesta.

I wanted to check on our press coverage on the web, and there was plenty. But this Googling is addictive and I soon found myself looking at articles I had written for a long-forgotten website several years ago, an interview I did for Motors TV about the state of World Championship rallying – in serious decline, I said. But as my search headed to page eight, I found a handful of comments in forums advising the world in vitriolic terms that I was one of the worst TV motor racing commentators of all time. I knew nothing, my delivery was rubbish and I was totally incompetent. One South African chap was particularly vicious. Different strokes for different folks, say I.

I was really depressed, but then I went on to my internet banking page to find my nice German client had paid me another decent sum for the previous month's DTM commentaries. So someone still liked me, but it did set me thinking about commentary cock-ups.

In another chapter, I discussed the perils of working the pit lane as the on-the-spot reporter. But I have also spent a good time in the commentary box over the years working on everything from Formula 1 to powerboat racing, rallying to motocross. Like most motor racing commentators I have, on occasion, said some daft things, misread race situations, stumbled over words and failed miserably on car recognition. Two of my worst cock-ups were commentating on motorcycle races.

The first came at a Mallory Park meeting for ITV several decades ago. The feature event was going to star Barry Sheene, but a horse race had been cancelled somewhere or other, so it was decided to add in a support 125cc race. Alongside me was the Bunteresque figure of Chris Carter and what he didn't know about bike racing you could write on the brown envelope that was slipped to Mr Sheene at the end of the race meeting.

In those days, the bike races were started by a push start and, on occasions, someone would get the kick instantaneously and, with a bit of luck, would emerge from qualifying grid spot 38 and lead into the first corner. Frantic looking down at the programme normally had the quick getaway artist identified within a few seconds and by lap three 'Freddy Fastarter' was back in the pack.

Remember, this Mallory Park broadcast was not on some current satellite station watched by an audience equivalent to the number of people who live in an obscure Cambridgeshire village. Back then, ITV World of Sport viewership was in the many millions as the population had nothing better to do on a Saturday afternoon. Or they were big fans of Dickie Davies. Which quickly reminds me of a phone-in show I once heard on which the hapless contestant was trying to name a TV sports star or personality from a set of clues. I think the answer was Murray Walker. The luckless contender was struggling and the radio host said: "Final clue: something you suck," thinking of the mints. Quick as a

Up close and personal with top IMSA team owner Wayne Taylor, always great for a strong quote. ***Fox Sports***

With former British F3 star Calvin Fish who has carved out an outstanding career as a TV commentator in the States. But when this shot was taken, he was still working the other end of the pits to me for the Speed Channel. ***Robin Thompson***

flash, she came back triumphantly, "Dickie Davies."

Anyway, back at Mallory. The race started and, yes, some guy in black leathers on bike 122 came out of the pack and into a lead. He was still leading as he headed through the Esses and up to the Hairpin. I looked down at my notes and entry list and there was no 122, or 22 or even 12. I looked at Chris and he made a face showing even he didn't know who the mystery rider was. But he knew the bike was a Yamaha, which helped a bit.

Five laps later, the mystery man was still out front albeit with someone challenging him. Still we had no idea who he was. Over the talkback we'd asked the truck to send someone to race control, but before we heard anything more, Mr Anonymous had the good grace to fall off his little Yamaha. We never found out his name!

On another occasion, I went to the British Motorcycle Grand Prix at Donington to catch up with some old mates and bumped into an Australian friend called Colin Young, although he usually went under the nickname of 'Woolly Hat'. He was commentating on all the races for Malaysian TV. "Join me in the commentary box for the 500cc race," he suggested. At the time, I was still up to speed on the Blue Riband category so I agreed. "In fact," said the woolly-hatted one, "come and sit in on the 125cc race just to get used to the talkback. You won't need to say anything."

This I duly did. There were about 10 minutes to go and 'Woolly Hat' welcomed the viewers in Kuala Lumpur but seemed a little hesitant. Apparently he'd been to some curry house in Leicester the night before and the vindaloo had taken a dislike to him. He was obviously in need of a trip down the corridor. "Take over," he mouthed to me, "I'll only be a couple of minutes." It was not something I had really bargained for and frankly I hadn't been following the antics of the tiddler bikes that season.

Fortunately, all the riders were on the warm-up lap and the grid caption was rolling so there was plenty to talk about. I found the section in the programme about the 125cc GP and threw in the odd fact. Now there was three minutes to go and Colin had failed to return. Two minutes to go and I had covered the weather, the grid girls, the excitement and the electric atmosphere.

With a minute to go I'd told the Malaysian viewers there weren't any Malaysians in the race, nor any Brits for that matter. In fact, half the field seemed to be Italian or Spanish.

Then the flag dropped and off they went and I was still on my own. They swept around Redgate like a pack of bees, down to the Old Hairpin where the leading bunch of about five all tumbled in one big heap. I was still trying to name the fallen riders when Colin returned with... well, let's say, a relieved look on his face. Fortunately he then took over – thanks mate!

A lot of commentaries are actually done not from a commentary box at the side of a race track but in a studio somewhere on an industrial estate behind Heathrow. The commentary box position was particularly important to a young director called Bill Hurtsman, who came from the States to look after the NBC broadcast of a round of the American Le Mans series at Donington. I was the executive producer and we had a cast of thousands – it was the biggest outside broadcast I had ever run. Bill had it in his head that the commentators' box had to be adjacent to the start/finish line.

There was a slight problem, because there was a grandstand in the way and Bill said it had to be moved – it was permanent and concrete. He then suggested we move the actual finish line, which Donington wasn't about to do. As it happened, on race day Bill failed to show having had some kind of nervous breakdown.

My first ever Formula One commentary for ITV also involved a commentary box scenario. It was the Dutch GP and certainly I was in a proper commentary box, in contact with the nearby control truck, or scanner as it is known, with all the APs and other TV land people running around. But all this happened not at Zandvoort but at Epsom Downs horse race course. In fact there were two commentary boxes, one for me and one for Brough Scott. Don't ask me why, but somehow it worked and I didn't get my Lester Piggots mixed up with my Nelson Piquets.

Of course, preparation is absolutely vital and these days I tend to have most of my notes on an iPad. But I do know commentators who do a great job with very few notes. I'm sure they have done a lot of prep and have a great memory. A strong bladder is also a key requirement. One of my former co-commentators had a maximum bladder span of about 75 minutes. It's either a trip down the corridor or bring in a bottle. I advised the former, I can hold the fort while you hold... well, you know what I mean.

There was one particular chap, no longer commentating on motorsport, but now runs a radio station, who obviously wasn't up to speed with the American Le Mans series. You may remember the Italian/American cheap-and-cheerful restaurant chain Olive Garden sponsored a bright green Ferrari 333 driven by Mimmo Schiatarella, among others. Our man decided that the driver was in fact, O-liv-e-ay Jar-dan, the French ace. The truth, I promise you.

On another occasion, the same guy, same series, saw a driver with a band across the top of his helmet with 'René Lezard' emblazoned on it. "René Lezard has just pulled into the pits for fresh tyres," he said, oblivious to the fact that René Lezard was actually the perfume brand that was the personal sponsor of the driver!

Of course, Murray Walker is famous for his occasional cock-ups, you can see them on T-shirts, coffee mugs and possibly even boxer shorts with, "If I'm not very much mistaken, etc" emblazoned on them. I am sure many of you have your own favourites, but mine is a sensory problem: "Do my eyes deceive me, or is Senna's Lotus sounding rough." Easily done I can tell you.

I get the powder puff treatment before presenting from the Silverstone TV studio. It made a change from door-stepping the show biz celebrities.
Hay-Fisher Productions

I was delighted to work with Murray a few times and co-commentated with him for Sky at a Race of Champions event at Wembley Stadium after he had retired from Formula 1. He was still up there on the rev limiter and had done plenty of research. A class act and full of some great stories from his advertising days where he was king of the jingles. Blame him for "Treats melt in your mouth not in your hand" or even Trill's "Makes budgies bounce with health."

He's not the only one to occasionally make the odd faux pas. BBC Radio's motor racing commentator James Allen, interviewing Ralf Schumacher, once asked: "What does it feel like being rammed up the backside by Rubens Barrichello?"

The veteran motorcycle commentator Jack Burnicle, talking about Colin Edwards' tyre choice at a World Superbike meeting, said, "Colin had a hard on earlier in practice and I bet he wishes he had a hard on now."

And here are a few more, just so you don't think it's only we motor racing commentators who make mistakes, or blurt out something stupid. The golf commentator Ken Brown commentating on golfer Nick Faldo and his caddy Fanny Sunnerson lining up shots at the Scottish Open: "Some weeks Nick likes to use Fanny, other weeks he prefers to do it by himself." The football manager-turned-pundit Ron Atkinson has several to his name, but I particularly like: "I never comment on referees and I am not going to break a habit of a lifetime for that prat!" or another Ronism: "He dribbles a lot and the opposition don't like it. You can see it all over their faces."

But my favourite of all time and it makes me smile every time was this from weightlifting commentator Pat Glynn: "And this is Gregoriava from Bulgaria. I saw her snatch yesterday and it was amazing."

OK, stop being silly. My first decent TV contract at World of Sport expired when the TV moguls decided to pull the programme. For them, I had commentated on Formula 1, World Championship bike racing, powerboats including the memorable live events at the London Docks (Sarah Ferguson was the PR for those events) as well as everything from near-clubbies at Mallory Park to Champ Car.

The Fox Sports pit lane quartet at the end of a Sebring 12 hours. Alongside me is Jamie Howe, Matt Yocum and Justin Bell. *Fox Sports*

Back then, the only TV opportunities were with ITV or BBC. But then along came satellite TV. Pretty soon I was at the WHSmith-owned Screensport and, while a lot of the work was voiceovers, we also did Le Mans live. Screensport was tough because it was broadcast in four languages. The commentary area, somewhere underneath Carnaby Street, had a separate booth for each language. I am not sure why it worked this way but sometimes when we were voicing to tape we all had to commentate simultaneously. If you made a mistake and wanted to stop and go back, everyone had to stop. The French bloke wasn't very popular.

Their English commentators were all freelancers, but they also had a group of full-time Dutch, French and German voiceover artists. Some specialised in just one sport like motor racing, but there were other guys who did both boxing and athletics and so on. The Dutch guys tended to be the most friendly with sometime historic race winner Allard Kalff as the lead and he was backed up on motor sport by a guy called Rick Bolt, whose previous job was handling baggage at Schipol airport. He'd lifted Jan Lammers' bag off the carousel a couple of times, so I guess that was good training.

One famous Sunday evening, I was there to call a Champ Car race at some mid-west oval. The top German guy, Stefan 'The Voice' Heinrich, had another engagement and then, at the last minute, his number two called in sick. The only German speaker on site was some burly bloke called Erich who had been there to do the earlier wrestling. Rumour had it that he was a former East German Champion who had defected. You won't be surprised to learn he wasn't exactly up to date with the latest on Al Unser and Mario Andretti.

In the five minutes he had to prepare, we sorted him out with an entry list and a CART media guide, patted him on the back (not too aggressively, you understand) and into the booth he went. After about half an hour we had the inevitable crash into the wall and out came the safety car. Pretty standard stuff.

Once it was all over and Rick Mears had recorded another win for Penske, we emerged from the commentary booths. "Erich," I asked, "how did you get on?" "OK I think, but I got a little confused after the crash and zat spectator got on the track with his Camaro, but fortunately all ze drivers knew something funny was going on so none of zem tried to pass him, then fortunately he pulled off. I told my viewers it was pretty unusual." Yes I know sometimes for the sake of a smile, I might just exaggerate a little, but this is 100 percent true.

While I was still very much in the sports marketing business with CSS,

I led a double life as a TV commentator and, increasingly, as a presenter. Sadly, Screensport was not making any money and left the airwaves but I was able to join Europsort, which at the time was in a commercial partnership with the Sky Channel, before it had its own sports outlets.

On my very first weekend working for them, I managed to be in two places at almost the same time. I commentated on a car race on the Saturday (I think it was a Grand Prix) and went back the next day and pretended to be in Suzuka for the Japanese motorbike grand prix.

On another famous occasion, there was a round of a World Sportscar race from Mexico City which we were voicing 'from the tube' when the local broadcaster switched to the commercials. The tech staff weren't quick enough to switch to our adverts and I had to try to fill over Mexican adverts for biscuits, Volkswagen and some foot powder.

I worked a Formula 1 season or two for Eurosport, sometimes commentating with John Watson, but missed the German race and suggested my then protégé James Allen as my substitute. Come the end of the year, I got a call from Richard Russell, the then-boss. The gist of it was we think you are great but James is even better, so goodbye. Lesson learned – don't recommend a stand-in who is any good. Actually, I got burned again several years later, but for a different reason.

Luckily, I then got a call from ESPN is the States to be their Formula One pits reporter with Bob Varsha and David Hobbs upstairs, as they say. Back then we were allowed our own cameraman in the pits and could interview the drivers as they climbed out of their broken cars.

Later, thanks to the huge support of Roger Moody, Sky's Deputy Head of Sport – who I had known since his Radio WM days – I moved on to a mainly production role at the channel which lasted well over ten years and during which I created and produced such weekly magazine programmes as *World Motorsports*, *Rally Fever* and *Mowlem's Racing Travels*, as well as running the studio based broadcasts for all the Indycar races and many NASCAR events plus Le Mans. For these we often had a studio, sometimes with relevant cars, guest panels and usually with the late David Bobin, former motorcycle racer Keith Huewen or the emerging talent that was Leigh Diffey in the host's chair.

The Daytona Victory Circle is always an exciting place to be. I've interviewed everyone from Dale Earnhardt to Derek Bell here. ***Robin Thompson***

As well as being an outstanding sportscar racer Johnny Mowlem – seen here after setting pole for the 2015 Rolex 24 – was a well-informed studio guest for the Indycar shows I produced at Sky. ***Andrew Marriott***

I could embarrass Keith about the programme he forgot he was hosting. I managed to find him 100 miles from the studio at a Donington Park race meeting about five minutes before we went on air. By then, I had found a young rugby presenter in the canteen to act as Keith's stand-in – his name, Simon Lazenby. He seems to be well into motor racing these days. Keith still holds the record from Donington to Osterley in a BMW, and he arrived in time to host the second part of the show. Regular guests on these shows included Johnny Mowlem, Jonny Kane, the controversial team manager Paul Cherry and, to add a bit of class, Christopher Tate.

The Sky management left me alone to manage and produce these hundreds of programmes. In fact, I think I only got called by them twice. Once was when the then Head of Sport Vic Wakling phoned me the following day after an Indycar show as a tape operator had complained that a certain Sky assistant producer had been drunk in the gallery and the other involved a reindeer.

We had shown an Arctic Rally where there was some fleeting on-board footage of the leading car hitting, and it has to be said, killing a wild reindeer that had wandered onto the track.

His rally ended right there and I thought it was relevant. But a viewer had apparently written in to complain that his daughter had been so upset by this she couldn't sleep at night. I was duly chastised.

We had some great commentators for the weekly *World Motorsports* show, particularly the man who is now the voice of the BTCC and World GT racing David Addison, as well as Ben Constanduros, Jonathan Green, drag racing commentator John Price and short oval man Dave Richardson. But I did quite a lot of it and the most challenging was the European rallying which came from a Belgian producer called Chris Courteyn.

Chris was supposed to include scripts plus translation of the foreign interviews. And usually he did. But sometimes he ran out of time. If they were Polish we were OK because the talented sound engineer Marek helped us out, but on more than one occasion we had someone like the Bulgarian Rally Champion banging on for a minute or so. Now it can be told: I just used to think what the bloke would probably say in that circumstance and just make it all up.

One of our main strands was the DTM – the German Touring Car Masters, Germany's premier series contested by teams from BMW, Audi and Mercedes. This was at the time of a huge change in the technical side of the television industry. Tape formats were changing to the groundbreaking Digi Beta and then to what is the norm today – just streams of data. The Cologne based Wige TV, which produced the DTM output, used to send the highlight tape via courier on the Monday night after every race weekend. We had some anxious moments but I don't think we ever lost one. Then they suggested they would send it via the internet. Common practice now, but groundbreaking less than twenty years ago.

Most recently I have worked on organising rather than conducting interviews for Noah Media. Here is Torqil Jones interviewing Jody Scheckter in his museum for a forthcoming film about Gilles Villeneuve and Didier Pironi. ***Andrew Marriott***

Sky Sports' very first programme which actually originated from a data stream rather than tape was a DTM race from the Norsiring. As I was the oldest Producer at Sky, I put that down as a success and it made up for showing the deer slaughter.

But I was never on the actual staff of Sky Sports, although I had my own desk there and enjoyed the best breakfasts in West London in the canteen. When CSS Television transitioned into Pit Lane Productions, we moved into offices at the back of the Sky building which were above the Bentley and Rolls Royce dealers Frank Dale & Stepsons. The smell of Castrol R occasionally drifted upstairs which was appropriate.

Over the years, I had the pleasure working with some great staff starting with Gaye Grinstead – who now has a very important job with the Olympics TV outfit – then Shanet Lewis. The 'lioness' Caroline Samuels from South Africa was my right-hand woman for eight years and there was also Stephen Slater, Ben Constanduros, Elise Biesek from Brazil and finally Hayley Squires. Most of them stayed in TV but Hayley now runs a successful London music venue and manages reggae bands.

We used Sky staff and facilities to make most of our programmes and the standard of cameramen, audio engineers and editors was top class, but I have to pick two people. The first is editor Bob Clarke, who now runs a terrific charity, the Mama Youth Project which helps troubled youngsters find a career in television production and cameraman Andrew van de Waal. We worked with many Sky cameraman but Andrew is the best, as long as you could cope with his South African humour.

But all good things must come to end and, after Sky decided to can World Motorsports as they were revving up for their huge Formula 1 commitment, we shut the office down. Despite that, I have had the occasional programme aired on one of the many Sky Sports channels in the past couple of years. They were challenging days, but there is no finer place to works in sports television than at Sky.

Chapter 17

DIESEL DICERS AND A CHILLING TALE

Truck racing, stunts and record breakers. The juggernaut jousters drew huge crowds.

He sat in front of me in my central London office with a very peculiar look in his eye. His two front teeth were missing and he told me his name was Steve Majors. He had seen the publicity I had been circulating in a bid to find stuntmen wanting to break Guinness World Records at the 1986 Multipart British Truck Grand Prix at Silverstone.

The 1985 event had been a big success, following on from the inaugural race at Donington Park the year before and the very well attended events at Brands Hatch. As the Promoter and Chairman of the British Truck Racing Association, I wanted to further ramp-up the second Silverstone event. The addition of associated events between the races was proving to be hugely popular.

I had already secured the services of a dashing Frenchman called Richard Almet who would attempt the world record for a high speed motorbike wheelie. Staying with the wheelie theme, sponsors Multipart had commissioned the build of a brand new wheelie truck called Skytrain in which Yorkshireman Steve Murty was keen to attempt a similar record. Gilbert Bataille was going to establish another record, circulating the full Silverstone GP circuit with the truck on two wheels but this time with the Leyland leaning sideways.

Someone called Wing-Commander Ken Wallis, DSO, MBE, said he could establish some record in his Autogyro, although I can't for the life of me remember exactly what it was while a mad inventor called Peter Pellandine would be stoking up his steam car in a bid to break a long-standing speed record for steam car. Sadly it failed to move an inch on the day.

I'd also arranged for the Kronenbourg Royal Marines parachute team to attempt a World Stacking record if weather conditions were favourable. Plus, a bloke was going to attempt to lift more beer barrels than anyone before him – or was it truck tyres? Thirty-five years dims the memory.

What was certain was that a chap called Mike Rouse was going to attempt to crush more cars than anyone before him with a ridiculous vehicle called Sky High. Mike sat in the bodyshell of a 1986 Ford Transit van which perched on a huge chassis. The machine was suspended on 16 huge Monroe shock absorbers controlling huge axles from a 5-ton military vehicle. The tyres were from a quarry dumper truck and were more than 5ft high and 4ft wide.

This rig was powered by a 7.5-litre Ford V8 motor producing 400bhp with massive torque, driving through a three-speed auto gearbox. When he wasn't crushing cars, he was going to rip them apart because I had hired another smaller car crusher to help pull some rust buckets into two – Sky High pulling one way and Sampson the other. More of that later. In the programme, I gushed "We are sure of one record already – the biggest ever truck racing meeting with 71 racing trucks entered – definitely a World Record".

Among the entry was former World Motorcycle Champion Barry Sheene, his mate Steve Parrish, top lady racer Divina Galica, rallycross hero Rod Chapman, historic racing star Willie Green, ex-F1 driver Slim Borgudd, Hot Rod World Champion Barry Lee, not to mention the truck racers like defending champion Richard Walker.

But let's go back to the man sitting in my office. Steve told me that he was Britain's top roller blading stuntman and had appeared in the 1982 movie *Blade Runner*. He also said he had jumped over four double-decker buses on his rollerblades. Indeed, I found a fuzzy video on the internet the other day of him doing exactly that at Long

I talked my way around Silverstone at the British Grand Prix while Gilbert Bataille two-wheeled the Leyland truck as a promotion for the forthcoming Truck Superprix. ***Leyland Vehicles***

Eaton stock car track. I was suitably impressed. He told me he wanted to set the Guinness record for high-speed rollerblading and he could do this around Silverstone with a truck as a wind break. He reckoned he could get up to 100mph. As it happens, he was something of a visionary in a way because that's what Guy Martin did in 2013 on Pendine Sands behind a truck driven by the son of one of the racers from 1986 Silverstone truck GP. Except Guy was on a push bike.

Steve then told me that he would need to practice a bit – and then I started to wonder about the missing front teeth. Had he already tried rollerblading behind a truck and got a little too close? I suggested we could find an hour at Silverstone before the event and arrange a truck. We agreed this was a good idea and I was pleased I had another record attempt in the bag and another headline for the *Star* newspaper which was our media partner – but I felt a little uneasy. He had a peculiar look about him and was just a bit weird.

A week later, he called me to say he had been thinking about it and he wanted a whole day at Silverstone to practise. So I told him politely that it wasn't an option. He became quite agitated so I said forget it. I went back to worrying where I could get enough cars to be crushed by Sky High. But Steve Majors subsequently phoned me two or three further times and finally got abusive. Definitely no World Record for him, and I thought that was the last I would hear of him.

Come the weekend of 16 and 17 August, we didn't miss Steve. On the Friday afternoon, all the racing trucks lined up nicely in the paddock and a stream of beautifully painted trucks, some with wonderful murals, were assembling for what we called the Convoy d'Elegance.

Meanwhile, a small team of us including my truck right-hand man

Steve Murty does a flame-out in the wheelie truck which was built to perform at truck events. ***Multipart***

Jonathan Reeves had assembled on the Stowe Straight for the first record attempt – Monsieur Almet's wheelie attempt. He seemed very confident. Guinness had sent along an adjudicator, a quarter of a mile was measured out, and the wind speed was definitely within the allowed limits. Watched by his girlfriend Isabelle Guyard, who also performed stunts with Richard, the red and yellow Kawasaki was fired up.

In short order, M Almet made two passes in opposite directions with an average speed of 127mph (204kph) with the front wheel about three feet off the deck. We had our first record in the book. Over the weekend, Richard, with Isabelle on his pillion, performed various other stunts. Richard is still thrilling crowds with his daring deeds.

Unfortunately, some of the other stuff did not go quite so well. Mike Rouse in Sky High did indeed crush a record number of cars but the pulling asunder of random old bangers went less well. At this point, I should explain that the other monster truck/car crusher device called Sampson had been built by Bristolian truck racer Reg Hopkins, partly from the proceeds of helping to build the M4 Motorway – as you do.

Sampson looked good but was powered by a Commer diesel engine giving about 100bhp. So we have Sky High with its 400bhp V8 chained to the front of a Vauxhall Viva and Reg's Samson chained to the back of it. I had seen something similar in the States.

I had not worked out two vital elements to this stunt. First, the car that is going to be ripped into two pieces has to be secretly weakened around the middle by some judicious angle grinding so that most of the work is already done. Second, you need two monster trucks of similar power for the deal to work.

You have probably guessed it by now. The signal was given. Both monster trucks made lots of noise and smoke but the Viva refused to be ripped apart. Instead, both it and Reg's Sampson were pulled along, churning up a load of grass and mud. The Viva remained intact and we were a little red-faced.

We sussed it out for the Sunday and the Viva was virtually collapsing in the middle while Samson was securely tethered to the ground. Finally, Ellesmere Port's finest snapped into two with the crowd roaring it on.

Meanwhile, Gilbert Bataille in the Leyland Roadrunner truck did break his record but I was pretty sure he would. The previous month, to promote the truck event, he had practised the stunt on the morning of the British Grand Prix. I was installed in the cab, complete with the radio mic and strapped in. In front of 100,000 fans, Bataille zoomed the six-wheeler along the pits straight onto a ramp which kicked the truck onto the nearside wheels and off we wavered for a complete lap with me commentating all the way round.

The one problem I had was that it was a bench seat and I was on the side of the truck which was up in the air. It took all my strength bracing my feet against the dashboard to stop sliding down into the French stuntman at the wheel. Anyway, we knew the good Gilbert could repeat the feat at the truck event and the record was broken.

I think we did crack a few other records, too. The Multipart and later ATS Silverstone Truck Grand Prix continued for another three years but without any more record breaking, except for lap records on the track. Actually, for the 1988 and 1989 events we changed the name to Truck Superprix – I suspect a certain B Ecclestone had mentioned something about using the words grand prix!

In November 2000, I received a call from a man called Detective Constable Tim Snuggs from Kensington nick who was working on something called Operation Oxborough. This was an investigation into the death of the TV personality Jill Dando. He asked if he could come and see me. I was completely mystified, but he said it was something to do with truck racing.

Anyway, PC Snuggs duly turned up the following day. He asked me if I knew someone called Barry George because they had found a scrap of paper in this guy's flat with my name and number on it, plus the words 'Silverstone truck race'. Then Snuggs said that this guy had been a stuntman and sometimes

Richard Almet with his assistant Isabelle Guyard pops a spectacular wheelie. *Richard Almet*

used the name Steve Majors.

His face and name had always stuck in my head, so I told him the story that Majors had come to see me 13 years earlier wanting to perform a stunt and that he was rather strange.

Subsequently in 2001, Barry George, who had a history of stalking female TV presenters, was convicted of Jill Dando's murder and was sentenced to life imprisonment. His conviction was finally quashed, on appeal, seven years later. I am rather glad that I denied him the chance of putting his name in Guinness Book of Records.

But let's spin the clock back a few years to 1984 and tell you how this crazy truck racing started. One of my clients at CSS Promotions was Leyland Vehicles, the truck, van and tractor manufacturer based in Lancashire. We handled their sponsorship of the Williams GP team and we enjoyed a very fruitful relationship with them.

Their marketing guys Andy Buchan and Peter Chambers (a sometimes TVR racer) phoned me one day and asked if I knew anything about truck racing which they heard had survived an initial meeting at Zandvoort, run by a fellow called Bertus van Holland. Another meeting was scheduled for Paul Ricard and they thought we should go and check it out as they were looking for a major promotion for their new parts operation called Multipart.

I have to tell you I thought the whole thing sounded both daft and dangerous in equal measure – did the trailers get sideways on in the corners? – but who turns down a trip to the south of France in the spring? Once we arrived, I quickly realised that the truckers had parked their trailers in the paddock and there was definitely something in the idea. I thought both the safety and the sporting regulations were too loose, but we were definitely onto an idea which could work well for Multipart.

Truck magazine publisher Andrew Frankl was quickly on board with his great contacts and enthusiasm, and so was John Symes, formerly track manager at Brands Hatch but then of the British motorsport governing body. He proved an invaluable ally. These days he is one of the FIA's main circuit inspectors. We founded something called the British Truck Racing Association – I think I might still be the President – to sort out the formalities.

To cut a long story short, we hired Donington Park for the inaugural race in 1984. Add into the mix a huge publicity campaign combining *Truck* magazine, *The Sun* newspaper – back then selling four million copies a day – and the massive listenership of Radio 1.

My girls – Helen, Lydia and twins Emma and Verity pose in front of Reg Hopkins' car crusher Samson. Sadly the Bristolian-built machine was no match for Sky High. *Jonathan Reeves.*

Touring car racer, the late Mike Smith, was the BBC breakfast show host at the time with a huge audience and was up for what he called racing "a block of flats". There was already a core of racers in Europe, mainly French, Italian and Dutch who were up for it. There were also several regular racers who were in the truck business and, importantly, we were able to persuade several truck manufacturers to join in. Ford backed Mike, DAF already had a promotional deal with Barry Sheene, so he came aboard, Mercedes got behind Barry Lee and Steve Parrish, Renault hired Martin Brundle and ERF had top sports car/historic racer Willie Green as their chosen man.

To enhance to the occasion, we added a truck concours, a charity van event, tractor pulling, laps by a V8 Formula 1 powered Transit van and personalities like Page 3 girl Linda Lusardi to keep the fans entertained. We knew from advanced bookings we had a success on our hands – but everyone underestimated the interest.The Saturday was pretty big but we coped. Come Sunday, so many people headed for the track that the gate staff were overwhelmed. The tail-backs went all the way back to the junction with the M1 and this meant that, for a while, access to East Midlands Airport was blocked and flights had to be delayed. It was estimated that over 100,000 people were in attendance, but quite a few got in without paying.

The track action was great and my knock-out system leading to a 'Grand Final' worked well. Multipart and the other sponsors were pleased and so were my fellow directors at CSS; this was definitely adding to the bottom line. In the following days, both Jimmy Brown at Silverstone and John Webb at Brands Hatch asked us to arrange similar events at their tracks the following year. Finding sponsors to back these events proved no obstacle; we had Lucas and Mobil at Brands Hatch, ATS/Michelin at Silverstone and even Yorkie chocolate bars. For the next five years or so, truck racing was a huge success.

I have already recounted the tale of the 1986 Silverstone race, but without question the most bizarre scenes were those that followed the conclusion of the race the previous year. The date was 18 August 1985 and, after a series of knock-out heats and even a Last Chance race, Italian Gaudenzio Mantova crossed the line, after 15 furious laps of the Grand Final, to take victory in his Scania 142.

The sometime single-seater racer had beaten a disparate group of drivers, which included Barry Sheene, Steve Parrish, Barry Lee, Willie Green, rally drivers Andy Dawson and Russell Brookes and even former Formula 1 World Champion Alan Jones.

Indeed, Mantova had started as one of the favourites. His regular racing background included winning the Italian Formula Ford Championship and even competing at Formula 2 level.

While Donington and Silverstone hosted some excellent truck events, Brands Hatch was probably my favourite venue and the track suited the racing. Circuit boss John Webb was and Track Manager John Symes were great allies. Here at a Mobil Truck Superprix Richard Walker powers into the lead with his Lucas sponsored White. ***Jonathan Reeves***

Earlier in the year, he came to Brands Hatch and won the first Lucas Truck Grand Prix. He put his success down to his mother's spaghetti, prompting *The Sun*, which had really got behind truck racing, to come up with the classic headline "First Pasta the Post".

But something wasn't quite right at Silverstone. The Italian had stopped his truck near Becketts Corner apparently out of fuel. He was picked up by a course car and brought back to receive the garland, the trophy and a cheque for £5000! The large crowd, estimated at close on 50,000, at what was only Britain's third ever truck race, was appreciative, although it would have preferred the win had gone to second-placed Richard Walker, a Nottingham based haulier with some minor rallying success. But the Italian had won fair and square – or had he? At Becketts, an eagle-eyed marshal had spotted something curious after Mantova had brought the truck to a halt. He thought he'd seen a match struck. He suggested the scrutineers take a look. As the Italian was heading back to the podium and the spoils of victory, the technical officials climbed up into the cab of the Scania and found a crime scene.

Mantova had been boosting the power of his Swedish diesel with a crude system involving some plastic pipe and a bottle of nitrous oxide. He had then attempted to burn the pipe, which seems rather more complicated than chucking it out of the window.

What followed was pure farce. As he stepped down from the podium, with the large shiny Multipart Trophy in hand and the garland around his neck, the dreaded call to report to the Clerk of the Course echoed across the paddock. The soon-to-be-disgraced Gaudenzio spoke not a word of English but the organisers, seeing eight Italians on the entry list, had hired a rather fetching Italian lady to act as translator.

Together with myself and a scrutineer, we approached the sweaty racer to tell him that there was a problem. Gaudenzio certainly got the message, and still clutching the trophy turned on his heel and was off like a robber's dog and we lost him in the crowd.

Repeated messages over the public address for him to join the stewards failed. His small team, including his pasta-baking mother, had no idea where he had gone, or if they did they weren't letting on. The stewards duly met and Gaudenzio was guilty as charged and stripped of the victory – thus handing it to crowd favourite Richard Walker, but the saga wasn't quite over yet. Mantova's Scania had been brought back to the scrutineering bay and the evidence confiscated. The paddock cleared, darkness descended but still the truck remained there, its hapless owner and driver presumably still in hiding somewhere behind a Silverstone hangar.

Shame-faced Mantova returned to his cab the following morning and when the few remaining officials had their heads turned, he climbed aboard and disappeared in the direction of his native town of Como, never to be seen at a truck race again. He was subsequently stripped of his racing licence and forever has a place in the often-bizarre history of truck racing.

The crowd knew little of this. They had enjoyed the racing, the jet truck, the wheelie truck, the tractor pulling, the stunt driving and the celebrities. Some great characters emerged from the racing, too. I have already mentioned Reg Hopkins – better known as 'Radiator Reg' – as the owner of the car crushing Samson.

Reg was one of those guys who found the accident that was happening close to him and joined in. He got the epithet 'Radiator Reg' following an incident when he attempted to repair a front bumper, which had been damaged in a fender-bending racing incident. Back in the paddock, Reg swung the sledge hammer, missed the bumper completely and planted the 14lb into his radiator with an accompanying hiss of steam!

Right from the beginning, I knew we had to make truck racing populist and hence I wanted to give some of the drivers catchy nicknames. Mel Lindsay became 'Meatman'. His day job was driving trailerloads of New Zealand lamb across the breadth of Britain. Lindsey was an inspiration character. At the initial Donington event, which he entered without any previous motor sport experience, he was hopeless and finished dead last. He phoned me the next day and said "I made a complete prat of myself but I had the best day of my life. I want to improve, what should I do?" Two years later he was the European Truck Racing Champion with full sponsorship from Perkins Diesel, GKN Chep Pallets and Shell.

He also got me out of an embarrassing situation at the 1988 Mobil 1 Truck Superprix at Brands Hatch in 1988. I had come up with the concept of a Trucker's Mate race as part of the programme. The idea was two-fold; drivers could give their hard-working mechanics a race at the end of the day, but I could also borrow a few trucks and place 'personalities' in them as part of the publicity machine.

There were quite a few 'stars', but by far my best pick was hapless plasterer turned ski jumper Eddie 'The Eagle' Edwards who was at the height of his fame. Eddie would race Mel's Leyland T45 truck and we even arranged a test day for him complete with Thames TV cameras in attendance.

It was tumultuous day. Steve Murty managed to overturn the Multipart Wheelie truck on the front straight and was trapped in the cab for a while. Not half an hour later, a guy called Chris Tucker took down a load of Armco barrier on the back straight and brought out the red flag. One sheet of Armco had speared right though the cab, inches from Chris. All this meant the whole meeting was running very late and, as I said, the Trucker's Mate race was the last of the day. Eddie had qualified about eighth for the race and the fans were full of expectation, well wound up by the commentators.

But as the trucks were being warmed up, Eddie's manager found me and told me that the Eagle had a very lucrative personal appearance gig back in London that evening and he couldn't wait any longer. He would be back tomorrow. The large crowd had stayed on to witness the Eagle's first ever race so I took a snap decision. 'Meatman' Mel was with the truck in the warm-up enclosure waiting to give the ski jumping hero some final words of wisdom – like don't bend my truck. I quickly explained to Mel the problem and told him that he would drive the truck instead and pretend to be Eddie. Of course, Mel had the speed to win this race easily so I told him just to finish fourth. Thus he wouldn't have to go on the podium and our dastardly plot would not be revealed. Nobody else, including the commentator, was in on this.

Off they went and from eighth, Mel was in the lead by the end of lap one and the commentator was going absolutely berserk – and so was I. This wasn't the plan. By lap three of the ten laps, I was on the pitwall hoping no one saw me giving Mel the slow down signal. Professional that he was, he threw the T45 into a half spin at Druids with a lap to go, several of his rivals passed him and he duly finished fourth. However, there was a Trophy for the fastest lap and 'Eddie' had won that. The commentator was screeching for him to come up to the podium. I gently explained that Eddie had to leave immediately after the race as he had an appointment in London.

The following day, the real Eddie did race, finished about tenth after a spin and then signed a very lucrative deal to race a truck in Canada. They thought they had signed a winner. Meanwhile, we successfully exported truck racing to Australia where CSS had a subsidiary company. Here, with the huge help of Ingrid Roepers, we ran meetings at both Calder Park and Oran Park.

Aafter seven years of trucking exploits, the FIA got very involved in truck racing and, to my mind, messed the rules around. Brands Hatch's new boss Nicola Foulston told us in no uncertain manner she could run truck racing better than us and Jimmy Brown decided not to continue after someone's rear axle dug a big gouge out of the track. So we stepped back, as they say.

These days, truck racing continues to provide great entertainment, particularly at the Nürburgring but also in the UK. But times have changed and I doubt the diesel dicers will ever attract the huge crowds of the 1980s.

The race that changed his life. 'Meatman' Mel Lindsey finished last in his first truck race but went on to win the European Championship a few years later. He was also a willing partner in crime in the great Eddie the Eagle scandal. ***Jonathan Reeves***

Chapter 18

DRAIN THAT SWAMP

The muddiest racing on earth and the only place racers might end up in the Sippy Hole.

Let's talk dirty, and I mean really dirty. No, this isn't the porn chapter based on shades of grey – more shades of brown. We are talking about the muddy, grubby, dirty sport of swamp buggy racing, which I first witnessed at the concluding round of the 2011/12 Budweiser Cup for Swamp Buggy Racing.

Swamp Buggy Racing is just about the most esoteric racing series in the world. There is only one track, at the Naples Sports Park on Florida's Gulf Coast, and they only have three race meetings a year. Hardly a tough schedule but, of course, it takes a while to dry out man and machine after ploughing through the Sippy Hole.

On arrival at the track, I was anxious to find out more and quickly acquired a copy of the Official Souvenir Program for the princely sum of $4. It was a steal. I sat down in the bleachers and got up to speed with all the latest swamp buggy news in a bid to learn the technical details of the machines which I knew rejoiced in such names as Hi Tech Redneck, Dat's Da One, Evil & Wicked, Spider's Dream, Radical Rabbit (driven by Vicky Rabinette, incidentally) and even No 123 Wet Willy and No 112 Pump it Out.

Page one of this publication featured an introduction by the President of Swamp Buggy Inc, a certain KC Hornbach – we are left to guess what the KC stands for – but he did promise us 'the muddiest racing on earth.' Page two of the publication listed the Board of Directors and then on page three we had a complete list of every Swamp Buggy Queen since the whole extravaganza started back in 1949, with a few exceptions.

In 1949, Joan Talbert was crowned the first Queen, but for the next years the winner is listed simply as 'local woman'. Then we have a succession of Dollys, Cindys, Kittys, Kimberleys until 1987 when we are informed: "No Queen Chosen".

At the humble end of Swamp Buggy Racing come the Jeeps complete with passengers. ***Andrew Marriott***

What happened in 1987 and for the next two years? Were the local girls simply not pretty enough? Perhaps the word had finally got around the local high schools that – and I kid you not – the main reward for becoming the Swamp Buggy Queen is that once the racing is over, the overall winner scoops you up in his arms and literally throws you into the Sippy Hole complete with your crown, gown and sash.

Anyway, the tradition restarted in 1990 and since then Ashley, Christa, Courtney, Megan and most recently Jennifer have been tossed into the swamp. The year I was there it got a little complicated because the Budweiser Champion turned out to be a woman called Lorrie Johns. In the end, she finished up in the swamp together with Jennifer and her car builder, who rejoiced in the name of Barefoot Bobby Williams. At least he didn't get his shoes wet.

Thumbing through the programme – all in glorious black and white despite the price tag – I was anxious to learn more of the top drivers but the next page was dedicated to a profile and three photos of Race Queen Jennifer who, we learn, "Feels she can make a positive impact on society by being a role model, she wants to show anything is possible by supporting Swamp Buggy Racing". She is training to be a vet. Perhaps she could start with some of the fish she found in the swamp.

Now, I can just about get my head round a page about Jennifer but the

Making waves, Lorrie Johns in Lady Liberty ploughs through the Mile of Mud on the way to winning the Budweiser Championship Cup in 2015. *Andrew Marriott*

next page in my souvenir programme profiled the three girls who were the runners-up – Alexandria, who wanted to be a nurse, Ashley who had this dream of working in the fire brigade and is studying for a bachelor's degree in fire science and Riley who is still at college and apparently, "Enjoys girl days with mom". Oh dear. Also I'm a bit worried about someone studying fire science – they don't even have a course for that at the University of North West Milton Keynes.

After a couple of pages of adverts for Sylvester Excavating, Sunshine Sanitation, and JCM Cattle & Fencing, not to forget the Good Time Diner, there was another page of editorial with the headline 'Girls – We Need You'. Evidently the organisers did not want to go back to the bleak days of the late '80s without a race queen. The article advised that if you are between 16 and 24 you can apply, make new friends, learn a choreographed dance routine and have the experience of a lifetime. Presumably that's being thrown into a muddy swamp by a sweaty racer. Furthermore, there was the prospect of a College Scholarship, crown and sash, trophy and a gift basket – containing we know not what.

This is all very interesting, but I wanted to find out more about the torpedo-shaped devices I had spotted in the paddock complete with huge narrow wheels, cockpits at the very front tip of the machine and thundering 800bhp NASCAR engines, sealed in the rear compartment. To be fair, the programme did outline some of the classes and had listed the World Champions and from this I can tell you that the Lewis Hamilton of Swamp Buggy racing back then was the late Eddie Chesser. He won the title from 1995 to 2000, again in 2004 and in 2010 and 2011. That's a total of nine, so even more titles than Lewis. However, the programme was pretty sparse on other details of drivers or their machines, so I set off to investigate.

On the way, I caught up with the sounds and smells of the concessions – one featured a Republican called Tim Nance who was bidding to be the County Commissioner District 5 who seemed to be standing on a pro-all terrain vehicle ticket and had a banner proclaiming: "I will LISTEN". If you've heard 800bhp of Chevy blasting through the deepest part of the swamp, then you'd realise that however much listening he did, he was only going to hear V8 grunt.

Next door was the stand selling the T-shirts and other gear for one of the top entries, Fatal Attraction. The startling pink colour scheme was carried all the way through to the cockatoo hair-do of the 18-stone woman manning the stand, so I quickly passed by and also gave a wide berth to the stall selling turkey thighs the size of a small Sumo wrestler. I was fascinated by another concession that offered me either sweet tea or un-sweet tea, not to mention fried pickles, chicken tenders and mozzarella sticks. I briefly wondered if they sourced the latter from Jody Scheckter's Laverstoke Park but came to the conclusion, after sneaking a quick look, that the supplier was the local plastics factory.

The choice of food at Swamp Buggy Racing is somewhat eclectic – what are Shoestring Onions? ***Andrew Marriott***

The large crowd was certainly enjoying the day and the spasmodic action. Some had undoubtedly tackled more than one of the massive turkey thighs and had definitely passed on the un-sweet tea in favour of large amounts of beer. This is not the sort of crowd you'd normally see at Silverstone and I believe it would be best described as 'blue collar'. Many had set up their own grandstands or perched on the bonnets of various jacked-up Jeeps and

Even the current Formula 1 stars have tried their hand at Swamp Buggy Racing. Max Verstappen and Yuki Tsunoda got down and dirty in Naples prior to the 2022 Miami Grand Prix. ***Red Bull***

other off-road vehicles. They lit camp fires, sparked up barbeques and were generally engaged in displaying the fine art of the local tattoo parlours of South West Florida.

The original Swamp Buggies were built on Jeeps with big balloon tyres for Sunday hunting expeditions deep into the Florida Everglades. One thing led to another, and one hunter challenged another to a race through a muddy bog on a potato farm, which was described as "The biggest hole in the vicinity of Naples".

The first official Swamp Buggy Races were held in 1949 and, with the keen spirit of competition, both the vehicles and the track quickly evolved. The track itself moved to a new venue a couple of miles away as the owner of the potato field decided he could build some nice homes there – including, as it happens, one that I own. Four bedrooms, nice pool, private estate. Available for rent folks.

Anyway, the new track became known as the Mile O' Mud which is kind of stretching the point as it is a seventh-eighths of a mile oval, but that said it has a one-eighth of a mile diagonal cut through. The depth of the mud is hard to gauge because brown swamp water covers every inch of the track, but most of the way it is only around a foot deep but in three spots it drops to five or six feet. The smaller Jeep-based class cars disappear up to their steering wheels as they plough through these sections. The largest pit is the famed Sippy Hole named after 'Mississippi' Milton Morris, who never made it through without stalling.

While the Jeep classes race together, the prototypes compete drag race style with two competitors racing head to head. A race consists of the start on the Grandstand Straight, a left turn via a cut through and then one and a half laps clockwise around the oval.

As well as getting thrown in the Sippy Hole, the Race Queen doubles as an interviewer. ***Andrew Marriott***

The overall winner is decided drag race style, going through eliminators, quarter, semi and then the grand final. It certainly builds the tension.

The top category is called the Pro-Modified, but the technology does not seem to have changed much in 20 years. Most of the racers seem to rely on 8.0-litre Chevrolet V8 motors, although there are a few Fords. There are categories for both two- and four-wheel-drive. You would think that four-wheel-drive would help but there were only three cars in that category. One of them was multi-champion Eddie Chesser but when I went to check out his machine, I noticed he had discarded the front driveshafts.

The chassis, which are Top Fuel dragster length, are all square-tube spaceframes in the Pro-Modifed class. Unlike the Jeeps, the general idea is for neither yourself nor the inner workings to get wet. By the front wheels are horizontal barge boards which apparently help the turn in. Yes, finally we are getting technical.

One innovation, however, is in the area of tyres. Until recently, most of the top contenders took giant and very expensive tractor tyres, cut the middle out of them and vulcanised them back together again. The middle ring of the tyre was discarded, or at least sent to be cooked along with turkey thighs. However, one of the top drivers, Troy Ortega, was surfing the internet and happened upon a Chinese site selling tyres for tractors that run in paddy fields. Guess what? They are the perfect size for a Pro-Modified Swamp Buggy. Troy is now importing crate loads of them.

Accidents seem few and far between, although mechanical breakdowns are common, particularly among the smaller classes. The Jeeps churn through the difficult parts of the track at snail's pace but the big Pro-Modified are hugely impressive at speed with huge plumes of muddy spray behind them.

The season starts in October, round two is held in January with the champions crowned in March. When I made my visit, the champion was Lorrie Johns who races a vehicle called Lady Liberty – she's only the second woman to take the title. After she had emerged bedraggled from her swamp dunk, she told the local newspaper she would celebrate by tucking into a Twinkie – whatever that is!

Swamp Buggy Racing is certainly a unique motorsport experience, which I would thoroughly recommend. And don't forget to buy the programme!

Chapter 19

TALES FROM THE LANE AND OTHER LE MANS STORIES

My round the clock experiences at La Sarthe.

The Japanese enthusiast was snuggled down in his sleeping bag in a dusty spot under the shadow of the main Le Mans grandstand, right opposite pit out. Toyota looked as if they might win the race and the battle at the front had raged on through the night. This chap was deep in his dreams – perhaps a night with geisha girls, or maybe a sushi blow-out or even a Sumo wrestling hold – but he was missing the action which might lead to a great Japanese victory.

I was in playful TV mode, presenting the 24-hour race for Sky, one of only two years that they actually covered the world's biggest sports car race. Earlier, I'd done a feature on the different memorabilia you could buy from trackside vendors. This finished up with me purchasing a pair of knickers emblazoned with the formidable upper body of a certain Samantha Fox. At the time, Sam was *The Sun*'s top page three model. I am not sure what it had to do with Le Mans but it made a change from a Steve McQueen T-shirt. Subsequently, it turned out Sam preferred women to men but not before she was in a relationship with the bloke who helped the Blairs buy their son's first flat in Bath. I recently learned that he has gone on to become a multi-millionaire. But that's a different story.

But back to our Japanese fellow, and it still astounds me that he could actually sleep so close to trackside with the cars blasting and screaming past a few yards away. I thought a hilarious way to introduce our 8am programme would be to bend down, shake him and wake him with the advice that he was missing a classic Le Mans with Toyota in the lead. Cruel, I know.

It didn't go as well as I'd hoped! He woke up all right, but I reckon he thought it was a nightmare. As I advised him of the race positions, he stood up rigid still in his sleeping bag and, to paraphrase one of my favourite comedians 'Blaster' Bates, "You cannot run at 20 miles per hour in the Le Mans stands in a sleeping bag." He fell over and he wasn't excited about being on British television – in fact, quite the opposite. I don't know much Japanese but I have since found out that 'hakuchi' is roughly translated as retard. Actually, I also recognised the word 'kimi' which was strange because, at the time, the Finn hadn't arrived on the motor racing scene. I have since found out that when Japanese use the word kimi, it is to show disrespect for the person they are talking to. Funny, that.

But I should really start at the beginning. As a cub reporter at *Motoring News*, I was sent to cover the great race for the first time back in 1965. To be absolutely truthful, I wasn't that excited about it. At the time, I was a dyed-in-the-wool single-seater man, reporting on Formula 2. I hadn't really been touched by the Sarthe star dust. But once there, I absolutely loved it and it helped that one of my Formula 2 heroes Jochen Rindt won the race with Masten Gregory. As you have surely read, they were convinced that the NART Ferrari 275LM would never make the finish and drove it as hard as it would go, but the Maranello motor kept on running.

Many years later, I met a man called Ed Hugus at the Bahamas Speedweek Revival who claimed to me that not only was he the reserve driver for the car, but that in the night he actually drove the Ferrari for a two-hour stint. According to Hugus, who seemed a very modest man, Gregory came in with his glasses misted up and didn't want to continue and Jochen was sleeping somewhere, so Hugus jumped in the car. Indeed, he had raced at Le Mans several times before so the story seemed feasible. Subsequently, I have seen this story repeated in a couple of American magazines as well as Quentin Spurring's ACO-authorised Le Mans book. I asked Ed why he wasn't on the podium at the end of the race. He said he had tried to get there to join Jochen and Masten

Ready for the start in full Fox Sports race suit. Even dressed like this people asked me "Who are you working for this year?" ***Fox Sports***

It is great to be in the thick of the action. Somehow during this Toyota pit stop I managed to both commentate then take this photo. But you really need to be on your toes and not get in the way of the crew. ***Andrew Marriott***

but the officials stopped him because he didn't have the right pass.

I went away from the conversation with Ed having convinced me that I had missed a massive scoop. But then quite recently I had the pleasure of meeting Luigi Chinetti Jnr, son of the owner of the NART team who ran the winning car. I told him about my missed scoop and basically he said there was no way Hugus drove in the night – if he had, he would have known. Chinetti said that Hugus told lots of people this winning Le Mans story, but it simply was not true. I hadn't missed the scoop after all. But then someone else suggested that had Le Mans realised an unauthorised driver took part, they might disqualify the car so NART denied the story and have stuck to the story ever since.

After 1965, I returned to Le Mans reporting the race for *MN* as a journalist before switching to TV with Screensport – the channel owned by the WHSmith newsagent organisation. This was thanks to a good friend Alan More, who was producing the show. Originally, Al had been an excellent cameraman and shot the film when the Lotus 49 made its debut at Zandvoort. Initially, I was commentating but then I moved into the truck producing the round-the-clock coverage, on the 'bench' alongside a brilliant director called David Jackson and a great back-up team of editors and production staff. Our on-air reporters included the outstanding Neil Crompton, who we flew in from Australia.

A memorable year, in more ways than one, was 1992, the year Derek Warwick won for Peugeot. In those days, the TV compound was actually in a public area, along the wall that runs behind the ACO building. You know the place, where they sell silk 24-Hour ties for £50. Our vehicles and Portakabins were at the end of a line with the Japanese Asahi channel next to us.

We were into the final three hours of the race when, without warning, the whole truck shut down – no power, it was pitch black in there. There were anguished calls from London. "We've lost your signal!" Switches were switched, curses were cursed and then director 'Jacko', who'd rushed outside to evaluate the situation, burst back into the truck. "Get the fire extinguishers," he shouted. The old transformer half way up a telegraph pole had burst into flames and knocked out our electricity. It was a couple hours before we had a back-up generator in place. We brought our own generator the following year. It was Jackson, incidentally, who implored his cameramen during the victory ceremony after Johnny Herbert won the 1991 race in the Mazda, to "Give me weeping nips." He'd probably be in trouble these days for such political incorrectness. I am not sure what the director was saying in the Asahi TV truck, but indeed our cameraman did find Mazda personnel in floods of tears. It was many years later that Toyota became only the second Japanese company to win the race.

I had wondered for a couple of years why the wall we parked against had yellow stains and algae on it. In 1992 I found out; the wall is basically a public toilet, it was highest up the wall for half a franc. We got pretty fed up with people relieving themselves and then, as they zipped up, grinning at us through the Portakabin window as we crafted our next feature or update. So one of the TV techies rigged up a couple of wires and in French and English added a notice which said: 'High Voltage – Live Electrical Cables'. We weren't troubled so much after that, the fans found another wall!

This reminds me of another story, and this one involves a fellow commentator who shall remain anonymous. The said fellow had headed off for lunch at the little café near Arnage station. If you know the chap, you won't be surprised to learn that he'd had more than a couple of glasses of madam's cheapest *vin rouge*. He needed to do what the chaps had done in their bid to turn that wall a nice shade of yellow. He wandered off, and returned a couple of minutes later with a relieved smile on his face but announcing that he couldn't find the light switch in the little room. This was a long time ago, before mobiles, and another member of his party needed the phone. He returned a little later announcing he had got through OK but the telephone cabin smelt rather unpleasant!

Which reminds me of the old Le Mans pits which some of our older readers will recall. They were absolutely disgusting, cramped and had terrible facilities. In fact, in the 1970s they were no different from 40 years earlier. Thankfully, they were subsequently transformed into the magnificent facility they are today.

I have had experience of working both the old and the new. It's difficult to believe now, but I remember in my *MN* days wandering down the pitlane, notebook in hand and watching the 7.0-litre Ford Mk4s race past, Dan Gurney and Mario Andretti, side by side at 200mph. The only thing between me, the rest of the pitlane and the cars was a white line!

I learned an interesting lesson in 1987 when the podium was in the middle of those old pits where the famous Dutray clock hung. I had the job of interviewing the winner Derek Bell, as did an American broadcaster working for ESPN; I think it was a guy called Marty Read. "Let's toss for who goes first," he said, and I agreed as he produced a dollar from his pocket. He tossed it and called heads and won. I found out later he had this special coin – heads on both sides.

For the best part of 15 years, it was my good fortune to be part of the Speedvision, then Speed and later Fox Sports team reporting from the pitlane. For many reasons, it doesn't get much better than that. Sadly, another channel then won the contract in 2017 and they decided to cut costs and use just the international feed. But over that decade or so it was always an exacting, exhausting but thoroughly enjoyable task but not without its frustrations. I worked with some great commentators including David Hobbs, Sam Posey, Bob Varsha, Calvin Fish, Brian Till, Chris Neville Justin Bell, Jamie Howe, Dorsey Schroeder, Greg Creamer and Leigh Diffey plus an outstanding Producers in Greg Oldham and Frank Wilson.

In the earlier days, there were as many as six commentators and four pits reporters. A group like this is packed with ego, but somehow everyone worked as a true team. The logistics were pretty complicated too as we had our own cameramen, took extra on-board feeds while all the graphics and some of the features were played into the show from a TV facility in Charlotte, North Carolina. Every Friday evening before the race, we used to spend hours doing what is called a 'fax check', basically a technical line up. You waited around with your microphone and transmitting kit for ages before someone in America asked you to count to ten. Then half an hour later the same thing but you had to start at ten down to one. One year, after this had gone on for well over two hours, I feigned illness and said goodbye. Otherwise I would have missed an outstanding dinner reservation a group of us at booked at a Michelin starred establishment in La Fleche.

When Speed was the main US broadcaster they took the race very seriously and 'the talent' as we were called could be as many as ten people. Left to right are Bob Varsha, Greg Creamer, Justin Bell, me, Leigh Diffey, David Hobbs, Calvin Fish, Brian Till and Jamie Howe. What a team! ***Speed Channel***

The channel's US based staff weren't always as steeped in European motorsport as you would hope. Indeed, 2010 was something of a watershed, thanks to the economic situation. Instead of having a staff of about 30 on site, it was decided that the whole show would be produced back in Charlotte. The commentary team would be there 'calling it off the tube' but, of course, the four pits reporters and a skeleton crew would be on site. It has to be said that being a pit reporter in the Charlotte studio car park would have been a challenge.

Yes, the late TV Producer Brian Kreisky did host a Dakar Rally programme from a sand dune on the beach of Douglas, Isle of Man, and pretended he was deep in the African desert, but we weren't up to tricks like that. Through the wonders of modern TV technology, I had the commentary team of Leigh Diffey, Calvin Fish, Scott Pruett et al in one ear and the pits producer – whom I hadn't previously met – in another.

This guy was, of course, in Charlotte and I guess he knew the name of all Mark Martin's children plus the nickname of Tony Stewart's dog, but pretty soon I knew it would be a long night. A few minutes before the start I offered him an interview with the FIA's then President. "Can you spell that?" crackled the message into my headphone. " T.O.D.T." I shouted.

"First name?" came the enquiry "J.E.A.N." I added. "Is the president a woman?" he enquired quickly followed by, "I think we'll pass on that but can you get me an interview with Terry Borcheller." In our final couple years, the crew on site was down to just myself and Justin Bell.

One of my annual tasks for US TV at Le Mans was to get the winners' interviews. More recently, this has become much easier, very well organised with a bull pen arrangement before the podium ceremonies. These interviews can be taken live and it is a great feeling to share the joy of victory with Tom Kristensen – on several occasions – but also people like Nick Tandy, Brendon Hartley and Earl Bamber.

But it wasn't always like that. Up until about 12 years ago, the interviews had to be conducted in an ante-room in the Race Control building which leads out to the podium gantry. All the officials, top team members, and the top three driver squads from every class packed into this small area – and remember, that meant the best part of 50 drivers.

There were three main problems. To gain entry you had to have a special letter – which some security guard took about five minutes to read, and there was only a window of ten minutes or so before we came off air. The building had lots of steel girders in it, so we could not transmit live. We are back in the days of tape here. Thus I would grab a driver, get some breathless excitement, the tape would be pulled out of the camera and a runner would then push through the crowds, over the rackety bridge and to the TV truck. Here, it was crammed into a VT machine, it was cued up – and played out as live. We had a string of runners, so sometimes we got three or four tapes back before the end of the show. If I had got the main winner interview and I knew we would be off air in five minutes I would take the tape myself. Talk about an adrenaline rush.

The colour, the speed and the noise are all enhanced at night. A Ferrari GTE car blasts through the darkness. ***ACO***

Sorting out your credentials at Le Mans can often be a bit of a challenge. A few year ago, they suddenly decided to put barcodes on them, not only the plastic credit card dangler thing around your neck but also the car pass as well. They had finally cottoned on that a lot of folk were getting more than one person in on the same pass by having someone else take it outside and hand it to a mate. Now, can you imagine anyone would do that! Anyway, the first year didn't go very well because half the time the barcode readers didn't work. If you came in the front entrance and went out the back, the computer got confused and the clever paper they printed the car pass on actually went black when it was exposed to sunlight – and it was a very sunny year. Just so you know, they've cracked it now.

That doesn't mean we don't have problems with access to the TV area. The TV compound is now situated on the last bit of the Bugatti circuit before it turns back on to the pits straight. To reach it from the paddock involves passing through a gate in the catch fencing, then climbing over some very temporary and wobbly steps over the Armco barrier and finishing up in a gravel trap, which may have been visited in the past by some errant Moto GP rider.

I probably went through the gate about 30 times every day, and a rota of security people patrol it day and night. I realise this must be a very boring job and you don't get the brightest of folk doing it. But one particular fellow still didn't recognise me, even by Sunday lunchtime. Each time it wasn't just a cursory glance to see if I had the vital number eight on my pass, he closely scrutinised it each time.

You would think that somewhere in his brain he would realise that some old bloke dressed in a race suit with Fox TV on it, holding a microphone in his hand and a headset on his head with a large aerial sticking out of it and a bundle of commentator notes and media books, wasn't actually trying to get into the TV compound for some nefarious unauthorised reason.

Gateman one also had a brighter mate who spoke good English and I happened upon him when he was in the process of denying three-time Le Mans winner Marco Werner access to the TV compound where he was supposed to be doing some colour commentary for Eurosport's German channel.

"He won the race three times in a row," I said, and I have to admit I was getting a little hot under the rather sweaty race suit collar. So I was surprised by his answer. "I am a fan, I know that," said the gate keeper number two, "but I'll get sacked if my boss finds out." Turns out the lad was doing it because he was a big enthusiast and, after I agreed to take the rap if he got into trouble, Marco gained access.

But it didn't stop there. On Sunday morning as Porsche, Toyota and Audi were all in with a chance of victory, I headed out of the compound for my final pit lane stint to the said gate and the dim bloke was on. He seemed to be surrounded by several frustrated TV people. He'd managed to slam the gate shut and it had locked itself and nobody knew where the key was. I trudged around a longer secret way out, through one of those strange compounds you find at race circuits where they store road sweepers and new pieces of Armco. And do you know what I found? The gate into that didn't have anyone checking if you had a number eight at all. If I'd known I could have got Marco in that way.

At Le Mans, you tend to bump into a lot of people you don't normally see the rest of the year. They like to catch up and most of them always seem to ask me the same two questions. The first one is: "This is my 23rd year, how many have you been to?" The truth is that without a trip into my dusty loft to look at old brown-tinged *Motoring News* copies, I don't know the answer. For many years, Le Mans clashed with the Canadian Grand Prix and I can't remember which of the two races I went to. I've got fed up explaining this, so last time I was asked, I said 50, which seemed a nice round number and was probably close to the truth.

Iconic photo on the film poster. ***Andrew Marriott***

The second question I get asked is: "Who are you working for this year?" I explained earlier that I worked for the same American TV group for over a decade and, although admittedly it has changed its name three times. But you know Americans, they love uniforms! So there I am wearing a Fox Sports hat, a Fox Sports-logoed polo shirt, and I have a pass, which says Fox Sports on it. Well, I am not working for Eurosport, am I? As my American colleagues would say: "Go figure".

I have never been to the race as a spectator, but I can't help but be impressed by the professionalism of the fans these days. Years ago, I remember seeing a Triumph Spitfire, which had been painted in Silk Cut Jaguar colours which seemed a rather strange and unique thing to do.

In recent years, driving back to the Eurotunnel, I couldn't help notice the number of British fans who had spent hours logoing up their various cars as if they were in the race themselves. They have outline maps of Le Mans, team allegiances that mainly equate to campsite groups and even their own names neatly affixed to the side of the cars, complete with a little Union Jack, or whatever their nationality might be.

One guy I passed had his name on the rear quarter light of his Hyundai complete with the union jack and underneath it – he was obviously on a bonding trip with his son, 'Little Un'. But instead of our national flag, there was a little McDonald's flag. Obviously they hadn't eaten in the newly Michelin-starred restaurant on the Loire at La Fleche, then.

A drophead BMW right behind me on the Channel Tunnel train bore allegiance to Team Langoustine – apparently these lads camp somewhere near Tertre Rouge and obviously eat in style. They even have their own website.

A few of the names surely are not real. Some are very laddish; a smart white Golf was crewed by 'Coops' and 'Wilko' and also stuck on the rear of the car one of the Pro stickers – exactly the same as the GTE Pro cars have to carry. I also noticed in the Channel Tunnel loading lane opposite a nice blue Cobra replica carrying the number 13 and crewed by 'Little Block' and 'The Beast' who were running in convoy with a magenta one driven by 'Big Block' and 'Al Col Hol'. I told you some of the names were made up.

I am not sure if I owned a very nice Bentley Continental GT that I would want to cover it in decals and claim to be 'The Sweeper' and 'The Spin Doctor'. In fact, they were in the lane other side of me and I asked the guy the meaning of the nicknames. I didn't really get a coherent answer. But I think they had enjoyed themselves and had seen a bit of the race. 'The Sweeper' asked me who'd won! Also, just behind it was another Bentley but from a different era – it was a beautiful white 1925 3-litre Bentley. I am pleased to report it had no decals on it at all.

There is a huge buzz from interviewing drivers and team bosses in the middle of a major event and it is funny how Le Mans changes even top drivers. In Formula 1 these days, if you want to interview any driver you have to go through a whole process with the team's PR and sometimes also their personal assistant. You have to be there at a set time and you only have eight minutes etc. But it is different when they get to Le Mans. A few years back, in the middle of the night, I was hovering in front of the Porsche garage as their battle with Audi and Toyota for the lead raged on. Mark Webber spotted me from the back of the garage, wandered over and said, "Do you need me, mate". Got a good interview, too. I have written separately about good and bad interviewees, but this reminds that the cyclist Chris Hoy – who had a go at the 24 Hours – was absolutely brilliant on the mic.

My most recent outlet has been Radio Le Mans, the remarkable business built up by John Hindhaugh and Eve Hewett. These days, of course, they cover hundreds of different races around the world, but the big one is still Le Mans. I am rather glad I didn't work for them a few years back when the pit lane reporting team was sponsored by Jiffy condoms. Back in the mid-1970s, I was heavily involved with Durex – as sponsors of Team Surtees – as well as Speedway events etc. The boss even sent me a silly telegram to be read out at my wedding. They did use the sponsorship programme brilliantly and their advertising agency Benton and Bowles came up with some superb catchlines like Small Family Car under the picture of Alan Jones in the TS19 and Crowd Stopper under a great speedway shot. Anyway, I have had enough of condoms.

Radio reportage is definitely a different challenge to television and probably an easier discipline. You don't have worry about where your cameraman is or whether you are looking pretty on camera, but you do need to be more descriptive. Plus working with Radio Le Mans, they are absolutely on top of the action, so if you offer up a story or interview they know immediately why and if it will fit in. With American TV, it was a very different story. Often you had to actually 'sell' an interview to the pits producer back in the States. Then the interview had to fit with the general traffic which included VT inserts, promotions for other programmes and advertising breaks every ten minutes or so. I found the freedom RLM offered most liberating.

Le Mans fans decorate their cars with packs of decals bought from the internet. I spotted this Cobra replica and the Bentley at the Eurotunnel terminal. ***Andrew Marriott***

Working the pit lane can be physically quite demanding. You can cover lot of ground up down the quarter mile or so of the lane, dressed in thick race suit and with all the transmission equipment. Sod's Law says that if you have a story at one end of the pit lane, the next one is at the other end. You also have to watch out for cars flying in, mechanics bustling around, wheels flying when they are changed. With your headset on you can't actually hear the sound around you, either.

Many years ago at the 1968 Race of Champions Formula One race, Denny Hulme in a McLaren nailed me when, in an angry moment, he let out the clutch in practice while looking behind him. I landed behind the car on all fours, fortunately with hardly a scratch. It didn't affect him too much, he finished third. And he did apologise.

At Le Mans a few years ago one, of the freelance Speed Channel cameramen got knocked down by an Audi and finished up with a broken pelvis. So it can be really dangerous. Since then, camera crews have to have a minder with them but I have been close to having tyre marks on my Sparcos a few times. You really do have to be careful. Most broadcast outfits have a rota system, so you usually spend say three hours on three hours off. After three hours, you are usually ready for a bit of a rest.

Radio Le Mans' coverage has a massive audience, far outweighing the numbers the US TV ever obtained, and John and Eve have assembled some great commentators and reporters – like Joe Bradley, Jonny Palmer, Bruce Jones, Nick Damon, Diana Binks, Shea Adam and the master of stats Paul Truswell. All have their individual strengths and styles and happily egos are left in the Portakabin. They even let this old bloke have his moment of glory – I was pleased to fight off the masses and get the first interview with Fernando Alonso seconds after his 2019 Le Mans victory. I also found find out why the sister car had made a mysterious last-minute pit stop which lost it the race.

Despite the hard work, I always enjoy Le Mans and my Twitter account tends to light up more in those few days than the rest of year. Three years ago I got a message from someone called Chloe Clairborne who tweeted "@Pitlaneandy [that's my handle by the way] is the cutest old man I've ever seen lol. Will you please be my Grampa?" Not sure quite how to take that but I think I'm pleased.

Well, I suppose if you've worked at 50 Le Mans races (maybe), what else can you expect?

Chapter 20

BALL OF STRING, DOUBLE EGG AND THE HONEY BADGER

Many motorsports personalities have nicknames – from humorous to just plain cruel.

In the next chapter, I will write about pseudonyms but here I will discuss nicknames which Wikipedia informs me are 'A substitute for a proper name, person or place, commonly used to express affection and endearment although this is not always the case'. Most pseudonyms tend to lack humour, but with nicknames it is a different story. They can be bestowed not only on drivers but also engineers, mechanics, journalists and other racing personnel. Even cars have had nicknames and so too do tracks, teams and even individual corners.

Nicknames are nothing new and way back in 1303 were known as ekenames, literally meaning additional name – eke being derived from the old English word for also. By the 15th century this changed to nekename and so on to nickname. They have been bestowed on all kinds of sportsman, politicians, musicians, military men and even blokes down the pub. Some are very creative, others associated with a particular name or trade – thus we have lots of Chalky Whites, Bunny Warrens and the occasional Spud Baker.

But is it only men who have surnames? The fact that Mark Webber nicknamed Nico Rosberg 'Britney' because he had Britney Spears-type locks doesn't really count. Of course, different people have different ideas of what a nickname is and, indeed, I have even created two sub-categories to help. I call one the descriptive and the other the alliterative. In the first category, we have the likes of 'Quick' Vic Elford, 'Brilliant' Bob Wollek, and in the second the surname drops away and you have the likes of Thorkild Thyrring, often known as 'Tireless Talking', although the Danish Le Mans racer probably fits into both categories.

A lot of so-called nicknames are really just shorted versions of the surname with -y, -ey or -ie added on the end. Think street artist 'Banksy' or even former team boss 'Pricey', as in Dave Price. The 1980 World Champion Alan Jones was often 'Jonesey' and British Grand Prix winner John Watson was usually 'Wattie'. But after one particular meeting where he did a lot of moaning about the set-up of the car, the mechanics actually – and very unkindly – changed the name on the side of McLaren to John Whatswrong. Anyway, the adding of the -y or -ie does not always work – 'Vestappenie' doesn't exactly trip off the tongue. Anyway, the NCB (Nickname Control Board) doesn't count this form of lazy nickname. To a lesser extent, you can add 'O' to the surname, but the only one I can think of just now other than David 'Hobbo' Hobbs is the trade union leader who brought British Leyland to its knees 'Red Robbo', aka Derek Robinson.

Let's get down some decent descriptive motor racing ones. Nicknames also have to be in common use and, when used, leave no one in any doubt about who is being discussed. Back in the heyday of '70s Formula One, if you said 'Chopper', everyone knew you were talking about the woodyard-based Ken Tyrrell. Lord Alexander Hesketh was the somewhat self-styled 'Le Patron' and Colin Chapman was 'Chunky', although he hated it. In fact he was quite svelte, so it was a little unfair. Whatever, in 1970s racing circles if you mentioned 'Chunky', everyone knew who you were talking about. Bernie Ecclestone was often referred to as 'The Bolt', stolen from the TV programme *The Golden Shot* but curiously sometimes he was referred to in long form – Bernard Charles. Formula 1's top medical man for many years, Professor Sidney Watkins, was almost universally referred to as 'The Prof', while Alan Prost was 'The Professor' due to his cerebral approach to racing.

The commentator who, for many years, was the English Public Address voice of Formula 1, Anthony Marsh was referred to as 'Bunter' and I have to say he had a particular talent for being at the front of any queue where free sponsor's food was available. His successor Bob Constanduros was called 'Dormouse', after falling asleep at his *Autosport* desk on more than one occasion.

One of the first motor racing nicknames came before WW2. The great Tazio Nuvolari was known as the 'Mantuan Flyer' and Britain's first World Champion Mike Hawthorn was the 'Farnham Flyer'. Plus we have all those Flying Finns – although the rally driver Rauno Aaltonen claims to have been the first.

Dave 'Beaky' Simms picked up his name at Team Lotus and more recently was the Team Manager for the Risi Competzione Ferrari team based in Houston although he recently hung up his head-set. ***Gary Critcher***

Two now defunct Formula 1 teams – Team Lotus and Hesketh Racing – were particularly fond of nicknames and we can start with an excellent story from the latter. A new mechanic turned up at Easton Neston Stables and his main attribute seemed to be a very shiny brand new toolbox. Spurred on perhaps by the late Harvey Postlethwaite – known as 'The Doctor' – a couple of the established mechanics decided to take a look inside at the array of tools when the chap stepped out for a so-called comfort break. They were highly amused to see the sole contents was a neatly rolled ball of string. After that, the hapless fellow was only ever known as 'Ball of String'.

Meanwhile, Hesketh design engineer Martin Read, who sadly died recently, rejoiced in the title of 'Cream Bun', his desert of choice. This merry band's Team Manager was 'Bubbles Horsley'; nobody called him Anthony, and I have no idea where he got that nickname from. Someone said it was rude, but I can't imagine why.

It was the journalist Mike Doodson, who first wrote their driver was 'Hunt the Shunt'. I believe in the same *Motoring News* report in which Ian Ashley became 'Crashley'. Mike himself was always referred to by Jackie Stewart as 'Scoop' but by others simply as 'Dood', while I had to be content with 'Hunt the Shunt' calling me only by my *MN* initials 'ARM'. His '76 World Champ partner Barry Sheene always referred to me as 'Moriarty' – he was a fan of the famous '50s and '60s radio programme, *The Goon Show*. Mike dished out quite a few nicknames, including bestowing the title of the 'Monza Gorilla' on the burley one-time Austrian GP winner Vittorio Brambilla.

As we said, Team Lotus also had plenty of nicknames, some of them rather cruel. Team Manager Peter Warr was often referred to as 'Blind Pew', a character who featured in *Muppet Treasure Island* – it was based on Peter's initials. His wife was known as 'Sweety', his affectionate term for her. However he also had, shall we call her a friend, who came to races when 'Sweetie' didn't attend and the mechanics named that lady 'Saccharine'.

Those mechanics included the venerable and long-serving Bob Dance, known as 'The Vicar', thanks to his love of tea. More tea vicar? There was Dave 'Beaky' Simms on account of his nose, Derek Mower who was able to sail under the title 'Joe 90', the cartoon child spy and indeed he bore a striking resemblance to Derek. Then there was the junior Team Lotus wrench who subsequently kept his nickname longer than anyone else: Mike 'Herbie' Blash. Apparently that title was bestowed on him when was worked for F1 team boss Rob Walker. When he first joined the team, some of the lads through he was a right Herbert – so he quickly became 'Herbie' and it stuck. When he moved to Lotus, he announced himself as Mike but the nickname had followed him up to Norfolk and has stuck through his career at the FIA. Team Lotus's group of mechanics also included 'Dr Kildare' and 'Carnoustie'.

Over at McLaren there was the hirsute Kiwi number one on James's car – Ray Grant, universally known perversely as 'Kojak'. For the younger among you, Kojak was a TV detective played by the bald actor Telly Savalas, while Ray had what I am probably no longer allowed to call an Afro.

Back in the late '60s, there was a Spanish Formula 2 team whose drivers were Alex Soler Roig and Jorge de Bagration. The English lads on the team quickly named them 'Twelve Volt Solenoid' and 'Jorge de Buggeration'. 'Twelve Volt' got to start in six Grands Prix but never finished one sadly; maybe the electrics let him down. A couple of off-the-wall ones. A mate of Bernie Ecclestone's who traded in racing cars was known only as 'Monkey' Brown and nobody knew his forename – well,

I expect his mum did, but racing people certainly didn't. Another chap I knew could have been in the previous chapter as well – a very fast Mini racer who raced under the pseudonym of 'Harry Martin' but was often referred to by the nickname 'Twinkle'.

In a slightly later era, I enjoyed chatting with the guy I mentioned in the introduction, Torkild Thyrring, the Danish sports car racer who always had a lot to say for himself and thus became 'Tireless Talking', although he could boast of a second nickname as he was also known as 'Tiewrap'. Another Scandinavian with a good epithet was the Formula 2 racer turner driver manager Eje Elgh, known throughout the paddock as 'Double Egg'. Ronnie Peterson was known as 'SuperSwede' with very good reason.

Apart from most of the Finns being 'Flying', some of their names were tongue twisters, or at least that was the US F2 team owner and Chevron importer Fred Opert thought – he obviously hadn't come across any Sri Lankan racers. Anyway, he decided nobody could pronounce the first name of his driver Keijo Rosberg and re-named him 'Keke'. It certainly stuck and I doubt if many current F1 fans even realise that 'Keke' isn't his real name.

Following suit, but at the hand of Marlboro's spin doctors, came 'JJ' Lehto – real name Jyrki Juhani Jarvilelehto. So why was he not 'JJJ' Lehto, then? Quite a few World Champions had nicknames. There was 'Black' Jack Brabham, Denny 'The Bear' Hulme, Jackie

Danny Rick or the 'Honey Badger'? ***McLaren***

Nico 'Britney' Rosberg. ***Mercedes-Benz***

Stewart was either simply 'JYS' or the 'Wee Scot', Nigel Mansell was known by his is Italian fans as 'Il Leone' but in the UK as 'Our Nige'. Sometimes the nicknames could be cruel. Privateer '70s Formula 1 racer Mike Beuttler was usually referred to as 'Blocker', because he was rather good at making his March very wide.

Among the current crop of Formula 1 drivers, there seems to be fewer nicknames – or maybe I am more out of touch these days. But I do know Australian Danny Ricciardo is often referred to as the 'Honey Badger' – a beast that is vicious and strikes when you don't expect it – or sometimes 'Danny Rick'. Kevin Magnusson is known as 'K Mag', at least by racer/commentator Paul di Resta. Nico Hulkenberg is 'The Hulk'. But I bet he has never been put in a headlock by Hulk Hogan – see chapter 10.

Perhaps the most used current F1 nickname is 'Checo', as Mexico's Sergio Perez is universally called, but I have never really got to the bottom of that one. I don't think Sebastian Vettel has a nickname – although he is often called Seb – but he sometime gives his cars nicknames or at least names. He has done it every year, starting at Toro Rosso in 2008 with 'Julie'.

The following year, having moved on to Red Bull, he called his first RB 5 'Kate', but later in the season there was 'Kate's Dirty Sister'. Others that followed included 'Luscious Liz', 'Randy Mandy', 'Kinky Kylie' and 'Hungry Heidie'. When he switched to Ferrari in

Tony 'Smoke' Stewart. ***Stewart-Haas***

2016, there was 'Eva', 'Margherita' and 'Gina'.

Kimi Raikkonen is known as the 'Iceman', although in US racing circles that is the nickname of multiple Indycar Champion, New Zealander Scott Dixon. Earlier, I mentioned my sub-category of the alliterative or descriptive which brings to mind Derek 'Dinger' Bell, although I am not sure that really stuck. Did you know that Le Mans Audi winner 'Dindo' Capello is actually Rinaldo on his birth certificate? Apparently, he used to live next to a church which had a loud peel of bells. The four-year-old Capello used to mimic the sound making the noise, 'dindo, dindo'. I know it is true because he told me himself.

There are plenty more. Racer turned TV presenter is 'Tiff' Needell because his brother could not say Timothy. The origins of the legendary Andrea de 'Crasheris' are obvious. Jody Scheckter was cleverly named 'Fletcher' by none less than James Hunt. If you have read the book Jonathan Livingstone Seagull, which the erudite Hunt must have done during his time at the upmarket Wellington School, you will know that Fletcher was the bird that tried to fly when he was too young.

There are plenty of nicknames that go back to the 1950s. The Frenchman who twice won the Monaco Grand Prix, Maurice Trintignant, was given one of the more unfortunate – 'Le Petoulet'. Let me explain. He retired from the Paris Grand Prix because rat droppings – *les petoulets* – were found blocking the fuel system of his Bugatti. Apparently, he didn't mind being called 'Rat Shit'. A racing contemporary, Jose Froilan Gonzalez, who gave Ferrari their first ever Formula 1 victory, was known by the British contingent as the 'Pampas Bull', but in his home country as 'El Cabezon', which translates as 'Fat Head'. Another great Argentine driver, Carlos Reutemann, was widely known as 'Lole' or 'El Lole', and the origins here go back to his childhood on the family farm. Apparently, he could not pronounce the name for little suckling pigs which were being raised by his family, presumably to go on the spit. They are called lechitos but Carlos could only splutter 'lole'.

The current top Argentine racer, Toyota WEC star Jose Mario Lopez, is known as 'Pechito' – it is even on his crash helmet. Again, this is another weird one. His racer father had a the nickname 'Pecho', apparently something he shouted at his rivals after a fierce battle on the track race. Literally translated, it is cold chest but means 'Scared cat'. The ito in Spanish or the inho in Portuguese indicates little or junior, so Lopez is 'little scared cat'. If I was called that, I don't think I would paint it on my crash helmet.

Meanwhile, his fellow Brazilian Carlos Pace was 'Moco'. That translates as 'Snot'. I kid you not. Apparently, before a race the Brazilian nervously picked his nose and put the deposits under the dashboard of race car. I must admit I never saw him doing it and he was a wonderful fellow. How about the former Formula 1 and Champcar racer Roberto Pupo Moreno, who often picked up rides when others were injured and was thus known as 'Supersub'? But that wasn't his only nickname – surely Pupo has to be the second? Wrong, it is his real middle name. But the diminutive Moreno was known in Brazil as

Sergio Perez even gets his nickname painted on the pit lane. *Red Bull*

'Baxinho', literally 'Little 'Un'. A man they all raced against was Jean-Pierre Jarier, fondly known as 'Jumper'. Earlier, the '50s British Formula 1 privateer Ian Raby was known as 'Puddle Jumper' as he was quick in the wet.

Even incidents get nicknames, most famously the 2008 Singapore Grand Prix after the incident caused by 'Nelsinho' Piquet – little Nelson – is universally called 'Crashgate'. Fans of the 1970s saloon car racing will not only remember Barrie 'Whizzo' Williams and 'Skid' Scarborough but, most notably the great Gerry Marshall, who didn't have a nickname but his Vauxhall racing machinery did. There was 'Big Betha' and 'Baby Bertha', both monster machines. The 1950 Cadillac which raced at Le Mans was also quite a beast and the French nicknamed it 'Le Monstre'. I even rallied alongside Andy Dawson in a factory Datsun we called 'Big Bomber'. The original pit reporter John Bolster, whom a I have mentioned elsewhere in this book, raced a special called 'Bloody Mary'. There must be hundreds more.

I haven't really touched on the NASCAR scene, which is rich in nicknames. The great Dale Earnhart was 'The Intimidator' for obvious reasons. How about 'Swervin' Ernie Irvan or 'Front Row' Joe Nemechek? There was 'Awesome Bill (Elliott) from Dawsonville', Richard Petty was quite simply 'The King', Terry Labonte was yet another 'Iceman' while Tony Stewart was simply 'Smoke'. This was not because he always left plumes of it when he accelerated out of the Daytona pitlane but because he blew up a lot of motors. Going back in time there was 'Fireball' Roberts. Germany has its own 'Smoking' Joe Winkelhock, but that was because the former BTCC Champion liked a cigarette or three after a race. The new FIA President Mohammed ben Sulayem, the umpteen-time Middle East Rally Champion, picked up the fine nickname of 'Dusty Bin'; just right for a guy who was quick in the desert.

I have not sure if it counts really, but some guys just get called by their initials, I already mentioned JYS, but David Coulthard is often just DC and Jenson Button just JB

But I want to finish with a story which might indicate the nickname could be a thing of the past. I found this story on a Formula 1 mechanics' chatroom. I rather hope it is not true because it about a team which for many years was led by Frank Williams, a man who, until his cars started winning, was known affectionately as 'Wanker' and had a Chief Mechanic known as 'Dobbin'. Anyway the team have, according to a post I read, banned the use of nicknames.

Apparently, one team technician was called 'Father Christmas' on account of his long grey beard. Allegedly after he took retirement he sued the Williams team because of the abuse and the hurt it caused him. Those in that chatroom discussion swear it is true.

What is this weird and wonderful world coming to?

Chapter 21

WHAT'S IN A NAME?

Sometimes drivers aren't who we thought they were.

My dictionary states a pseudonym is a name that someone – often a writer – uses instead of a real name. It is also sometimes known as a *nom de plume*, in the acting world as a stage name, or perhaps most appropriately for motor racing, a *nom de guerre*. A name of war.

Over the years, this practice has been used by everyone from World Champions to Le Mans winners. The reasons have varied from guys who had lost their driving licences through to drug smugglers, chaps trying to hide their racing activities from parents/wives/mistresses/children/shareholders/debtors (delete as appropriate) to one of the most famous drivers of all: his proper name was far too common.

I am, of course, referring to Ayrton Senna da Silva. As is the Brazilian and originally Portuguese tradition, Ayrton's full name included that of his mother's family name, Senna. However, his father's family name of da Silva is a very common in Brazil – the equivalent of Smith – so going into his second season in the UK, Ayrton dropped the 'da Silva' bit. I have no doubt that in the lofts of some of our readers are race programmes from 1981 with the full da Silva moniker shown. Senna's parents had a nickname for him, 'Beco'. So he could have adopted that, but Ayrton Beco doesn't quite have the same ring about it, does it?

The previous Brazilian World Champion, Nelson Piquet, also shortened his name but for different reasons. He, too, adopted his mother's family name. On his birth certificate, the son of Brazil's one-time Minister of Health is named as Nelson Piquet Souto Maior. Nelson's dad, Estacio, was so keen on him becoming a top professional tennis player that he even sent him as a teenager to an expensive Californian tennis ranch. In fact, Nelson was pretty handy with a racquet but what he really wanted to do was race.

So to hide his racing from his father he adapted his mother's name and in his earlier events actually raced as 'Piket', but once this ruse was discovered he changed the spelling back to his mother's name. I have no explanation as to why, but Brazilian football stars seem to be referred to under just one name – there is even one called Emerson. I can only presume his parents were fans of Emerson Fittipaldi. In fact, and not many people know this, Emerson was named after the American essayist and poet Ralph Waldo Emerson, who was much admired by Emerson's father, the journalist Wilson Fittipaldi Senior.

Much more recently, Michael Schumacher's son, in an attempt to ward off the pressure and scrutiny, started racing in karts under the assumed name of Mick Betsch, his mother's maiden name and then switched to Mick Junior. However, as he moved up the ranks and won the Formula 2 title he has raced as Mick Schumacher and everyone knows now that he is Michael's son.

Of course, it is well documented that the first ever winner of the Monaco Grand Prix in 1929 was the French-born but British driver, W Williams, sometimes just referred to as Williams. A remarkable man, he was actually christened William Charles Frederick Grover, but later his name was changed to Grover-Williams. To keep his early racing on a motorbike secret, he

'Williams'. The war hero who won the first ever Monaco Grand Prix in his Bugatti. He raced under a single name but was christened William Charles Frederick Grover. ***CSS Archive***

Mick Schumacher competed under a pseudonym when he started racing using the name Mick Betsch, his mother's maiden name. ***Haas F1***

entered as W Williams and he kept this pseudonym as he switched to car racing. At the time of his Monaco victory, he was a rather upmarket chauffeur for the famous portrait painter William Orpen. He was later involved in espionage in World War Two and was eventually killed by the Gestapo. To learn more, I can thoroughly recommend Joe Saward's book, *The Grand Prix Saboteurs*.

But Williams wasn't the only driver in that inaugural Monaco GP not to use his correct name. The man who finished fourth, was on the entry list as 'George Philippe', but was actually Baron Philippe de Rothschild of the banking dynasty.

I mentioned that some Le Mans winners did not use their own name and famously 'John Winter' had his cover blown when, together with pasta heir Paulo Barilla and Klaus Ludwig, he raced to victory to the 1985 Le Mans 24 Hours with the Joest Porsche 956, at which point his mother found what her son Louis Krages had been doing most weekends! The story does not have a happy ending, as Krages moved to Atlanta, Georgia, and set up a toy business, which got into difficulties and he took a gun to his head.

Another Le Mans winner not to use his correct name was, of course, 'Johnny Dumfries'. Johnny who died in 2021 was a super guy and in his younger days I believe he thought that his chances of gaining sponsorship would be hampered if companies knew he was actually John Colum Crichton-Stuart, the Earl of Dumfries. He was probably right and, at the time, he had no access to the family fortune. So he liked to be known as Johnny Dumfries; he even adopted a London accent, so if you met him back then you would be hard-pushed to know he was an aristocrat. Later he became the 7th Marquess of Bute, but preferred to be known as John Bute.

Then, of course, there were several occasional F1 drivers with assumed names. 'Mike Sparken', actually Mike Poberejsky, 'Gimax' (proper name Carlo Franchi) and who could forget 'Bern Nacke' (real name Gunter Bechem) who competed in a couple of 1950s German Grands Prix. I rather hope he didn't happen upon his new name following a fire in the cockpit, if you see what I mean.

The 1970s Ensign and Brabham F1 driver Frederick 'Rikki' von Opel, grandson of the founder of Opel cars, started his British Formula Ford career as 'Antonio Bronco' and, though I knew him quite well, I never quite plucked up the courage to ask if he had found the name on a piece of toilet paper. Yes, really it was a famous brand and even used the slogan 'for the bigger wipe'. Anyway, when he switched to the Ensign Formula 3 team, he used his proper name.

I never knew until I started researching this chapter that 1961 Ferrari Formula 1 driver Count Wolfgang von Trips, started his racing career under the pseudonym 'Axel Linther'. Another of those aristocratic things, you see. He also had the nickname – which is entirely different – Taffy, although he had no Welsh connections. Students of German can probably fill in the details. Actually, his full name was quite a mouthful: Wolfgang Alexander Eduard Maximillian Reichsgraf Berghe von Trips. Try putting that on a credit card application form.

The most prolific almost serial pseudonymist (probably not a real word but you know what I mean) was Friedrich Glatz. He raced as 'James Bald' in German Touring Cars, in sports cars as 'Frederico Careca', in Formula 3 as 'Umberto Calvo' and in Formula 2 as 'Pierre Chauvet' The latter surnames translate as bald as he was deficient in the hair department.

At one stage, it was almost de rigeur among Italian racers to have a pseudonym. I have already mentioned 'Gimax', who tried to qualify for the 1978 German Grand Prix, but who can forget touring and sports car racer 'Pal Joe' which sounds rather like a name I would give a budgerigar. Actually, after a career spanning 16 years, Gianfranco Palazzoli went on to become the Osella Formula 1 team manager. Another Osella driver, 'Amphicar' (real name Eugenio Renna) won the 1976 Targa Florio but also won in an Italian sports car race at Enna in the same year. Those of you who have been to the Sicilian track will know it circles a big snake-infested lake. With a name like Amphicar, I just wonder if he took a short cut on his way to the win.

Two other Italian pseudonymists 'Tiger' and 'Geki' perished in the same tragic race at the appallingly dangerous Caserta road circuit about 25 miles north of Naples in Italy. Both were leading Formula 3 drivers and the entry that day also including Clay Regazzoni and Ernesto Brambilla. 'Tiger' – now there is a decent pseudonym for a racing driver – was actually Romano Perdomi and 'Geki' was Giacomo Russo. Then there was 'Pooky', which wasn't former Long Beach Grand Prix organiser Chris Pook but Italian Vincenzo Cazzago.

'The Stig' has become very much a part of British pop culture through the massive success of *Top Gear*. But did you know that 'The Stig' actually raced? It was on the occasion when *Top Gear* ran a BMW 3-series for its presenters in the 2007 Britcar 24 Hours, complete with schoolboy humour pretend sponsors down the side of the car. I swear I saw Ben Collins' eyes pointing out of the famous white helmet and he seemed to be a lot quicker than Clarkson and co. Perry McCarthy was the first Stig, and I am pretty sure I know who the current one is, but I am not telling. I do wonder if the *Top Gear* people actually knew of World Rally Champion Stig Blomqvist or the broadcaster Stig Abell.

There are hundreds more. 'Pierre Levegh', who almost won single-handedly at Le Mans in 1952 and then crashed into the crowd in 1955 was actually Pierre Bouillon, although there is some controversy about the spelling of the name. Another aristocrat raced as 'Raph', real name Comte Georges Raphaël Béthenod de Montbressieux. In real life, Le Mans front-runner 'Beurlys' was Jean Blaton.

Then we come to the best pseudonym of all: 'Willie Eckerslyke'. Former 1960s racer Bill Allen was responsible for this. Bill was an associate of the Moores family who owned the Liverpool catalogue and pools company. Heir apparent Nigel Moores wanted to

Patrick Head, with Ayrton da Silva who raced under the Senna name. *ICN*

Monaco Historic regular Mister John of B with his beautiful Matra. Real name Jean Guittard. *Andrew Marriott*

race and could afford it but the family, fearing he may come to harm, said no.

Bill came up with the idea of racing under an assumed name, but what? Nigel had acquired a Jaguar D-type, but there were some quick and more experienced rivals so he probably wasn't going to take the winner's chequered flag. As Bill speculated, 'Would he win?' It was unlikely but you have to say the answer with a northern accent, 'Will he heck as like'. Which became Willie Eckerslyke – brilliant and sounds like a good Lancashire name.

The French don't seem to care much for pseudonyms, but there is the historic racer who calls himself Mister John of B. I have no idea what the B stands for. But Germans still favour pseudonyms and there are usually about a dozen or so of them on any Nürburgring 24 Hours entry list and at least a couple seem to be called Axel Shaft. Jürgen Stiftschraube (George Retaining Screw) is a also regular. Some just choose single names like 'Brodie', 'Max', and not forgetting 'Smudo'.

I suspect there are people out there even now racing under an assumed name that remain undiscovered.

Best ever pseudonym 'Willie Eckerslyke'. Liverpool Pools' heir Nigel Moores raced a Jaguar D-type. *Bill Allen*

Le Mans winner 'John Winter', aka Louis Krages. *Opel*

Cheers to the memory of 'Johnny Dumfries'. *Sue Weaver*

Chapter 22

BEDDING DOWN

The Grand Prix drivers who came to stay a while.

"Who was that on the phone?" shouts Mrs M. "Just an old flat mate," I say. "Oh," she replies, "which one of the sixty or so was that then?"

As I mentioned in an earlier chapter, my first resting place when I arrived in London was a room shared with a dismantled vintage motorbike and the damaged parts of a Ginetta G4. This was only a temporary arrangement and I quickly moved on to various rented addresses around Central and North London over the next eight years. But then I finally became a responsible adult, got married, bought a house in Muswell Hill in North London and climbed on the property ladder.

I have trawled through my memory and I reckon I lived in eight different flats and was also once briefly homeless, only to be taken in by the kind parents of a mate. For some reason, we never crossed the river. All the flats were to the north of the Thames, starting in Enfield and heading as close to the centre of the capital as Baker Street.

I was not a solitary sole and each of the eight flats was shared with a regularly changing cast of both full-time and occasional dossers. They numbered among them one who went on to be a Formula 1 World Champion, another who won the British Grand Prix, a former Gold Leaf Team Lotus Swede, two RAC Rally winning navigators, the original drummer of the Rolling Stones, and a man who went on read the sports news on Central TV. Then there was a fellow journalist who become managing director of Haymarket Publishing, another graduated to the position of Donington Park Managing Director, and yet another who ran an award-winning vineyard in the Napa Valley. Then there was the guy who dominated the passport photo business in London, a chap who later in life sailed a 60ft canal boat across the English Channel plus various other journalists and would-be racers.

Tragically there was one guy destined for Formula One, the hugely talented Chris Lambert, who perished in his Brabham Formula Two at Zanvoort after a clash with Clay Regazzoni. Clearing out his stuff, including parts of a kart engine he was building on the kitchen table, was not something I clearly remember, but reminded us of the fragility of life. Soon after, another member of that flat also died from an illness I have now forgotten, so I was happy to move on. I checked the place out the other day and it looked pretty seedy.

This group of aspiring fellow travellers were virtually all drawn to London by the bright lights, a pint or two in the Steering Wheel Club and were seeking fame and fortune in the world of motorsport. In those days, London was the only place to be, I suppose now there are similar groups in rented houses in Milton Keynes. But back in the swinging '60s, MK was just a load of fields near Bletchley, so wasn't really an option.

These various flatmates either came with or adopted nicknames which sometimes referred to their physical appearance or habits such as Twinkle, Hooter and rather disgustingly Bogey. Others had shortened versions of their names: the 'Dood', 'Oggers', 'Davers' and 'Aitch' come to mind. An early flatmate had a rallying Mini reg number BOJ 732 so he became known as 'Bodge', while ace racing car cut away artist Tony Matthews was most definitely 'Pencils'.

While these were primarily bachelor flats, various women passed through, some even became resident and they too had nicknames. There was 'Turtle' – named because she was helpless when on her back, according to that man who went on to sail the barge across the Channel. Then there was the alluring redhead just out of Hornsey Art College called 'Ginger'. There was 'PJ', because Petronella was far too long a name, and, lest I forget, a sometime visitor who went on to be Formula E and Ferrari ace Sam Bird's Mum, who was simply 'Di'.

As I mentioned in an earlier chapter, my first flat was in Enfield and, after a few weeks of enduring the lumpy mattress, landlord Ted announced he has found me a proper place to stay, with some bloke whose name now escapes me, but was a designer at Lotus in Cheshunt. Again, for some reason that I can't now recall, it didn't work out. I was hankering after the bright lights of London rather than the dubious suburbia which was Enfield. Briefly I was homeless but, as I recounted earlier, a mate called Martin Miles persuaded his parents to put me up in their luxury flat off Enfield Chase.

One of my first flat mates was Chris Lambert, a Grovewood Award winner who was surely heading for Formula 1. Here he is at Jamama in his P&M Preps Brabham BT21 leading Jo Schlesser. Chris was tragically killed the following year at Zandvoort. ***LAT***

So proper food, freshly ironed laundry and home comforts.

During this period, I somehow got wind of a flat inhabited by the aforementioned 'Bodge', who was sharing it with his then girlfriend. As a naïve 22-year-old from Derby, I found this pre-marital living together a trifle shocking. However, the location was good; 8 Bolton Road was just off Abbey Road, less than a quarter of a mile from the famous studios and the world's most famous zebra crossing. I was joined at various times by then *Autosport* reporter Simon Taylor, plus racer Chris Lambert (and the various kart engines he was rebuilding) plus Roger Willis, just about to be promoted to Competitions Manager at Castrol. I think one of the conditions of him moving in was that Castrol sponsored Chris's Brabham Formula 3 car.

Apart from the tragic death of Chris and the fact that it was a dank and dark basement, we all had a wonderful time, often dining around the corner at a marvellously cheap French bistro which played nothing but Edith Piaf over its music system. "*Je ne regrette rien*". We didn't.

'Bodge', and the lady who became his wife and later ex-wife, moved out and it was Mike Doodson, now a veteran Formula 1 journalist, who took over that bedroom. He brought with him a degree of sophistication from his days at Oxford to add that of Cambridge educated Simon 'Hooter' Taylor, who went on to great things in both broadcasting and publishing with the Haymarket group. The 'Dood' also possessed some skills in the culinary department when he wasn't trying to persuade us to listen to some obscure jazz trumpeter. There were plenty of other drop-in visitors or people who stayed the occasional night. On occasion, they come up to me to say and tell me they remember staying at this or that flat and some amusing incident that has since been erased from my memory bank.

However, one particular incident that remains vivid features the then rising star of Formula 5000 and subsequently historic racer Willie Green, who was staying the night. He was probably about to head for a meeting with Hexagon's Paul Michaels to tell him the brown hue of the F5000 Trojan he was racing for Michaels shared a description which compared with the car's handling.

Paul's response was to tell Green where to go and promptly, at our suggestion, hired a regular Irish visitor to the flat – John Watson. A few months later, Michaels ditched the recalcitrant brown racer and replaced it with a Brabham F1 car. Thus Wattie became a Formula One driver and Willy didn't.

Anyway, we were settling down for the night when there was the most piercing yell from Green who had stepped on a hornet, which promptly stung him. The somewhat over-the-top screaming was still continuing when there was a furious thumping on the door. With Green still yelping, we opened it to find our downstairs neighbour in his pyjamas and he had obviously woken from his slumbers by the screeching Willie. He was last seen limping as fast as he could go down Bolton Road with this fellow in pursuit.

As I mentioned, the Abbey Road EMI studios were just a few blocks down the road and so too was a house where another up-and-coming racer was holed up. That man was ace getaway driver and Great Train robber Roy James. Indeed, he was apprehended just a couple of blocks away from Bolton Road, skipping across the roof tops. Honestly, he never graced the doors of 8 Bolton Road, gov. In fact, I had reported on some of James's early races in the Brabham, which he had purchased with a suitcase full of fivers.

Flat mates at different times. On the left Mike Doodson, as MGD a colleague at Motoring News and Tony Chapman, former drummer, fine art shipper and hero of Chapter 4! ***Andrew Marriott***

He was a true talent and had he given up his life of crime he surely would have made it to Formula 1. He wrote a couple of letters to me from jail in his immaculate copper plate hand writing, which unfortunately my mother later binned.

Again for some reason I can't recall, but possibly to do with next door being demolished, I moved on to a much more salubrious flat at 49 Marloes Road, W8, in the heart of Kensington. I think this was at the instigation of one of the tenants, the redoubtable John Foden. Foden's career included inventing the Players No 6 Rallycross Championship, a long spell marketing Austin Rover's competition success and a stint at the helm of Silverstone's PR and Promotion Department. If you have an hour or three Fod, now resident in France, will tell you all about it.

As well as Mr Foden, this flat was already inhabited with various names of the rally world and included star navigators John Brown and John Davenport, plus journalist Richard Hudson-Evans. These days, RHE is an expert of classic car auctions but then was a certified daredevil and lunatic. From time to time, most of the top Finnish and Scandinavian rally stars passed through, Simo Lampinen being a regular.

But my strongest memory was of a particular party where Hudson-Evans, having consumed more alcohol than was good for him, decided to climb out of our front window. The flat was on the first floor. Outside was a four-inch ledge which went along to the Devonshire Arms pub next door which was the end of the block. This ledge continued around that establishment and then round to the back of number 49. About ten minutes after Richard had departed there was a furious tapping on the window at the back of the flat. RHE has circumnavigated around this perilous protrusion and there he was madly grinning and asking to be let back in. While researching this chapter, I took a look at Google Earth. I thought our flat was next door to the pub, but it wasn't. There were about three other houses between us and the Devonshire!

Probably because they put the rent up, in 1970 I moved to an even smarter address, 73 Baker Street, almost opposite the mythical home of Sherlock Holmes. Yes, we did have

Jody Scheckter arrived at 73 Baker Street and found a bed for a few weeks while Team Lotus racer Reine Wisell was an occasional visitor to 7A Netherhall Gardens. Sadly Reine recently died in Thailand where he had lived for several years. ***CSS Archive***

Japanese tourists knocking on the door asking if this was where the sleuth had lived. This was a slightly weird deal because the couple who were renting it to us were actually doing so illegally sub-renting it to us with a mark-up – something which took us about a year to discover. This place was palatial and, of course, very central.

Among the full-time residents was Robert Fearnall, then a journalist, but who went on to successfully run Donington Park race track for many years and Mike Doodson, re-joining me as a flat mate. It was here that Jody Scheckter apparently, according to his autobiography, 'lived like a dog'.

Let me explain. I met the future World Champion at a South African Motor Racing Club event near Kyalami where I was giving a talk. Afterwards, young Jody approached me and told me he had won a driver to Britain award, sponsored by Ford and would be heading to the UK to race in Formula Ford. I gave him my card and said to give me a ring if he needed any help.

A month or so later, at about 7.30am one day, the phone rang to be answered by Mike as I had been back to Derby for a Mallory Park meeting and also to present my mother with a load of dirty washing.

The phone call went something like this: "Is Mr Marriott there, he said he would help me. I am at Heathrow with my 'appie' [mechanic] and Mr Stuart Turner said he would be here to meet us with a car, but he isn't here and we don't know what to do!"

Mike, kind soul that he is, suggested that as the Head of Ford Motorsport, Stuart had better things to do at 7.30 in the morning than collect young racing drivers from airports and that the best course of action was get on the tube to Baker Street and find number 73. That is exactly what Jody and his mechanic did and they finished up sleeping on the flat floor for a month or so during which time I managed to do a deal whereby the so-called Magic Merlyn Formula Ford passed from the championship-winning hands of Colin Vandervell to Jody. Never did get the commission on that sale, Colin!

I said earlier Mr Doodson was then a handy cook and he is now hugely accomplished at the stove, but he wasn't always around, so the culinary skills passed to me. I was very good at peeling a few carrots and potatoes and opening a can of Irish stewing steak – very tasty, too. But Jody, somewhat traumatised by the fact that we didn't have a couple of maids looking after us, thought it tasted like dog food, hence his comment. Not that he complained about it at the time, nor the fact he lived rent-free until Mr Turner found him a place in Boreham. Or that the Merlyn was still a winner. Or that I recommended him to Phil Kerr and he got him a McLaren ride.

Anyway, while we were at Baker Street, suddenly outside were erected some posts called parking meters which were a pain in the backside. But we quickly discovered that the ring pull from a beer or coke can neatly fitted in the slot, logged up an hour's worth of parking time and jammed the machine in that position. The glory of this deal was that the parking wardens couldn't even see what had happened. Now we weren't the first to do this terrible deed, but we in part responsible for the kink you now see in ring pulls which stop them being used for this nefarious purpose.

It was here at Baker Street that James Hunt was a regular visitor; indeed, he came on occasion as a judge for some competition or other that I was involved with. I can't remember the details but I do remember, surprisingly, he took it all very seriously.

It was in the parking bay right outside number 73 that Mike took delivery of a road test Lotus Europa modified by Mike Spence Ltd. It arrived on a trailer and, once unloaded, Mike asked the driver to show him how to start it and the various controls. However, the Renault engine in the rear refused to fire, it was loaded back on the trailer and never seen again. Possibly the shortest road test in history.

Just before we were chucked out of that flat because of the sub-letting scandal, we got a bill and I was horrified to find the total was almost three hundred pounds, a lot of money back then. But then I noticed we were in credit and didn't owe anything. I called them saying we were leaving the flat and a fat cheque arrived. We could only assume the meter reading operative had previously been in the pub up the road or had left his glasses behind. It didn't need Sherlock Holmes to tell us to spend it quickly and we bought a magnificent square box called a Sony Trinitron colour TV. I presume the gas board found out the mistake later, but by then we had moved on to 7a Netherhall Garden, Hampstead NW3. I just looked on Zoopla and it is now worth £4.8million.

John Watson was a regular at 35 Alwyne Road when he raced this Brabham. ***Hexagon***

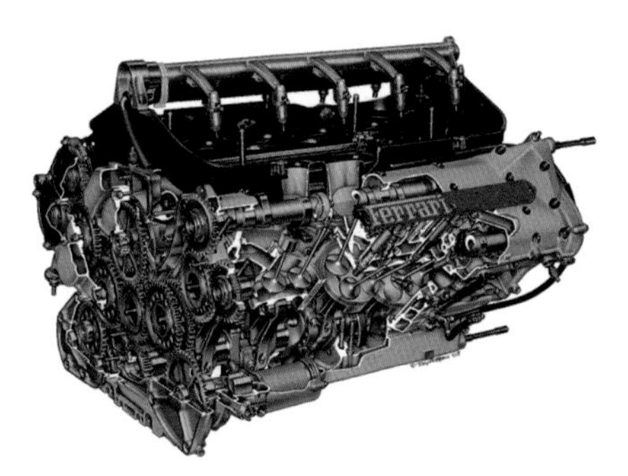

Flat mates Tony 'Pencils' Matthews was a brilliant illustrator and famous for his cut-away drawings while California Randy Lewis left lots of his decals behind. He went on to race at Indy and become an award winning wine-maker. ***Marriott Archive***

Since my occupation, it has had a huge amount of work done to it but back then the ground floor was actually a garage workshop with two floors of accommodation above it. The workshop was operated by Chris Coburn under the name of Coburn Improvements, tuners of Austin-Healey Sprites, Minis, and other rally cars. Taking into account that these machines weren't always that reliable, we unofficially renamed Chris's enterprise Cockup Impairments. Rally driving Chris was that man I mentioned who had a girlfriend called 'Turtle' and who sailed that barge across the Channel. His rally co-driver was a fellow called Rodney Spokes, whose named was emblazoned on the side of their Triumph 2000 rally car in letraset. Now I know this is childish, but we did laugh when we peeled off the 'S' from Rodney's surname. I think he spotted it before they headed off to take part in the Targa Rusticana or some similar rally.

It was here we held a press conference and demonstration of some new type of Nomex race suit that Chris was promoting. He dressed up this gear and we set off into the largely uncared-for garden at the rear of the workshop with various scribes in tow. There we had set up a large tray of petrol which Chris would then walk through. But all didn't go to plan. Somehow we lit it without it exploding but it burned so ferociously that all the nearby scrubs and bushes caught fire and we lost interest in Coburn and struggled to contain the blazing garden.

Again, various racers came to rest their heads on the spare couch. They included some who made it and plenty who didn't but were probably more fun. One regular was Team Lotus F1 driver Reine Wisell, he of the bright green crash helmet and Lotus 72 and BRM fame. While staying with us, he managed to win a Formula 2 at Crystal Palace. The following morning, we were surprised to read that 'Whistling Diesel' was the victor. It seems the copy taker at the *Daily Express* had mis-heard the name and the sub-editors never questioned the curious name.

Other F3 visitors included such forgotten names as Randy Lewis, who went on to race at Indy but found more success in the Californian wine industry, and Cliff Haworth, always known as Cliff Baby.

Through these various flats and moves, I never once remember having any legal disputes and we were safe in the fact that one early flat mate was top legal brain, and solicitor extraordinaire Duncan Rabagliati. He has, of course masterminded the huge success of Historic Formula Junior.

After the owners of 7A Netherhall decided to develop the place into the multi-million pound property it is today, Doodson and I headed a couple miles away to the Garden Flat, 35 Alwyne Road in the lush surrounds of Canonbury. Strangely, despite its name, we had no access to the garden itself. The whole magnificent town house was owned by a certain Nick Brittan, a man of multiple talents. He was a quick racer, first in karting then as the driver of the famous 'Green Bean' Anglia, and a works Frazer Imp. He was also one of racing's top PR guys and he later went on to be a very successful property developer and the father of classic endurance rallying. He moved to Australia and sadly took his own life some years later.

The flat had just two bedrooms. In one we installed another well-known journo, Clive Richardson, while Doodson and I, amazingly, shared a bedroom. Nothing funny, we just did, somehow co-existing quite happily. It was outside this flat that my Reliant Scimitar GTE's brake pedal literally snapped in two when I was doing a three-point turn. The management at Tamworth were neither surprised nor apologetic. "We've had a few of those go, rogue welder you see, we've sacked him. We will send you a new one free of charge." It was also at 35 that John Watson was such a regular visitor that, having tired of the lumpy mattress we offered him, actually bought his own camp bed.

These days the flat at 8 Bolton Road, close to the famous Beatles zebra crossing on Abbey Road, looks decidedly dingy but it was quite smart when our group of racers and journalists lived there.
Andrew Marriott

One particular occasion after a televised Formula 3 race at Lydden Hill, we had decided to hold a party back at Alwyne Road and over half the grid turned up. They included David Purley and his dad Charlie, then boss of the Lec Refrigeration company which went on to construct the eponymous Formula One car. But I was upset when said Purley Senior decided to sit on a coffee table which hardly took his weight and stubbed out his cigar butts on the wall behind him.

One fine day, Nick's wife Jenny announced they were moving to an even larger pad in Hampstead and so we would need to look for new accommodation. Then Nick appeared and said all was not lost as he was developing an old greengrocer's shop into three flats in a rather more seedy part of Islington just round the corner from Pentonville Prison. Guess what? He would give us a great deal. Subsequently, I bought the top two floors and Mike acquired the basement while Nick managed to sell the ground floor to a bloke who played principle clarinet for Rudolf Nureyev at the Royal Ballet.

When I recount these stories of the '60s and '70s, I am sometimes asked if we were stoned out of our minds half the time. Sorry to disappoint, but I don't believe there was much, if any, drugs at any of these flats. I certainly never got involved and don't remember smelling any weed being smoked, and certainly never saw any white powder. But there were a lot of cigarettes, beer, cheap wine, whisky, rum and even cider!

With that final eviction prompted by Nick Brittan, I became a home owner and no longer an itinerant apartment dweller and, obviously, a lot more grown up. These were wonderful and heady times and I am proud that I am still in contact with many of those with whom I shared a roof.

Chapter 23

THINGS THAT GO BUMP IN THE NIGHT

From ghosts to gourmet, my travels have taken me to some of the world's shabbiest and smartest hotels.

Whoooooah! I wrote this chapter after staying at The Kenilworth Lodge Hotel and it is rumoured to be haunted. This is not a hostelry in Kenilworth, Warwickshire, you understand, but right among the orange groves of Sebring, Florida. The Kenilworth was built over 100 years ago by the man who gave the town its name. George E Sebring was a pottery magnate originally from Ohio. The hotel was a huge establishment for the insignificant town of Sebring at the time, but George had big plans for the whole area. The hotel featured 200 bedrooms, a massive conference room, vast lobby and reception areas and such pleasant additions as an Olympic-sized swimming pool and even a dedicated billiards room. You don't get that up the road at the Econo-Lodge.

Outside on the veranda, there were rocking chairs where you can watch the sun set over Lake Jackson while sipping a Bud. In the Spring, the air is infused by the heady scent of orange blossom. As a pits reporter and thus part of what was, perhaps, optimistically called 'the talent' by Fox Sports, I was even allocated a suite.

This all sounds idyllic except the owners hadn't exactly spent any dollars on the place in years – the Kenilworth was, to put it mildly, down at heel and had seen better days. Back in the '70s it used to be the place to stay in Sebring but now the high rollers all check in at hotel built by the late Don Panoz and originally called Chateau Elan but now known as Seven as it overlooks the track's Turn 7.

In fact, until US TV budgets got slashed, we stayed there for a number of years. Panoz and his wife Nancy even had motor racing-themed the decorations, right down to the bedspreads. On arrival, there would be a bottle of Don's finest Georgian wine waiting in our room, complete with a custom-made label celebrating that particular race. I drank the somewhat dubious liquid long ago but I have saved the bottles hoping one day they might become collectors' pieces. The paddock and TV compound is only a brief golf cart ride away, which meant more time in bed, except that at Sebring they always seem to have a practice session for a Mazda MX-5 race starting at about 6.45 am. Now the MX-5 may not make the noise of the Japanese company's Le Mans winner, but 40 of the things buzzing past your window will quickly raise you from your slumbers.

After the bean-counters decided that we were being over-indulged at a $400-a-night establishment, we found ourselves sharing villas, actually privately-owned bungalows at a golf resort called Spring Lakes, which is only a five-minute drive from the track. It was a perfectly pleasant experience despite the warnings that there were alligators in the waters.

But then, the folk at NASCAR Travel – remember sports car racing in the States is now run by NASCAR – were a little slow booking them. So no room at the Lakes. They needed to find us alternative accommodation. You might think that the Kenilworth, with all its history and a lobby full of motor racing posters, would have also been full, but its now dubious reputation had gone before it.

So we got rooms, complete with dodgy plumbing and non-functioning wi-fi, while the only race team staying there was an outfit competing in a support event. The team, judging by their bright yellow race uniforms, appeared to be sponsored by some regional American sausage brand. Sadly, the Kenilworth's breakfast buffet featured neither their nor anyone else's sausage or bacon or even scrambled egg. I am not sure how these banger-backed boys got on, but any team that can find time to start doing a jigsaw puzzle at breakfast, handily provided by the Kenilworth management, probably isn't going to win much.

Anyway, back to the establishment's reputation of having its own ghost, and a story that was being circulated by my Fox Sports colleague Calvin Fish. Those of you with long memories will remember Cal racing in Formula 3 for Dave Price in BP colours back in the 1980s. Cal left our shores to find fame and fortune in America over 30 years ago and, while his on-track successes for

Perhaps the smartest place I stayed was the Villa d'Este on the banks of beautiful Lake Como and handy for Monza. These days it also hosts a major Concours event. ***Villa d'Este***

Ford were noteworthy, he really found his niche as a brilliant broadcaster and successful driver-manager.

Calvin had heard stories that things went bump in the night at the Kenilworth and he wasn't helped when his too-clever electronic key failed to open his suite, despite it clicking and the lock showing a green light. It seemed something or someone was the other side of the door pushing against it. Then at the fourth attempt, the door inexplicably opened and he thought he heard swift footsteps in his room! Calvin was sufficiently spooked to sleep with the light on that night. The fact that the same thing happened to a few of us would suggest that it was electronic glitch rather than an out-of-body experience, but it certainly adds to the myth.

I couldn't find anything on the internet about the Kenilworth Hotel ghost but plenty about a Brooklands one who apparently walks the hallowed British track's banking.

The famous and, dare I call her, veteran motor racing PR lady, Ann Bradshaw, later told me she stayed at the Kenilworth 15 years earlier and when she got to her next destination, she opened her suitcase and out hopped a present from the Kenilworth: a cockroach.

In fact, one of my worst ever motor racing accommodation experiences came at Sebring many years earlier when I was working for an Australian production company who pulled a late deal together to film for Toyota. I will spare you the detail but I finished up in some rented room in a kind of tin-roofed conservatory on a camp bed. It doesn't usually rain in Florida in March, but that year it did and I can still hear the plip, plop, plip of the rain above me.

When we racing people arrive at the track, be it broadcasters, journalists, trade, engineers, mechanics or even drivers, the default question as we meet our like-minded companions starts like this: first, of course, "How are you?" quickly followed by the inevitable, "Where are you staying?" This is usually followed by a long diatribe about the secretary, travel person or whoever, screwing up the booking one way or another. This can be as extreme as confusing the Nürburgring with Nuremberg and finishing up in a hotel 250 miles away from the track. This did actually happen a few years ago to a couple of Japanese journalists I met.

It didn't help that when they asked the staff at their chosen hotel to direct them to the race track they were instructed to head to the nearby Norisring, which is on the outskirts of Nuremberg. On arrival, they were rather surprised to find that while there were plenty of signs for Dekra, Bosch and the like, the massive concrete grandstand from

Sebring's Seven Hotel overlooks Turn 7 and was a great place to stay except when practice started at 7.30am. ***IMSA***

where Hitler gave those speeches, was empty. Adding to their confusion, they found that in the paddock there wasn't a racing car in sight. They had a long journey to the Eifel Mountains.

This kind of segues into my time as the English TV commentator for the DTM German Touring car series where I was working for a German production company called Wige. I never met the person who booked the hotels, but her knowledge of German geography was sadly lacking. We usually finished up at least an hour's drive from Hockenheim, Lausitzring, Oschersleben or wherever. I should point out that there is a hotel overlooking the track at two of the three tracks I mention. Actually there are two at the Nürburgring – and a casino as well. We, meanwhile, always stayed at a distant Center Parcs.

Frau Travel Booker also seemed to favour a German chain called NH Hotels – I have stayed in at least four different ones within distant striking distance of Hockenheim. The brand's USP seems to be the world's thinnest duvets, free internet but only in zee lobby and a free apple on reception; you vill eat it. I kid you not.

Frau Travel Booker had to work overtime when the DTM decided to strut its stuff in Shanghai and Moscow. In Shanghai we were booked into a Holiday Inn – unfortunately, she didn't tell us which of the two Shanghai Holiday Inns she had chosen. Needless to say, with a 50/50 choice, I went to the wrong one first.

Eventually I found the correct one and was delighted that the extensive buffet – very good value I might add – included such delicacies as fried chicken's feet. Not quite so popular were the police/army patrolling in front of our hotel and looking at us very suspiciously.

I have stayed at some other pretty swish hotels over the years, including the famous Hotel de Paris in Monaco's Casino Square and the handy-for-Monza Villa d'Este, the stunning five-star establishment overlooking Lake Como. It was here that a kind colleague altered the breakfast order hung on my door. I thought I had ordered porridge but I got cock-a-leekie soup. It is a mark of the hotel's ability that they were able to present a bowl of the said chicken and leek creation at 7.30 in the morning.

At this juncture, I should point out that I am not in any way connected with another famous hotel brand – Marriott. My family name seems a source of constant inquisition at car hire desks, by US customs officials and other random members of officialdom. If I have been asked once if I own this American group I have been asked a hundred times. I have stayed at a few of them too, and never have I been upgraded by a Marriott establishment. However, a lovely if dim girl at the Hilton Hotel in

In 2022 the former grand entrance to the Kenilworth Lodge looked like this, the plaque says it is on the National Register of Historic Places. A sad end to the 1916 dream of George Sebring. ***Andrew Marriott***

Another shot of Sebring's Seven Hotel, formerly Chateau Elan, shows how close Don Panoz built hotel to the track. ***Seven Hotel***

Cannes was so tickled that a Marriott was staying at a Hilton, she upgraded me to a terrific Junior Suite.

I did, however, pull off a sponsorship deal at the JW Marriott Hotel in Dubai when Andy Dawson and I were running a Middle East rally programme for Jeep. In return for some decals on the car and some decent publicity, I think I negotiated a hundred free room nights. Dawson and I both got suites in the executive section and they featured the best bathroom I have ever had the pleasure to shower and shave in.

This imaginary scene at Siebkins Resort sums up its reputation as the American racers favourite hang-out. How many drivers can you name? Roger Warrick's poster is still available to purchase. ***Guy Hobbs***

Perhaps the most famous racing hostelry of all is the Hotel de France in La Châtre-sur-le-Loire near Le Mans, recently taken over by an enthusiastic Englishman. Everyone from President Kennedy to Steve McQueen and Derek Bell has stayed there. Inside, there is a magnificent photo gallery of racing drivers who have rested their weary heads on their pillows and it is where the Triumph, Aston Martin and Gulf teams based themselves for Le Mans back in the roaring '60s.

But a firm rival for motor racing's favourite hotel comes from across the water. You may not have heard of Siebkens Resort in Elkhart Lake but there's not an American racing driver who hasn't at some time or other visited the place. Most have found their way to the bar, which is covered top to toe with photos, posters and other memorabilia. They say if your photo is not up in that bar, you haven't made it in American road racing. The likes of Englishmen such as Vic Elford, Brian Redman, John Fitzpatrick and David Hobbs have spent many a noisy night there. They even sell wine from Mario Andretti's Californian vineyard.

There is a postscript to my Kenilworth Lodge stay. In 2016, it had a small electrical fire which led to a routine fire inspection. The officials were horrified and found multiple violations including taped-over sprinkler heads, open electrical wires, obstructed fire exits and so on.

The building was condemned until everything could be rectified and the owners boarded it up. Vandals have since broken in and caused further damage. It still sits there rotting – even the ghost has left for pastures new.

ALL CHARGED UP?

Is the internal combustion engine history?
Formula E has proved a political success but they don't sound great.

I climbed out of the Avismobile, in the field next to Sebring's ticket office not so long ago and was assaulted by a wall of sound. The best noise in the world: racing engines at full chat. My drive across central Florida through scruffy towns like Immokalee and La Belle and then up the 17 Highway between the orange groves had been slightly delayed, so practice for the Sebring 12 Hours race had already begun.

As I stood in line (aka queued up) to collect my season hard card (aka season permanent pass), I wondered about a few things. First and foremost, why did I have to go to one of the seven windows for the hard card itself but a different window for the car pass?

Why do I still use the same photo from several years ago on the credential (answer: vanity) and why had someone at NASCAR Productions in Charlotte North Carolina booked me, and the rest of the crew, at a hotel in a place called Okeechobee, 45 miles from the race track?

From the Sebring Will Call Center – that's how they spell it – you can't quite see the race track but, as I said, you can certainly hear it. One of the outstanding aspects of sports car racing is the different and loud exhaust notes. Yes, that's definitely the new Cadillac, well I know the engine is a Chevrolet and the chassis is a Dallara, but nevertheless you can recognise the sound of that thumping 500bhp V8 in the back. I pictured the car, almost taking off over the brutal bumps of that challenging final corner – Turn 17.

Formula E may capture the zeitgeist but little compares with the sound of a big V8 in the back of something like this factory Corvette. ***IMSA***

But there were other contrasting sounds: the factory BMW M6 GT with its straight six motor. And surely that was the shrill sound was the AER engine in the back of the Mazda DPI. And there goes the Rizi Competizione Ferrari, unmistakable.

Surely I must be far from alone in experiencing the special thrill when you arrive at a race track and hear the race cars in the distance. I had it when I was a teenager arriving at the Mallory Park Hairpin and waiting to drive into the centre of the track, even using part of the race track to do so, and it is the same to this day.

We probably all have our favourite racing engine exhaust notes. I loved the sound of a 1.0-litre Cosworth MAE Formula 3 engine complete with megaphone exhaust. Or what about the Mazda four-rotor at Le Mans? Or a Cosworth DFV in the back of anything has always sounded pretty good. There's little to beat a Ferrari V12 Formula 1 engine vintage 1995. Let's not forget the sound of the Matra V12 either. Current F1 engines are a disappointment, of course; hopefully this will be addressed soon. Going back in time, there were great sounds like the BRM V16 and before that the supercharged six-cylinder ERA motors that someone described as sounding as if calico was being ripped. I have never actually heard anyone ripping calico but I know what they mean.

This all makes me wonder about Formula E. I know it is very well established now and among motor manufacturers, with a look to the future, it is the series of choice, but it just doesn't excite me. Call me a dinosaur, but I just can't see how it is ever going to catch the imagination of the fans. You arrive at some temporary street circuit,

Hugely technically complex, but Audi's latest electric Dakar RSQ e-tron racer still relies on a 2.0-litre turbo DTM racing engine to charge the batteries! ***Audi Sport***

park up and hear precisely nothing apart perhaps from the squeal of the Michelin tyres. Is that going to set the heart racing? I don't think so. As you get closer, you simply aren't going to say, "That's the fabulous whine of a Faraday Future Dragon Racing electric motor," or "There goes the Mahindra M3 Electro. I know the sound of the electro-magnetic inverter". It is just not going to happen.

I went to the original Formula E launch and just to remind myself of the background I have just checked out their official website and their Wikipedia page. Nowhere does it actually say what the E stands for.

We can, of course, assume it is for Electric. But it could be Formula Earner, because a lot of talented drivers who haven't quite made Formula One or passed through it, seem to be earning a very good living racing in the series.

It might even be Formula Empty, because that's what happens to the batteries at the end of a scant 75 miles. Or maybe just plain Formula Eccentric, because it is a pretty good way to describe how these cars look. It is certainly not Formula Elegant, that's for sure. Seriously though, I take my Trilby off to Mr Alejandro Agag for what he has achieved. Maybe he should be called Mr Agog, agog at the success he and his team have had at setting up street races at some fabulous inner city street venues in places like Buenos Aires, Berlin, Hong Kong and even Saudi Arabia.

Also let's not forget Agag and the gang pulled off a major coup by promoting a race in London's Battersea Park, something that I firmly predicted would never happen. But Agag persuaded Wandsworth Council and the event ran in 2015 and 2016 to what I would call limited success in terms of crowds and exposure. But then along came the Battersea Park Action Group, including a gentleman who was incensed he couldn't take his dog on its normal walk for a few days a year, and he managed to get the whole thing stopped. It wasn't the best track on the Formula E calendar but they made it work. Now they are racing in London's Olympic Park.

Mr Agag and his team must be wizards with the finances too. Quite how he balances the books, I am not sure. It costs a fortune to set up a street circuit, let along hire one like Monaco. From what I have seen on television and in the magazines, the crowds rarely look much larger than what you would expect at a VSCC Silverstone meeting. There was a suggestion a few years ago that the whole show was about to run out of money, but the Spaniard found a new backer just in time and has gone from strength to strength.

Agag has an interesting CV. He spent his early years between Madrid, Paris and New York, he speaks four languages and graduated from Madrid University. He was involved in politics from an early age and ran for a seat in the European parliament at the tender age of 23. He didn't win that time, but finally took a seat five years later as a member of the European People's Party, for which he became the Secretary General. A few years later, presumably having spent too many sessions in the European Chamber listening to Nigel Farage's rhetoric, he suddenly quit politics.

In 2002, he moved to London and started his own company, Addax Capital, and his first venture into motorsport was when he joined with Flavio Briatore to acquire the Spanish Formula 1 TV rights, just as Fernando Alonso was emerging. He bought the Campos Racing GP2 team and re-named it Barwa Addax. They won the title in 2008 and plenty of success followed.

British Formula E racer Jake Dennis of the Andretti Avalanche team jumps for joy – maybe because the salaries in the category are pretty competitive. ***Andretti Autosport***

Together with Flavio Briatore and Bernie Ecclestone, he bought Queens Park Rangers football club and, under their watch, the team was promoted to the Premiership in 2011.

His wife Ana is the daughter of the former Prime Minster of Spain Jose Maria Aznar and guests at the wedding included the King and Queen of Spain and Tony Blair. So you get the idea: this guy is well connected; a mover and a shaker.

But even so, I still can't help wondering if Formula E will finally go the way of A1 Grand Prix series. Admittedly, it does have the backing of several motor manufacturers, more so than Formula 1, but it seems a couple have already tired of it. I had lunch in Florida recently with the man who used to control Ford and later Jaguar's F1 budget and his stories made me realise why so many motor manufactures aren't involved at the Grand Prix level of motorsport.

The manufactures all want to prove their green credentials and, compared with running in Formula One or the WEC, Formula E is relatively cheap. So it ticks quite a few boxes and it is a very interesting exercise for the engineers, but there are elements that are still missing: for a start, all the cars look the same.

NASCAR snubbed its nose at technology for many a year. Not ten years ago, the race cars sweeping around the Daytona banking were still sucking in the gasoline from a great big four-barrel carburettor while all the spectators' cars had fuel injection.

The new delta shaped Gen 3 Formula E car which will race from season nine onwards. It has the equivalent of 470bhp. And be able to reach 200mph but still won't sound great. ***Formula E***

Flying high. Formula E spin-off Extreme E has provided some great action in remote venues and attracting Lewis Hamilton, Michael Andretti, Nico Rosberg and Jenson Button as team owners. ***Extreme E***

Am I anti-electric car? Not at all, I love the look of the Tesla and Jaguar models and I would even consider buying one as I am told they drive brilliantly, but I wouldn't purchase one until they have sorted out the fact that if I want to drive to Le Mans from London, I will have to stop at least once to charge up and it will take a lot more time than squirting 60 litres into the tank. A lot of very clever people are trying to increase the life of the batteries and making great progress, but it is never easy as they are fighting chemistry.

So it is a brave new electric world out there encouraged by the British government who are all for banning those horrible internal combustion engines. Nevertheless, when it comes to the track action I just hope everything doesn't switch to 'the juice'. However, I do hear that Porsche and several fuel companies are working on synthetic fuels which won't poison our atmosphere.

For that very reason I think all this electric racing might just be a passing phase. Bring on the banshee wail of a Matra V12 at full chat!

Mark Webber's protégé Mitch Evans has carved a great career in Formula E driving for Jaguar. ***Andrew Marriott***

Chapter 25

DON'T MENTION THE GIRLS

Why do so few women race? And why was the situation different in the past?

I am treading on eggshells in this chapter because I am going to be discussing women racing drivers and, as the father of four daughters, I have learned to be pretty PC. That said, just the other day I got into huge trouble with my eldest by referring to a group of racing PR ladies as 'the girls'. "You can't call them that, it is demeaning," she chimed. "You have to call them women." "Rubbish," I said, "it is just a figure of speech," and off I went, chuntering into my beer. You see what I have to put up with.

As you know, I have tried to raise a smile or two in this book and this chapter could be the opportunity for quite a few cheap shots at the expense of the fairer sex – I probably shouldn't say that either. But I do have some

Maria Teresa de Filippis was the first woman to compete in a Formula 1 Grand Prix. ***Maserati***

Hellé Nice was the 'Bugatti Queen'. ***CSS Archive***

credentials to discuss the motoring skillset of women. I once ghosted a book for the actress Hannah Gordon called *Woman at the Wheel*. It is definitely a period piece and has motoring tips like replacing a broken fan belt with a pair of tights or cutting a potato in half and rubbing in on your windscreen if your wiper falls off!

But back to the main theme, where are all the women racing drivers? I just cannot work out why there are so few of them. Obviously Formula W, introduced in 2019, has raised the profile of women racers, but has also highlighted the fact that the numbers haven't really increased in over 80 years. Back in the earlier days of Formula 1, we had the occasional lady competitor. Over in America, a recent highlight came in 2012 when as many as four women raced in the Indianapolis 500. But the 2020 the count was back down to zero.

The current lack of track success comes where the British females, in particular, are proving hugely adept at

Desiré Wilson won the Monza 1000Kms with Alain de Cadenet. ***Alan Wilson***

cricket, where the lady tennis stars earn the same multi-millions for winning tournaments as the men, where Arsenal ladies could probably beat Mansfield Town's men's side and a lady jockey can win the Grand National.

Bernard Ecclestone wound up the media on a number of occasions by calling into question the ability of women to compete at the highest motor racing level, both from a physical and mental angle, but I simply don't agree. In the challenging and sometimes dangerous sport of Three Day Eventing, women compete against and regularly beat the men. I think if we put Mr Ecclestone on Zara Phillips' horse Toytown he would find it would need tremendous concentration and strength to control the beast.

But while women/ladies/females/ girls are increasingly flourishing in other major sports, they are simply going backwards in motorsport. The first lady factory racing driver was Camille du Gast of France and that

The all-woman Formula W Championship, which now competes on the Formula 1 World Championship bill at some events, has seen some good racing. But double Champion Jamie Chadwick has been unable to move up to Formula 2. ***Formula W***

was back in 1900, preceding by a few years the first British professional racer Dorothy Levett.

Think about Le Mans, in 1935 there were no fewer than 10 female drivers in the race. These days, it is more like three or four. And there hasn't been a British woman there since Amanda Stretton, and that was over a decade ago. Back in 1935, six of those ten female competitors were driving in a trio of factory MGs and I think they all made it to the finish.

Before World War Two, one of the biggest stars of Brooklands was the Canadian Kay Petre and typically there were more ladies racing at the Surrey track back then than there are at a regular Silverstone meeting in the 2020s.

I did have the pleasure of co-authoring Desiré Wilson's autobiography and she was probably the best female racing driver I have witnessed. Let's not forget how quickly she went in the Tyrrell at the 1981 South African Grand Prix and, but for politics, she would have been in the record books as one of the few women to have raced in the World Championship. The South African was able to win Aurora Formula 1 races and also two rounds of the World Sportscar Championship in a de Cadenet. But all that was 40 years ago.

Side by side, sometimes literally with Des in various John Webb-promoted races, was Divina Galica, who also was never short on the bravery side and made it to the fringes of Formula 1. Divi is still hugely enthusiastic about racing and works with the Skip Barber School at Sebring. Touring car ace Yvan Muller's sister Cathy was another talented single-seater driver, who came close to the podium a couple of times in Indy Lights but that was 25 years ago.

Coming up to the present, another very talented lady competitor is Guildford's Katherine Legge. But she had to go to America to get

Janet Guthrie (left) was the first woman to race at the Indianapolis 500 but it was Danica Patrick who became the most successful woman racing driver in recent times and finished third at Indy in 2009. She started her car racing career in the UK. ***IMS***

fully recognised and there she won in Formula Atlantic and had four seasons in Champcar/Indycar. She has subsequently forged a great career in the IMSA sportscar series earning her position as a fully paid professional by right. She has also survived two horrendous accidents.

In Formula 1, we shouldn't forget the late Lella Lombardi who made history when she achieved her half point for a top six finish in the shortened 1975 Spanish Grand Prix, or Maria Teresa de Filippis who raced a Maserati 250 in 1958.

I mentioned the Desiré Wilson book so here is another must read and one of my all-time favourite motor racing books, *The Bugatti Queen* by Miranda Seymour about a former Paris stripper who competed as Hellé Nice. She became a factory Bugatti driver, raced Grand Prix Alfa Romeos, but after the war was mysteriously denounced by a hostile fellow driver, Louis Chiron, as a Gestapo agent. It is a terrific tale.

The last woman to attempt to compete in a Grand Prix was the cinema chain heiress Giovanna Amati. She failed to qualify for the first three races of 1992 in a Brabham but earlier in her life had made more headlines when she was kidnapped and later released after payment of a ransom of 800 million lire – it works out at about three quarters of a million pounds .

So far I haven't got round to mentioning the most famous female racing driver in the world, the one who has been on pole position at the Daytona 500, finished third at the Indy 500 and won a round of the Indycar Championship. I am, of course, talking about Danica Patrick. Her career in NASCAR was less successful, but she stands out as the best-known and certainly financially successful lady racer of all time. A site called celebritynetworth.com reckons she is worth over £50million.

Researching this chapter I Googled 'Top 10 Female Racing Drivers' and was directed to a site called 'Top Ten Hot Racing Drivers'. There I found that there were a number of 'sister' sites, such as 'Top Ten Bollywood Controversies' and 'Top Ten Hottest TV Babes', among others. There was even a link to some mature dating site.

Then I found a different site, which had a list of the Top 15 Hottest Racing 'Chicks', the majority of whom seemed to be drag racers and three were the daughters of John Force. Anyway, Danica was only 14th. The list included the surgically enhanced Venezuelan Milka Duno in sixth place, although I haven't seen her at a race track in almost ten years. Susie Wolff was fifth, but a lady called Madalena Antas topped the poll. Frankly, I had never heard of this Portuguese off-roader but, to quote the website, "She has excelled in the Dakar and many other rally events". Also "She can travel through dirt and dust in a Nissan pick-up at 120mph and flaunt her stunning body in men's magazines". A woman called Stephanie Whitfield wrote this, incidentally, and she should be ashamed.

But these lists, stupid as they are, served to remind me that for some reason both in the States and in Europe, there is a substantial number of absolutely top women drag racers. Why should that be? And I don't want any comments about they don't have to turn left or right or anything like that. Hurtling down the 1000ft chute in 3.7sec or whatever it is with about 8500bhp up your backside seems pretty brutal to me. Then they cross the line at 330mph and the girls (there I go again) seem to be just as good at it as the men.

Here is another question to ponder. Where have all the top lady rally drivers gone? Fifty years ago we had Pat Moss, Ann Wisdom, Sheila van Damm (who also managed to run the Windmill Theatre in Soho) and, a little later, Rosemary Smith. All of them were at a very high level, fully paid factory drivers who could win international events. In the 1980s, Michèle Mouton could drive an Audi quattro pretty well on the same pace as Hannu Mikkola and Stig Blomqvist and won World Championship rallies. A few years later, Louise Aitken-Walker was another lady rally driver who fully deserved her place in the factory Vauxhall team. Jutta Kleinschmidt did a very strong job on the Dakar in the Schlesser Buggies, but now who is there? Can you name me a lady rally driver of international note?

Michèle Mouton has been behind the FIA's Women In Motor Sport Commission which was created back in 2009 and, if you can go on the website, you can read the very laudable mission statement, but I am not sure it is having a huge effect.

I covered the DTM series on television for a number of years and, during that period, both Audi and Mercedes-Benz hired a number of women racing drivers including, of course, Susie Wolff, who now runs a Formula E team. Audi tried Vanina Ickx, Rahel Frey an Katherine Legge. Rahel still races and Audi GT3 car regularly in the Creventic series. Back in the 1990s, Mercedes ran Ellen Lohr from Mochengladbach (not many cities have four syllables) and she raced in the series for six years and remains the only female to win a DTM race – back in 1992. In the last couple of years or so she has not only raced in the NASCAR Whelen Euro series but also successfully in truck racing.

As I mentioned before, a few years ago the Indy 500 bucked the trend despite having previously discouraged lady racers. Female reporters weren't even allowed into the Indy pits until 1971. Janet Guthrie became the first woman to race the 500 back in 1977. In 2011, Danica, Sarah Fisher, Ana Beatriz and Simona de Silvestro all took the start while Milka Duno failed to qualify. Four women also took part in the 2011 and 2013 races. A special mention, too, for Britain's Pippa Mann who has raced the 500 on no fewer than eight occasions, most recently in 2019. In 2022, there wasn't a single woman on the grid.

But what of Formula W? A very smart lady called Catherine Bond Muir came on the scene after a career in the City which included brokering the sale of Chelsea Football Club to the Russian oligarch Roman Abramovich and Aston Villa to Randy Lerner. Like me, she couldn't understand why so few ladies were racing, particularly in single-seaters. So she decided to do something about it.

The South African Desiré Wilson was perhaps the most talented female racer to date. She is the only woman to have won a Formula 1 race – in the British Aurora series – won in sports cars and competed regularly in the Indycar series as seen here. ***Alan Wilson***

Her idea, of course, was to run a series called Formula W for women racing drivers in Formula 3 type cars and she raised an astonishing £30m to back up this idea. She also surrounded herself with some smart people like David Coulthard. In 2019, after a rigorous selection process, twenty women got to race without having to put their hand in their handbags. However, the idea was not without criticism; Indy racer Pippa Mann called it a sad day for motorsport – suggesting women racers should not be segregated. She wasn't the only one.

But the series went ahead with Britain having the largest contingent by country. Jamie Chadwick took the honours and was set to defend the title when Covid 19 quashed the series in 2020. For 2021 and 2022, the series returned with races on the Formula 1 under-card and it will be interesting to see if the new champion can move up the ranks.

Actually, however laudable the idea, I don't think Pippa Mann is completely out of order. If the 2022 champion moves up to Formula 2, she is going to finish up racing against a field of men. She will only fulfil Catherine Bond Muir's dream of making it to Formula 1 if she can finish regularly on the podium against the top men by beating them in Formula 2. To do that it will really need someone with the talent of Desiré Wilson – let's hope there is such a person.

Meanwhile the FIA, led by Michèle Mouton, has a rival scheme called Girls on Track with the winner being awarded a place in the Ferrari Driver Academy and a full season in Formula 4. So watch out for the recent winner, a 16-year-old called Maya Leung.

There is no question, we need to see more women performing well in motorsport at all levels. It is difficult to comprehend that there are fewer professional women drivers than there were 50 years ago.

Chapter 26

THE FAME GAME

Motor racing has attracted plenty of film and TV stars. A few have proved to be very talented racers too.

I would love to have been a fly on the wall the other year when the Le Mans organisers found that they had more celebs attending the race than parade up and down the grid at the Monaco Grand Prix. Well, for a start, none of the motor racing-loving band of actors and musicians quite fancied a trip to Azerbaijan for the inaugural round-the-houses race in the City of Baku. So kind of the Formula 1 authorities to arrange for it to be on the same weekend as Le Mans.

Or just maybe, the stars discovered that there wasn't a chance of being interviewed on the grid by Martin Brundle. Martin had decided the opportunity to race an LMP3 car in the Road to Le Mans support race was better than trying to fight his way through the selection of dodgy oil rich high-rollers from what appears to be a despotic state – albeit one that according to some sources paid more for its Grand Prix than even the Gulf States.

Anyway, the list of those who wanted to attend Le Mans in 2016 included the Kung Fu master himself Jacky Chan, who was certainly there with good cause having helped fund a Chinese-entered LMP2 car and, of course, Patrick Dempsey, who was likewise on hand as a team owner of the Dempsey Proton Team. Then there were at least three Hollywood A-listers. For a start there was a man who, when I first heard his name, I thought was called 'Piano' Reeves, on the misguided assumption he was some sort of actor/song-writer who tickled the ivories. It turns out that he is actually called Keanu Reeves – it is not a first name I had previously encountered and, surprisingly, he does have some sort of motor racing history.

You may know that, since 1977, the Long Beach Grand Prix held a pro-celebrity support race backed by Toyota. They finally pulled the plug after some thirty years of celeb excitement and bent panels. It seems that 'Piano' showed some speed and skill by winning it back in 2009. He'll never match the fellow who won the final edition, a certain Alfonso Ribeiro, of whom I know little except he also won the race in both 1994 and 1995.

Whatever, Keanu seemed to be enjoying his time in the pits and was welcomed into the Audi garage, while mortal pits reporters like myself, in my case trying to tell the US audience why the four rings was struggling, had our entrance barred by one of two very burly German gentlemen.

As well as Keanu, there was an English chap called Jason Statham. Call me naïve, call me out of touch, but frankly I simply hadn't heard of him. I now discover that he is the guy who narrated that terrific Audi documentary from a few years ago called *The Truth in 24*. But he is probably better known for appearing in *Lock, Stock and Two Smoking Barrels*, *Fast and Furious*, and the *Transporter* trilogy. I now understand that is nothing to do with what my US colleagues call a hauler, the vehicle that transports race cars to the track, but a film that includes some of the best fight scenes ever seen in a movie. Some of my better informed colleagues – and I have to put Justin Bell at the top of this list – were getting very excited that Jason would bring along his wife to be, a certain Rosie Huntington-Whitely. Strangely I had heard of her: I am quite good on super models.

Three stars connected with Le Mans but only one of them has raced at the track. Left to right: Keanu Reeves has waved the start flag, Steve McQueen made a famous film about the race but only Nick Mason has driven in it. He made five starts and was second in class in 1979. ***Marriott Archive***

Justin, a class winner himself at Le Mans, son of Derek and the father of an emerging TV star back in the States, was the other half of the Fox Sports pits reporting duo. Justin fancies himself a bit as a friend of the stars and, in the States, has worked with the likes of Jay Leno. That particular year, we were forced by the organisers to wear silly-looking skateboarding helmets, which made it almost impossible to also don the headphones and antenna that make it possible for us to hear our producer and the commentators who, just to make it easy, are buried in some bunker in Charlotte, North Carolina.

Anyway, we finally gave in and Justin wore his for the first time on his Brundlesque (is that a word?) pit walk. I was at the other end of the grid interviewing Chip Ganassi, who sounds like a rhythm and blues singer but most of you know is a mega team owner. Justin tells me that he was getting ready to interview the said Keanu Reeves, when the star of *Chain Action* and many other box office hits said to him what you could translate as "If you want to look a prat, wear a silly hat". JB was so distraught that he missed his cue to start the interview. Fox Sport went to the second of about 298 commercial breaks in its coverage. By the time the three minutes of commercial messages had passed, Keanu was on his way to the VVIP Hospitality Suite!

While Justin failed to get his man on the grid, I managed to get my microphone under the nose of Dempsey as the race moved into the second hour. Patrick has just finished filming a sequel to *Bridget Jones*, something of a departure from his long time TV persona as the neuro-surgeon Dr Derek Shepherd in the hit series *Gray's Anatomy*. I have to say he is a fiendishly good-looking chap which is probably why he has the nickname 'McDreamy'. He also had the good grace not to comment on my headgear.

Over the years, Dempsey has turned into a very quick 'bronze', and I am not referring to his tan. In 2015, if you recall he had a great run with Patrick Long and Marco Seefried to finish second in the Proton team factory-backed Porsche in GTE-Am.

Another VIP credential was prepared for the always under-stated and brilliant Nick Mason who, just in case you didn't know, is not only the drummer with Pink Floyd, but also competed five times at Le Mans and twice finished up with a class podium with the Dorset Racing Lola T294. It says a lot that Audi usually nominates Nick to drive the pre-war Auto Unions up the hill at Goodwood. While Nick had been invited as an ACO guest, he would have gone anyway to support his son-in-law Marino Franchitti, who was driving for Ford.

But none of these fine fellows, nor for that matter our great motorsport leader Jean Todt, who wisely chose La Sarthe over Baku, had the honour of actually waving that big Tricolour to start the race. That honour went to no less than William Bradley Pitt, known to his mates as Brad.

Now you can see what I mean about wanting to have been a fly on the wall in the ACO's offices when they had to decide which of its star-studded guest list would wave that flag. Will Keanu refuse to come to Friday's big dinner? Will Jacky Chan give the ACO President Fillon a kung fu flying kick boxing move and perhaps Jason Statham would turn on his heels and head off for his private jet? Anyway, everyone seemed happy, so the ACO must have turned on the charm offensive.

By the way, Brad Pitt waved the flag with gusto and 24 hours later was there again to peer down the road, chequered flag in hand, and was surprised to find he was waving it at a Porsche rather than a Toyota. Usually, the person who waves the starting flag isn't around on Sunday afternoon to wave another one. Certainly President Hollande didn't hang around a year earlier, but he probably had some French union to sort out.

Patrick Dempsey is a great supporter of Le Mans and finished second in the GTE-Am category in 2015. He continues as a team owner. ***Porsche***

Pitt is not the only star to have started the race by the way. French actor Alain Delon got the 1996 race underway. Famously in 1971, Steve McQueen was on hand as his Le Mans movie was heading to the cinemas, but he needed the help of the US Ambassador to unfurl the Tricolour.

Steve, of course, was desperate to race at Le Mans and to find out more you might still find the film I co-produced *Steve McQueen – The Man and Le Mans* on Amazon Prime or an aeroplane.

I still think that, of all the actors, musicians and celebrities who have been involved with Le Mans, and I include Paul Newman, Steve did more to promote the world's greatest race than anyone. However, it was wonderful that Le Mans creates so much interest year among the glitterati.

They can always go to Baku the next time it hosts the Eurovision Song Contest.

TRACKS OF MY YEARS

It is the big bragging rights question – how many tracks have you visited? Here's my tally.

Find a bar, perhaps in the British Racing Drivers' Club at Silverstone or maybe a watering hole close to a far-off race track, and the talk can often turn to the ultimate bragging rights question: "How many tracks have you raced on?" Or, for the journalists, officials, trade, engineers and mechanics amongst us, "How many race tracks have you visited?" There are probably also fans out there with some impressive totals.

I've been reporting races for over 50 seasons, which gives me something of a head start. I reckon there aren't many other media folk with my tally. It also helped that I competed in those early Tour of Britain events and the similar Tour of South Africa plus, in the past, I reported not only car but also motorcycle grand prix racing. So they certainly helped to build the total.

Ah, I hear you say, do motorcycle tracks count? So before you all start jotting down your list of tracks, we need to set some ground rules, but it could take all night to finalise the regulations! The redoubtable reporter Marcus Pye and I comprise the judging panel.

It gets tricky because many tracks do double-up for both two and four wheels, although some don't. Take the daunting Yorkshire track of Oliver's Mount – it is primarily a bike circuit but they did race cars there in the past and it still used on special stage rallies. So I say count the bike tracks, it is too complicated not to – and improves my score!

Rule Number Two is pretty clear. Silverstone counts as only one track, and so does Brands Hatch. No double-counting here. After all, those of us who have been to the Buenos Aires Autodrome know two things – it has a great steak restaurant and it also has lot of different configurations. Circuito Ocho is often the layout of choice. My schoolboy Spanish is good enough to tell me that this means they had at least seven other versions. Randomly, it also reminds me that, while Aintree only had two versions of its track – Grand Prix and Club (three if you count the Grand National horse track) – it also used to have an excellent fish and chip shop in the paddock. I seem to remember paying one and six for cod and chips. Youngsters, grandad will translate.

Two tracks both with banking. The California Speedway at Fontana and the Avus track in Berlin which just had the banking at one end of the Autobahn based track. I've worked at both but the banking had gone at Avus when I covered the Super Touring races there. ***Marriott Archive***

But now the rules can get a little tricky. Do you count Kyalami as one or two tracks? When they rebuilt the circuit, they slipped it down the side of the hill and away from the nearby prison but they still used a small section of the original. Then they rebuilt it in 2015 altering some corners. But you still have to drive through the original main gates to get in. I think if there has only been one main entrance, then you only count that venue as one.

So what do we do with the Miami street circuits? There is the Bicentennial Park track used in 1986 when Emerson Fittipaldi made his famous comeback in a March sports car and the Bayfront Park track, which hosted an ALMS race in 2002. I've been to both and I'm pretty sure that about 100 yards was common to the two circuits, although used in a different direction. I think we can count that as two because they definitely had different main entrances – as well as different pits and paddocks. We can now add a third with the Miami F1 track inaugurated in 2022.

Big Rule Number Three can be contentious, particularly for us non-drivers. You can only count a track if you attended when there was track action taking place. This means a race, qualifying, practice, test session, even a track or promotional day. Cars need to be going round the track at speed. Let's open it up a bit – if you visit a track where nothing has happened that week, it does not count

This rule therefore also covers street circuits when they are not active and all the grandstands have been taken down. So you can't count the Birmingham Superprix track because one day you happened to get lost driving away from the Bull Ring and suddenly found yourself zapping past the Bristol Street Motors showroom where the start line used to be. For that, score zero. Neither can you count Brooklands, just because some classic rally you happened upon is starting on the famous banking. I am not even counting the ultra-dangerous Belgian road tracks of Chimay and Mettet, despite being driven round them by the legendary Denis Jenkinson in his Jaguar E-type. Absolutely no counting of Monaco because you just happen to be touring the South of France and fancy a visit to the casino. You have to attend the Grand Prix, Formula E or historic event in race week.

There is a German journalist I know who, in his spare time from reporting the DTM, makes a habit of visiting venues that used to be race tracks, looking for the old buildings and so on. He recently made a pilgrimage to Nivelles, the Belgian track which briefly and ignominiously hosted a Grand Prix. He didn't find any pits but he found a nice supermarket car park – just about as underwhelming as the original circuit.

Maybe we could make it a separate competition, I know a few of you will have visited Rouen and Reims on your travels through France, but some of us older guys were there in period and only that counts. Some years ago, but over 15 years after it had run its last race, I stopped off at the Reims pits – before they has been renovated – and went up

Credentials from tracks around the world.

This old passport tells a few tales!

into the control tower. There were still some desks there and I opened one to find the results sheet of a Formula 3 race I had reported. It was a little yellow around the edges but still legible. At the back of paddock were the shells of what had been the champagne houses' hospitality suites. I think there where about four of them but sadly there was no sign of any champagne bottles left behind in a corner.

I have to respect Rule Number Four. You can't count drag strips – unless it happens to be Indianapolis Raceway Park where there is a race track alongside the drag strip. Also no kart tracks, no hillclimbs or sprint venues nor even short ovals. To be counted a track

Last on my A-Z list is Zweibrucken in Germany.

Jim Bamber's brilliant cartoon of Silverstone.

All Photos Marriott Archive

has to be at least 0.4 of a mile, so no counting Ipswich, Hednesford Hills or the other stock car venues. I have been to quite a few and I am not counting them. But at half a mile, I can count the wonderfully-named Kokomo Speedway in Indiana. I was there in 1982 and I still have the T-shirt to prove it. Also on my list are three dirt ovals, Indianapolis Fairgrounds, the awesome San Jose Mile in California and Ascot Park in LA which closed back in 1990.

The committee, such as it is, does allow private tracks such as Ascari in Spain or the Bedford Autodrome, but not tracks like MIRA, built primarily for testing road cars rather than racing cars. You also can't count

I have lapped Goodwood in a Can-Am car with World Champion Denny Hulme, an experience I will never forget. ***Mike Marchant/Gulf***

The Sebring fans love to dress up. ***Andrew Marriott***

autograss tracks but I am not sure what we should do about rallycross circuits. Obviously some serve as race tracks as well, such as Lydden Hill, but in Europe there are several permanent facilities dedicated to rallycross. My feeling is they should count.

Another grey area is stadium events such as the Race of Champions or those mainly forgotten DTM Munich Football stadium shows. I've worked at both but I'm not counting Munchen. The committee probably needs to rule on that.

I might up my score by one with a very unusual venue and one I believe I have written about in an earlier chapter. Back in 1974, I competed with Andy Dawson in the Marlboro Trans Chaco Rally in Paraguay. The start order for the rally was decided on the results of a time trial held at a rallycross course a few miles from Asuncion – at the Autodromo de Aratin

Among the tracks where I my cut my teeth as a young reporter were some of the airfields 'up north' that briefly served as circuits. My list includes places like Rufforth which really should have been spelled 'rough up', Elvington (which still hosts record breaking attempts) and even Ouston, although I never made it to Linton-on-Ouse. At Rufforth, I saw a man noted in the programme as JY Stewart win in what looked like a road-going Jaguar E-type. At Elvington, the only way to obtain the official results for the race report was to copy them off a sheet stuck to the side of an ageing race control caravan. At Ouston I saw Rodney Bloor win the main race of the day in a Brabham. While he was receiving his trophy the next race started – for motorbikes.

I mentioned that the fabulous event called the Tour of Britain – based on France's Tour de France Auto – visited various race tracks, as well as rally stages and hill climbs. On one occasion it even visited Santa Pod. There were four of these events altogether in period – three backed by Autoglass and the final one by Texaco in 1989. Over seven days, it visited 59 competitive sections, including eleven different race tracks in England, Scotland, Ireland and Wales. The Welsh track was Pembrey but the original Tour had taken in Llandow. One of the competitors was former World Champion Graham Hill who was being paid a sizeable amount to drive a Datsun Bluebird. I interviewed him after the race about the conditions. His moustache twitched and he came up with the all-time classic quote: "Slippery as snails' snot."

One circuit I don't want to go back to is San Carlos in Venezuela, which was the home of the Venezuelan Motor Cycle Grand Prix in the late '70s. I was doing duty both as a reporter and photographer. As I wrote elsewhere, I had a gun poked in my chest by military men.

Another bike track that won't be on many people's list is the former Finnish GP circuit of Imatra, a fiendish road course where, if you missed your braking at the hairpin, you finished up crossing the Russian border. I exaggerate, but the border was only about four kilometres away. This is the track where the much-missed Barry Sheene had one of his finest hours.

Appalled by the state of the toilet and shower block, Barry crept in one evening and deposited some primed thunder flashes. What he hadn't calculated was the amount of methane accumulated in the crude wooden building. In the words of the famed stand-up Cheshire comedian and demolition expert, 'Blaster' Bates, "Up it went, height of Blackpool Tower, no messing". The organisers were not amused but the culprit could not be found. They might have got a clue from the prize-giving when Barry, who won the 125cc Grand Prix, got a

Our rules allow oval tracks if they are half a mile or longer – this sensation shot is of the San Jose Mile which I visited back in the 1980s for flat track motorcycle racing. ***Norm DeWhit***

bigger cheer than the bloke who took the 500 honours.

While we are engaging in toilet talk, I recall Graham Hill staging a campaign to get doors put on the Indianapolis toilets in the late 1960s. Meanwhile, US motorbike aces Kenny Roberts and Randy Mamola caused consternation when they urinated on the side of a toilet block in Spa because they hadn't quite embraced a certain Belgian custom. You know the one. The toilet blocks are cleaned and defended by a lady of senior years, who has eaten too many frites and needs a shave. Her demand for 10 Belgian francs to use the facility tipped them over the edge. Actually, they were bursting for a you-know-what just before the start of the race and you tend not to have either Belgian francs or Uncle Sam's dollars tucked down your leathers.

Back in the 1960s and 1970s, some far-off tracks really did welcome you, particularly those looking for plenty of publicity. One chap I know was part of a very small band of journalists to attend an early Mexican Grand Prix. On the first night in the hotel he received a knock on his bedroom door. His provocatively clad visitor announced, "I am yours for the night, compliments of the Autodromo." I received a few presents from race tracks in my time, but boringly they were mainly odd commemorative coins, a rustic hessian bag and a green music case from Paul Ricard (I still have them) and from Mugello (or was it Misano?) a curly salami. It festered in my fridge for about a month before I chucked it out. If I'd kept it I could probably sell it on eBay now for £35!

Now I haven't yet told you my circuit count yet, but if you make your list in alphabetic you probably finish up with Zolder, but I can go one better than that because I reported a German Super Touring race at the bumpy track of Zweibrucken. The same series also took me to the German equivalent of Rufforth and Elvington – Mainz Fithen and Diepolz. For Formula 2, I was at another airfield track, Austria's Tulln-Langenlebarn.

There have recently been quite a spate of new street circuits thanks to Formula E, but otherwise very few permanent new venues have been built in the past five years – The Bend in South Australia being the most notable. Formula 1 has some new temporary venues with Saudi Arabia recently coming on stream. I was surprised that Lewis Hamilton's stand on human rights allowed him to race here.

I originally wrote this chapter as an article for the BRDC *Bulletin* and there was quite a lot of discussion among fellow journalists and colleagues about who had been to the most tracks. I think it was generally acknowledged that the wonderful boss of Schnitzer – the late Charley Lamm – came out on top with over 150 tracks. But I reckon I am still the leading scribe, although I have only added two or three to me count in the past few years.

But using the rules I have outlined, I think I am on 139 tracks. Because of Covid I wasn't able to increase the number so I don't think I will make it to 150.

Chapter 28

A PASSAGE TO INDIA

The world's largest democracy has yet to produce a World Champion but my travels to India convinced me it is only a matter of time.

Did you have a wonderful time? Did you go to a concert at the Sydney Opera House? Or prop up the Leaning Tower of Pisa? Or even lose money in the Monte Carlo Casino? Those are just four of the many questions I have been asked by non-racing friends after what they consider to have been an exotic trip abroad. In reality the trip has probably been fraught with hassle and even a couple of all-nighters, and probably compounded by lost baggage.

We racing folk know the reality is as follows. Airport-track-hotel-track-hotel-track-hotel-track-airport. I admit that back in the earlier pre-email, pre-iPhone, pre-text days of my 20s, we did sometimes stay out between Grands Prix and had great times in places like Ilha Bella in Brazil or lazing around the Kyalami Ranch pool.

Karun Chandok made it to Formula 1 and has since become an outstanding TV analyst for Sky Sports. *Motorsport UK*

But for most of my journalistic and broadcasting career, it has been very much the airport, hotel, track deal, although a handful of years ago on the way back from a DTM Hockenheim race, I did stop at an asparagus farm to buy some fine white shoots. That was about as adventurous as it got. At Cologne airport, they insisted on putting them through the X-ray machine.

Anyway, over the years I have been promising to go back to the places I should have visited if I hadn't been gunning the hire car back to catch a plane. Or perhaps actually visit some places on the bucket list that are nowhere near a race track.

Finally, with my commitments now reduced, I have started to tick off that list. I've done Shanghai and Moscow – actually thanks to the DTM – but then, after watching a TV programme featuring a certain chef from Padstow and his search for a perfect curry, I took it into my head that I wanted to go to Kerala in Southern India. Mrs Marriott agreed, particularly when I told her there wasn't a race track or even a rally there. Usually she is pretty suspicious of the places I suggest. Let's go to Austin, Texas, I suggested recently, I hear there is a great music scene. But somehow she had heard of the Circuit of the Americas. I must hide *Autosport* when it pops through the letterbox.

Truth is, I had been to India once before, on the way back from Hong Kong in the days of the 555 Rally. The smoky folk at BAT had asked me to meet with Nasir and Katie Hoosein who, at that time, ran India's biggest motorsport event, the Himalayan Rally.

I remember it as a whirlwind 36 hours and I have vivid recollections of Nasir and Katie taking me to a cricket stadium to witness the bizarre spectacle of scooter racing, their elegant flat in Bombay, and observing the abject poverty of India in the 1980s. This included the sobering sight of people converting a discarded concrete drainage pipe into their home. In the end, the tobacco people decided not to sponsor the rally so I never returned to India and had little desire to do so.

But Rick Stein's TV programme changed my mind, so off we went and had a great time. In a reverse of my opening comments, motor racing folk kept asking, "Did you go to the Buddh track? I hear they spent $400 million on

This must hurt. Pulling a truck with hooks in your back in Tamil Nadu. ***Andrew Marriott***

We saw this on one of Kerala's trunk routes. The elephant seems to have left a message. ***Andrew Marriott***

it." The answer was no as it was a plane flight away from the marvellous beaches and bustle of Kerala.

In fact, after that initial trip, we decided to return again but this time to be a little more adventurous. They say you have to see the Taj Mahal at dawn before you die, and friends who are Sub-Continent regulars also suggested we should visit the Red Fort at Agra and so on.

Life and motorsport has many mysteries, and having spent another two weeks in India, this time embracing six different towns/cities including New Delhi, I can't for the life of me understand why the country hasn't produced a string of World Champions. There is no question that several of our F1 stars should be sent by their teams to tackle the Indian traffic and learn how to drive millimetres away from the other vehicles without actually hitting them.

The driving everywhere is amazing. At first it seems completely crazy, head on crashes are averted by fractions, drivers cut each other up yet no-one seems to lose their cool. It seems there is some unwritten priority pecking order. Top of the list comes the elephant, although there are not many of those on the trunk routes (sorry!), then, certainly in the North of India, the cow comes next. In places like Jaipur the streets are full of them and they are given room although their passage is somewhat erratic.

Next up is the camel then the truck, followed by the bus, car, tuk-tuk, then motorbike. There seems to be a sub-section here. Motorbikes have preference over each other based on how many family members are aboard. I counted five on a rather clapped out Royal Enfield. It is the same with tuk-tuks: I saw one with 15 school children on it and another which carried so many bananas they could have filled the shelves of the local supermarket for a week. By the way, they have red bananas in Kerala. Anyway, the tuk-tuk with 15 school kids – all in neat uniforms – had preference over the one with three grannies, the one with 10 second-hand truck tyres and definitely the one with the bananas.

After the tuk-tuk in the road priority pecking order comes the moped, the hand cart, the pedestrian, the goat and finally the dog. Of all these, by far the most agile, other than the surviving dogs, are the tuk-tuks. Although these little three-wheel, half motorbike half dustbin machines were originally developed in Italy and can be found all over the world, they seem to thrive in India.

One of our drivers even had the logo "Need for Speed" emblazoned down the side of his machine, although this was one of the new four-wheeler Tata versions. It even had a gear change and a steering wheel. It also had a button to start it rather than the lever you crank to fire it up.

But the good old scooter-based ones with their handlebar front end can turn on a sixpence and some of the drivers have the same bravery and skill level that takes Lewis Hamilton flat through Eau Rouge on full tanks. In fact, I read that Mercedes-Benz in India has been running a competition to find the next Karun Chandhok/Narain Karthikeyan/Jehan Daruvala.

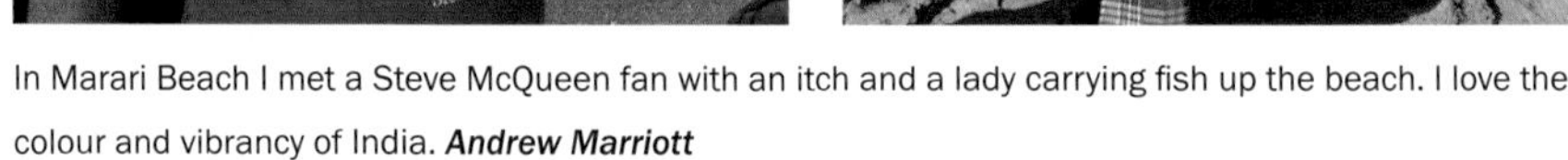

In Marari Beach I met a Steve McQueen fan with an itch and a lady carrying fish up the beach. I love the colour and vibrancy of India. ***Andrew Marriott***

Another of life's mysteries, incidentally, is my wife's attitude to danger when in India. When she is in the UK she is one of the worst back-seat drivers I have ever encountered: "Watch out", "Careful", "Slow down" plus regular intakes of breath every time I apply the brakes hard. But in India, she happily rides in the tuk-tuk with not a murmur, as the guy weaves through traffic, motors though decreasing gaps with millimetres to spare and she thinks it is all "marvellous". I just read the other day that marvellous is a word that is falling out of favour and is being replaced by the awful 'awesome', so I just wanted to use it.

Another of life's great motor racing mysteries is why Force India didn't have the biggest budget in Formula 1. It doesn't matter where you go in India, you only seem to have two choices of beer, Kingfisher Premium or Kingfisher Strong. Actually about 40 percent of all the beer drunk in India is Kingfisher, which is made by United Breweries Group, the company still partially owned by the former owner of Force India, the fun-loving Vijay Mallya. After the problems with his bankrupt airline, he is subject to an extradition order from the UK, served by the Indian government. But I would have thought with his beer profits he could have sorted this and had a Ferrari-type budget. Of course the team has now passed from Indian beer magnet to a Canadian clothes and handbag entrepreneur.

The first Indian racing driver I ever met rejoiced in the name of Diwan Rahul Lal, although he went by the name of Kinni. He raced for none other than Frank Williams back in the 1968 British Formula 3 Championship. Even back then, Frank's cars were immaculate, the chocolate brown Brabham BT21 for Kinni and a crystal white version for his other driver Sverrir Thoroddsson of Iceland set the standard in the F3 paddock.

I took to Wikipedia to see if I could find out what happened to Kinni and came across a page called Indian Racing Drivers. Staggeringly, at the time, Wikipedia only listed a grand total of 13 for the second most populous country in the world, although last time I looked the numbers had more than doubled. The original list included my rally organiser friend (and now FIA steward) Nazir Hoosein, Kinni, Karun, his dad Vicky, Narain, a bloke I saw racing and crashing Volkswagen Sciroccos in Europe, two other guys who raced briefly in A1 Team India and a girl called Alisha Abdullah. She has recently switched from car to bike racing and is now about to make her Bollywood debut in a film called *Iron Horse*.

I promise that I hadn't any intention of visiting India's former F1 venue as Mrs Marriott would not be happy. But researching our route from New Delhi to Agra to visit the Taj Mahal, I realised that our driver 'Mr P' in his trusty Toyota Innova MPV would actually use the Yamuna Expressway. This is

Two different forms of transport. Mr P with his Toyota and this guy who basically set up his smoothie station on his pushbike. ***Andrew Marriott***

Who said I was a charmer! I check out this Cobra in a street right in front of the Red Fort in Agra. ***Caroline Marriott***

the $2.1billion super highway built by the Jaypee Group which was also responsible for the Buddh International circuit. Just after the start of that Expressway, some 40km out of Delhi alongside to the Highway is the track, part of an emerging sports complex.

Indeed, we spotted signs a few kilometres in advance and then the impressive facility itself came into view. But Mr P was not in a good mood. On the way out of Delhi, a truck had crisply severed the left-hand wing mirror, adjustment wires and all. A genuine Toyota replacement was going to cost him a week's wages so he was grumpy. Anyway, visiting the track wasn't on the itinerary so I couldn't get him to drive off the slip road and down to the paddock entrance but at least he stopped for me to take a couple of photos.

The FIA's signs for International Media and so on were still in place, but with no Indian Grand Prix for several years, following some political interference and unpaid bills to Formula 1 Management, the place is starting to look a little forlorn. Checking on its website, I see that it is open for 'Happy Hour' most days from 9.30am to 10.30am and 5pm to 6pm. It costs £80 for cars and £60 for bikes, and for that you get 50 minutes on track. Quite what happens in the remaining 10 minutes I am not sure.

This magnificent facility quite recently hosted some truck racing, with a few British drivers making the trip, but the majority of the racing activity is still at club level. For a world class facility, that is a disaster.

Actually, the Yamuna Highway itself provides plenty of adrenalin rushes. Although it is similar to our M1, there is a constant stream of motorbikes and scooters travelling down the hard shoulder in the opposite direction to the main traffic. Mr P muttered something about bike riders being killed on the road every day. Neither was he happy about the three tolls, which totalled about £1.20. Motoring in India will always be an adventure even on their most modern highway.

Our trips to India have been a highlight of our more recent travels – we just love the colour, the smells (well, some of them) and the vibrancy of this massive nation. I am confident that India will produce a World Champion in the future. Wouldn't it be wonderful if he had learned his driving skills on a tuk-tuk?

Chapter 29

ANYONE FOR GUINEA PIG?

Peru is a fabulous country to visit particularly if you know their most famous racing driver.

As we swept into the lobby of our hotel in the upmarket Miraflores district of Peru's capital Lima, the doorman eyed the old racing mate of mine who was parking his car outside. In a reverential tone he said, "Is that the racing driver Jorge Koechlin?"

Amazingly Jorge Koechlin Von Stein (to give the him his full name) is still remembered in Peru for his successes back in Britain and Europe, relatively modest though they were. A second place in the opening round of the 1982 Aurora British F1 race in the Ian Dawson-run Amazon Team Peru Williams FW07 was the best result of eight years or so racing in the UK and Europe.

Back in Peru, Jorge did win one of the world's most dangerous motorsport events and the one with possibly the longest name – the Grand Premio de Carretera dos Caminos del Inca.

Back in 2017, I returned to South America for the first time in 35 years.

Jorge Koechlin in his Williams FW07 racing in the Aurora F1 series. ***Jorge Koechlin***

The Continent had always fascinated me and I had reported races in Argentina and Brazil and rallied in Paraguay. Now I had planned a fabulous trip and, as well as visiting two new countries for the first time – Peru and Uruguay, I would also revisit Buenos Aires.

Of course, Jorge is not the only Peruvian motorsport person to make it overseas. Ramon Ferryros, who based himself in the early days at Andy Dawson's Silverstone workshops, competed for eight years in the WRC and was a front-runner in the Production class. These days Ramon is proud to run Peru's biggest chain of Hyundai dealerships and Hyundai tops the sales charts in Peru.

More recently another Peruvian, Nicholas Fuchs, was a regular in the WRC and in 2013 won the Production Cup. Watch out for rising Peruvian star Matias Zagazeta who finished second in the 2021 British F4 series.

But it is Jorge who continues to write the headlines. Following in the footsteps of his father, 'George' as he is sometimes known, recently stood to be a senator for the province of Lima. In conversation with him, he seems to have a sneaking respect for Donald Trump: his slogan "make Peru great again" obviously borrowed from Donald.

Jorge originally pitched up in the UK back in 1974 with $50 in his pocket, the address of Brands Hatch and a burning desire to be Peru's first F1 racer. He had no racing experience other than unofficially hurtling around the awesome street circuit in the south of Lima, half of which is sheer rock face on the inside with a long drop into the sea on the other.

His Latin American charm and good looks soon paid dividends. Somehow he got a seat in a Merlyn Mk20 Formula Ford car before Peter and Brian Hampsheir at Elden took the aspiring racer under their wing. He even debuted their long-forgotten F3 car as well as racing the factory Formula Ford.

He found lodgings in West Kingsdown at the home of the famous 'Red' who provided a roof over the head of several aspiring racers, including Indy 500 winner Danny Sullivan and the finest Welshman ever to sit in a racing car, Tom Pryce. Jorge has fond memories of Tom, Mawdwyn as he called him, and recalls that his English was little better than his own, as Tom's native tongue was Welsh.

Heaven knows how, but Jorge was introduced to Lord Howe, who immediately had him made a member of the RAC Club in Pall Mall – the club's sole Peruvian member, he only relinquished his membership a couple of years ago. Through contacts there, he found sponsorship and a drive with Heini Mader Racing in Switzerland in the 1975 Formula Renault Championship in Europe, competing against the likes of Arnoux, Schlesser and Pironi who he remembers had the

This poster from 1958 is actually on display in the Revs Institute in Naples Florida. ***Andrew Marriott***

Roasting the guinea pigs by the side of the road. They are then waved at passing motorists looking for a culinary experience. ***Andrew Marriott***

biggest transporter, a spare car and lots of women around him.

Now, my mate Jorge would remember this because he is a hit with the opposite sex. He is the archetypal Latin Lover from Lima. His stories would fill a book. His first marriage to a Bunny Girl actually made the front page of the *Sunday Express*. "Famous racing driver ties knot at Chelsea Registry office" etc. There was a subsequent wedding to an Irish aristocrat, a liaison with the wife of a Prime Minister (not a UK one, I hasten to add) and he was once smuggled into a Middle East country in the boot of a car to 'service' the wife of a member of the royal family. This, I promise you, is not fantasy.

When he wasn't sweeping the opposite sex off their feet, he moved on to a one-off start in a CART race and then a distinguished career in publishing, television commentary and the internet. Now based in Los Angeles, he remains one of the greatest characters I've met in motorsport. Whether his bid to join the political elite of Peru will be successful remains to be seen, but I wouldn't bet against it.

My trip to Peru was prompted by an email from Jorge's brother Joe offering preferential rates at the Inkaterra Hotel group, which he owns. Thus we set off, not only to see the stunning Machu Picchu historic city but also to visit some of Peru's incredible Inca sites at places like Arequipa, Cusco and to witness the majestic and effortless soaring flight of the vast condors over the Colca Valley.

On the way to the Colca Valley, the route included one of the most fabulous roads any one could wish to drive – sadly I was just a passenger in a minibus, but even so one could see what a wonderful strip of tarmac it was. But the climb out of the throbbing city of Cusco was far from promising, peppered as it was with other tour buses and countless US-built trucks off to collect copper ore.

But then we stopped at a junction with a tiny restaurant/café where they tried to sell us wooden piped instruments and fed us on rib of alpaca. By now, thanks to our guide, we knew the difference between sheep and llama – pretty straightforward – but also llama and alpaca and alpaca and vacuna. Alpaca seems to be the most versatile. Like a sheep, you can use the wool and eat the meat, whereas llama is too tough to eat and the wool is a bit rough, while the vacuna has the softest wool and is kind of sacred, so doesn't finish on the dinner plate.

Anyway, the point is that after our lunch halt, all the copper trucks headed

Peru's most famous racing driver stood for election in Lima Province – Honesty, Action and More Honesty was his slogan, but he wasn't elected. A great character. ***Jorge Koechlin***

off in a different direction and suddenly ahead was this fantastic strip of empty road is. As a backdrop, you have a string of volcanoes and towering mountains. Because it is a tourist route, the Peruvian government had invested millions in a beautifully smooth blacktop.

But as you approach Colca, you start to breathe deeply. We stopped to look at a volcano, still active with a mushrooming plume of smoke above it, and a helpful tourist information board told us we were at 4700 metres above sea level. That is higher than anywhere in Europe; we'd be looking down on the peak of Mont Blanc.

Finally we started to drop down again and our guide starts mentioning those delightful little pets, the guinea pig. You know the ones you bought your kids because the hamsters seem to meet an untimely end with monotonous regularity. This either had something to do with being left out of the cage, thus providing the next meal for the family moggie or – in the Marriott household case – by having a traumatic seizure. Ultimately, in our experience, the life span of the guinea pig was only marginally longer than a hamster. Better though than in Peru, where the cuddly little creatures are considered a delicacy.

Jorge gave us the grand tour of the sights of Lima in his Jeep. ***Andrew Marriott***

They have been eating the furry little beggars for centuries, even before they started eating alpacas, and apparently they breed like mad, need little maintenance and are very high in protein. All good so far.

Jorge with his ESPN commentator Mexican Adrian Fernandez. Adrian was the runner-up in the 2000 CART Championship. ***Jorge Koechlin***

But then we motored into this village, apparently a sort of Guinea Pig-eating capital of Peru, to find that about 10 of the local restaurants along the main road were offering the little devils as the *plat du jour*.

How did they do this? Well, first they roasted them a golden brown. If you are squeamish stop reading now. Then they took a metal stake and rammed it up the little furry friend's backside until it came out of its mouth and I swear they still had their whiskers and tails attached. Then each of these piggy palaces had their prettiest waitress stationed by the side of the road waving the delicacy at us. "Drive on", I shouted. I was looking forward to alpaca stew.

Mrs Marriott is an adventurous soul and, while we did not stop at the roadside, she did subsequently order guinea pig *a la mode*. Do you know what? She absolutely hated it. I had one mouthful and agreed. Stringy, and a cross between pork and a damp dish cloth.

In the past, I had heard tales of marvellous classic cars being rescued from the remote reaches of Latin

An Inca agricultural terracing experiment near Moray. ***Andrew Marriott***

America, so I was on the lookout, hoping maybe there was a pristine, if dusty, Hispano Suiza in the next village, just looking for a buyer. Well if there were, they have all gone now. During my 10 days in Peru, I saw one very down-at-heel and not very old Volvo, a very scruffy Morris Minor Traveller, a rust rotted Austin Cambridge and quite a few Volkswagen Beetles which had seen better days.

For the car enthusiast, the roads in Peru may be fabulous but the cars are not. As I mentioned, Hyundai is the top selling make, followed by its Korean bedfellow, Kia, and there are lots of Toyotas, Mitsubishis, Suzukis and Mazdas, plus a few rather dodgy Chinese cars, the badges of which I didn't even recognise but were probably called Flying Pigeon or maybe even Roasted Guinea Pig. The aforementioned Jorge Koechlin von Stein took us to a very swanky Lima eatery complete with pre-Inca ruins next door and valet parking. It was the kind of place you might expect to see the odd Ferrari or McLaren. But the best motor in the parking lot was a new BMW X5. The valet parking guy, of course, recognised Jorge and asked for a selfie.

The extraordinary salt fields in Maras near Cusco teeter on the side of the mountain. ***Andrew Marriott***

The Condors are a huge tourist attraction in Arequipa. ***Andrew Marriott***

From Peru, we flew on to Argentina and then took a ferry to Uruguay. In the former I met up with another old mate, who used to be a gofer for the Shadow team but is now the most important executive in sports television in Latin America. In Uruguay, by complete chance, I happened upon an old street circuit that was used for the Sud-Am Formula 3 Championship and included a section where the cars raced around a derelict bull ring. I was told the vibration of the cars was so bad that it caused chunks of brickwork to fall from the decaying circular structure. It must have been true because when Formula E visited Uruguay in its opening season, they disregarded the ready-made layout of Colonia and spent millions instead racing at Punta del Este. And I doubt if they knew it was James Hunt's favourite seaside resort.

I can thoroughly recommend a trip to the marvellous country of Peru, even if the cars are boring and you have to run the gauntlet of the guinea-pig-on-a-stick wavers. One thing is for certain: drop Jorge Koechlin's name and you will probably get an upgrade!

Chapter 30

KYALAMI CAPERS

South Africa's top track deserved a return visit but didn't offer much of a welcome.

Kyalami has always been a special track for me, the venue for the first so called 'fly away' grand prix I ever reported. South Africa was always a great place to start a Formula 1 season. Remember, back in those distant days of the swinging '60s and super '70s, most of the World Championship races were held on European tracks with just a handful of races requiring a flight of more than a couple of hours.

So when the chance came to attend the Johannesburg wedding of former employee Caroline Samuels, I jumped at it not only because the nuptials would be fun (plus trips to a game reserve and Cape Town), but also because there was the chance to see how the old track was progressing, as I had heard it had passed into new ownership.

What I hadn't expected was a building site. A gentleman called Toby Venter purchased the facility in 2015 in an auction, no less, for about £10million. Among other things, Toby is the Porsche importer for South Africa and, while some reports suggest it was Porsche that has actually purchased the track, in fact it is Mr Venter's company, LSM Distributors.

He quickly realised the place needed a bit more than a lick of paint, so he had pledged another £10million to refurbish the place, lengthening the main straight, adding a new corner or two and building a tunnel under the track. So far so good, but I am a little perplexed that the new corner is called Crocodiles, although I suppose it is appropriate if you have someone snapping at your heels. Another corner has been renamed Cheetah, although taking into account some motor racing practices, I wonder if he has the spelling right. He is also resurrecting some of the names from the original 1970s like Barbeque Bend, the naming of which I never understood because in South Africa, a barbeque is a *brai*!

Some older readers will remember the original track was rebuilt and was basically slipped down the hill for the 1992 Grand Prix. Only a short section of the original track was used and the general opinion is that the later layout lacked much of the appeal of the original. I believe the 2015 changes have addressed that as the circuit proved a popular venue when international sports car racing returned there in 2019.

My visit to the track was when the circuit was going through its rebuild

Apparently Kyalami welcomes you but the gate was kept firmly shut when I visited during its 2015 re-build. It is still one of my favourite tracks. ***Andrew Marriott***

James Hunt and Graham Hill find time for a game of backgammon at the Kyalami Ranch Hotel. *LAT*

and I was keen to check out the progress so I presented myself at the entrance under a sign that said 'Welcome to Kyalami'. Unfortunately, this was not a warm welcome and two burly guards told me that not only could I not come in, but that I couldn't take photographs nor park my car outside. I patiently explained that I was visiting for the first time in almost 25 years. But it was, you guessed it, more than their job was worth (which looking at the state of their uniforms was not a lot) to let me in.

Although South Africa is a pretty high tech place these days, these chaps didn't quite latch on to the fact that I wasn't just holding my phone at a funny angle but actually snapping happily away at what looked more like a building site than a race track.

Visiting Kyalami, albeit briefly and from the wrong side of the fence, also brought home how much Johannesburg has expanded. Even back in 1992, you drove out of Jo'burg and pretty quickly you were in farming land and the track sat in a wide open space just the other side of the Juskei River. Now the 15-mile or so drive is packed with housing, factories, warehouses and a massive shopping centre called Kyalami Corner.

Long gone, to make way for a housing estate, was the famous Kyalami Ranch where most of us stayed in the thatched cottages. Around the pool you could find World Champions like Jackie Stewart, Graham Hill and Mario Andretti, as well as Francois Cevert looking like a god in tight swimming shorts and, of course, wives, girlfriends and wannabes. There were a few rivalries, but largely everyone got on and shot the breeze. For the journalists and TV reporters, there were no PR people waving recording devices and limiting the length of your interview to exactly three and a half minutes. You just chatted and, if you were lucky, picked up the odd scoop. In the evening, we sat down and had dinner with a group of drivers.

Every so often there was the rasp of a DFV, as the hard-working mechanics fired up an engine at the track and that heightened the anticipation of the days to come. But even the mechanics had the chance to relax at the pool once their work was done.

The race was held on a Saturday, of course, and post-race we all looked forward to the official prize-giving in the garden of the magnificent home of Francis Tucker, the head of the organising committee. Here a sumptuous spread was laid out and the top three called up to receive the trophies on Mr Tucker's veranda. However well his race had gone, Graham Hill always found his way to the front and to deliver not only a heartfelt thank you from all the drivers but also some of his best if bawdy tales.

While the Kyalami Ranch was the hotel of choice, some of the sponsors and high rollers used to stay at the Balalaika in Sandton, an upmarket suburb of Johannesburg. Sometimes, pre-race events were held in its beautiful gardens and again it stood out on a dusty road in fields. I always fancied staying there, so for my recent trip I pushed out the proverbial boat and booked a suite with the added bonus that, in these days of globalisation, I would even receive some Marriott reward points.

South Africa's Desiré Wilson is, in the opinion of many, the most talented female racing driver in the history of the sport. She took part in her home Grand Prix in a Tyrrell in 1981 Grand Prix but also famously won an Aurora British F1 race at Brands Hatch and rounds of the World Sportscar Championship.
Alan Wilson

I am not sure what the opposite of déjà vu is but, as the taxi drew up, it didn't appear to be the place I remembered at all. I walked into the lobby and nothing clicked, it was if I hadn't been there before. Opposite was a huge corporate building and the place was surrounded by office blocks, apart from the plot next door, which had been a shopping centre, built since I last visited. Except, when we got to our room, I realised they were still actually knocking it down. They were even smashing concrete at 8am on the Sunday morning.

Wandering down the corridor, I happened upon some framed press cuttings and realised why I didn't recognise anything. The hotel still had the same name but it wasn't the same building. Like the shopping centre next door, it had been razed to the ground and rebuilt twice the size but without its characteristic thatched roof.

Denny Hulme in the Yardley McLaren M19 on his way to victory in the 1972 South African Grand Prix.
McLaren

Kyalami indeed brings back many memories including some terrible ones, including the death of Tom Pryce. Another outstanding driver of that era, Peter Revson, also lost his life at the circuit due to a mechanical failure.

I have covered both car and bike race at the track. I was there for the 1983 South African bike grand prix where I was commentating for ITV. Barry Sheene was making his GP return after his horrendous Silverstone practice crash. I don't know why, but for some reason I was terribly nervous about this broadcast and it was back when there was just one commentator and no pits reporter. It was just me and voices in my headset. Anyway, I tried to calm my nerves and went a bit too far with the Chenin Blanc. Although nobody mentioned it, I am pretty sure I was half cut. Perhaps somewhere on YouTube the evidence is there for all to hear.

Talking of the drink causing problems, you may recall that back in the late 1970s, Williams had sponsorship from Leyland Vehicles which also included its tractor division, although the glorious 1979 Patrick Head-designed FW07 was anything but agricultural. Leyland was still a big player in the South African tractor market and the Leyland marketing team had a marquee to entertain their guests where the beer and wine certainly flowed.

Alan Jones retired from the race and decided to join the Leyland gang to drown his sorrows. He had downed a beer or two when he was approached by one of Leyland's customers who had been in the tent all day. If he had known anything about AJ, he may not have addressed him in the way he did. It is not recorded what he said, but Alan didn't suffer fools and landed a heavy Australian punch in a stout area close to where the beer lay. The guy crumpled to the ground and AJ turned on his heels muttering that it made up for retiring from the race. I'd like to tell you that the guy put in a big order for Leyland tractors the next day, but I would be making that bit up.

Peter Revson lost his life at Kyalami after leaving McLaren and joining Shadow. ***McLaren***

This was not the first time I had been involved in an AJ punch-up. One Italian GP when he was driving for Williams, he turned up at Monza with a heavily bandaged hand. Frank Williams decided we should issue a press release to explain the injury and the fact it wasn't going to affect his driving. It appears AJ had been involved in some road rage incident with a chap in a Transit van in Chiswick. I think the guy subsequently regretted it. Sadly the PR blurb did not give the correct details; I think I wrote he had slipped on the bathroom floor and smacked is hand on the tiling.

The Intercontinental GT Challenge has brought top level sports car racing back to South Africa. Here Dutch racer Yelmer Buurman sets the pace in practice for the Kyalami 9 Hours. There is even a rumour that Formula 1 could return. ***BPR***

For some reason I can't remember, we usually flew to Kyalami on a South African Airways Boeing 707, but they weren't allowed to cross over the bulge of Africa back then. So we had to head first to the Cape Verde Islands to refuel where we were all allowed to get off and stretch our legs. On one occasion, I was sat next to the lady who became in short order Suzy Miller, Suzy Hunt and Suzy Burton. Returning to the plane after the stop, she couldn't contain herself as she settled into her seat. "Do you know what, ARM [James Hunt always referred to me by my *Motoring News* initials], a big black man flashed me in the ladies' loo! I am not sure now that James really measures up."

I hear there is a chance that Formula One may return to South Africa and Kyalami. I quite fancy another trip, and I could even make it past the front gate this time but I might have to find a new hotel – I expect the Balalaika will be having another rebuild.

Chapter 31

RUSHING AROUND

A trip to Moscow came with quite a few surprises, from the press room cuisine to the visa regulations.

She had scrutinised my passport for perhaps a minute, bleach blonde and unsmiling. Then she looked up sternly with an expression which made me realise I was a very naughty boy. Her English was limited to three words: "You no visa". Well, I did have a visa, it filled a whole page of my dog-eared passport and it had cost me over £100, express VIP next-day service you understand. *Please note this chapter was written before Russia invaded Ukraine.*

It had also taken about two hours to fill in the application form and two trips to a rather strange office just round the corner from London's new high tech valley, Old Street, and not a million miles from the old *Motoring News* office. If any of you are considering going to Russia, maybe even to Moscow Raceway which was my destination, be prepared to fill in this incredible form. Someone told me they make it particularly difficult for the British because we make Russians jump through hoops to get into the UK. This does not really explain why they seem to be buying all our football teams and large mansions.

As well as the time-consuming form-filling, be prepared to walk through memory lane. You have to list every country you have ever visited in your life. In my case this was somewhere around fifty. I am not sure what I did in Paraguay forty-odd years earlier was really of any concern.

Then you had to list your parents' professions. How does it help them to know that your father, who in my case had died 50 years ago, had worked for the Ministry of Supply in 1957? In fact, I didn't fill in 'civil servant' or anything similar as I thought it might prejudice a visa being granted. "Look Vladimir, we can't let this motor racing journalist into Russia. In Stalin's time his father used to work for the British government." Anyway, I put veterinary surgeon, it seemed safer! He liked dogs.

But the best bit of the long form was your employment record. It asked you to list every place you had ever worked, the name of the boss and, somewhat alarmingly, the reason for your dismissal.

Anyway, I must have done alright with the form. They didn't contact the governing body of British vets to check if my dad actually was one. So I got the visa, which meant I could fly to Moscow for round six of the DTM race series at the Moscow Raceway. I later found out to my cost that it is just off the M9 Baltic Highway and virtually half way to Riga in Latvia. That's an exaggeration of course, but it is a long way from the centre of Moscow.

The race had happened – more of that later – and I was now on my way home. The problem with my visa was the fact that it had run out seven hours before I presented it to immigration. It didn't matter that it was still yesterday in Hawaii. Your visa is supposed to be for the exact period of time you are in Russia and no longer. This doesn't take into account that you might just miss the last plane out of Domodedovo Airport – which is what had happened to me.

The blonde controller of departures lifted her phone. A minute later another woman appeared who looked as if she had served time in the KGB. She was stern and her English was double that of her colleague. She led me to a little office, scrutinising my passport as she went. "You no go London today," she told me.

I tried to explain that I was really sorry but you must know how bad the Moscow ring road traffic is, so I had missed the plane and spent the night in an agreeable airport hotel. I also told her the Moscow subway system is brilliant, I thought Lenin looked great in his tomb etc, but I wasn't sure if she understood any of it. I even tried a bribe, I uttered the word dollars. She wasn't impressed. They must pay Russian immigration staff too many roubles these days.

This was a classic Catch 22 situation. I could not leave because, quite simply, I didn't have a visa to stay. Simple really. I was ushered to sit down. So I sat down opposite her somewhat communist period desk. Suddenly she found more English. "No, no, no, no here, go outside."

Over 45 minutes later I was still sat on a bench with a couple of other miscreants and, on at least three occasions, saw my passport transported between two different offices. Finally I was ushered to yet another part of the immigration holding area and I was even allowed to sit in front of a desk. They gave me a long form, which I had to sign, except it was all in Russian. For all I know I have signed up to go

Brazil's Augusto Farfus makes the sparks fly from his BMW in the inaugural Moscow DTM race. ***BMW***

to the salt mines. This official was also short on English vocabulary. Finally my passport was presented back to me with the instructions: "You go see EasyJet, their problem." EasyJet have stopped flying to Moscow these days and I can understand why.

So I hopped back to the airline desk, still without a visa to leave and presented myself. Thankfully the station manager knew a man in the consular office at the airport who might just issue a new visa for the remaining hour I had left in Russia for £30 (and I got a receipt) always assuming I could make the plane on time. Maybe it had something to do with the fact that they already had my bag in the hold of the aircraft but I just made it, the last person to board. Anyway, that is another page of the passport full. So I finally managed to leave Moscow and I am not sure I'll be going back in a hurry. In fact, I think the form I signed probably said I couldn't return.

But let's rewind a little. As I mentioned, I was there to provide commentary for the DTM International English TV feed – the first time the German-based series had raced in Russia. At the time, they were spreading their wings Internationally and also had a Chinese round.

I had taken some time out, together with my wife, to do some sight-seeing, including a trip by an impressive TGV-style train to St Petersburg. I wasn't telling fibs to the immigration person, the Moscow subway is excellent but I didn't actually see Lenin in his tomb. You have to be in a queue in Red Square before 12 noon and, although we were there at 11.55, that was, apparently, too late. He has to rest for the remainder of the day.

Having enjoyed a couple of luxurious and expensive nights in the Crowne Plaza Hotel at the World Trade Centre, I waved goodbye to Caroline and headed off for the rather less luxurious Hotel Aquarium, strategically placed on the ring road as part of a kind of National Exhibition Centre, except there weren't actually any exhibitions on. I'd rather fancied a look round the Russian Catering Equipment and Clothing Symposium which was taking place in September.

Strangely, the Hotel Aquarium did not have, as far as I could tell, an aquarium, although my room was furnished floor to ceiling with Ikea items. Actually, I have to say it was a pretty efficient place. Most of the guests were teenage athletes taking part in some student games, plus our group of 50 or so German TV engineers, producers and technicians.

My bosses from the German TV company Wige greeted me with the news that we were all going to the track in a pair of coaches for the Saturday practice and qualifying, departure time 6.30am the next day. That's racing.

It was only about 40km to the track, but traffic is such around Moscow that I endured 90 minutes surrounded by snoring German technicians who, I found out later, hadn't left the circuit the previous night until 1am.

The track itself is rather typically Herman Tilke design and indeed the man himself was there; perhaps he was collecting the final instalment of the €130million he had been paid to design and build it. Actually, I've got a few suggestions for an improvement or two he could make, but I'll come to that later.

Certainly no improvement was needed in the media centre though. The wi-fi worked perfectly, there were plenty of desks and you could see the track well. But the pièce de resistance was the lunch. It was crowned by the most wonderful delicacies – hand-crafted macaroons of many colours, there were coffee ones, strawberry ones, Earl Grey tea ones and probably ones with a blend of vodka and caviar, for all I know.

It's not normal in the UK to feed the media, although at the Brands Hatch DTM one year they did actually provide a few of Mr Huntley and Mr Palmer's best biscuits. This reminds me that back in the days of the Birmingham Superprix, where I was the Media Director for all of its five years. I did a deal one year with McDonald's. It had a location at the first turn and I managed to arrange for it to not only sponsor the corner, but provide the media with Egg McMuffins for breakfast. The staff got a bit carried away and there were so many of the egg thingies that even the massed ranks of the press couldn't polish them all off.

So the Moscow Raceway food certainly comes top of the DTM list, far ahead of the Hockenheim wurst, the Valencia paella and even the meal we had the first year we went back to the Red Bull Ring. There for the Saturday lunch time, waitresses came to each media desk and effectively laid a table for you and then served a three-course meal.

Anyway, back to Moscow where the paddock talk was mainly of the previous race at Norisring. We arrived with the news that the DSMB (Germany's answer to the Motorsport UK) had decided that nobody had won the race. Not one of the 22 cars could be declared the winner. Swede Mattias Ekström had taken the chequered flag first, but during the parc fermé celebrations he had said something in Swedish to his dad. Ekström senior promptly opened a bottle of water and stuck it in his son's race suit pocket and emptied it down his leg. Possibly this was some strange Scandinavian ritual – or maybe not.

The resultant pool of water at the winner's feet made it look as if the Swede had got over excited at his first win in over 18 months. The Stewards took the view that it had violated the parc fermé rules and promptly disqualified him and promoted Robert Wickens to first place. It wasn't the way the Canadian wanted to score his first DTM win. Not surprisingly Audi protested, Ekström remained excluded, Wickens put back to second and there wasn't a winner. It defies logic.

Back on the Moscow race track qualifying began. If you have followed the DTM (which is now a shadow of its former V8 growling self), you will know that the session is run on a knockout basis. However unlike Formula 1, the final four then go into a one-lap shootout. So here I was, happily

I was the lead commentator for the DTM's TV World Feed for a number of years and it took me as far afield as Shanghai and Moscow. During the period I saw a lot of Audis race and win. ***Audi Sport***

It will be a while before the track welcomes back the International series for which Herman Tilke designed it at great expense. The BMW passes the pits. *BMW*

commentating knowing that, with typical German efficiency, Q4 would start in five minutes' time. Except it didn't. Ten minutes went by and still no action but a message from race control on the timing screen advised that the safety helicopter couldn't take off, it was grounded. Was there a technical failure I suggested to our viewers?

Then my producer came over my headset. "It's Putin," he said. "The President's plane is in our air space, so the chopper is banned from flying." Q4 was abandoned and indeed Putin's Illuyshin jet had been about 50 miles away.

There were even conspiracy theories. One media guy told me that he's heard that Putin hated the oligarch who built the track, so deliberately had his plane fly in the direction of the track simply to mess the guy around. Frankly, I didn't buy this.

Imagine the scene in the Kremlin. "Comrades, let's stop talking about Crimea we have more serious matters. That swine Alexi has a big race going on at his track this weekend. I happen to know that the DTM Q4 will start in 30 minutes time. I am going to jump in the jet and muck up the air space. I know they will stop the qualifying if the medical helicopter can't fly and I don't much like the look of that Gary Paffett either. They didn't even find a car for my mate Vitaly Petrov to race, just made him drive one of those DTM taxi things. See you all later."

Anyway there was no Q4, and frankly it didn't make much difference. The following day saw another 6.30am start, although this time I was only surrounded by snoring German TV techies for less than an hour.

Now let's get back to Mr Tilke's €130million race track. As I mentioned, it was just a few hundred yards from the M9 Baltic Highway. You might have thought they would have built a nice big roundabout or even flyover system so you could enter or leave easily. You could peel off into the track smoothly. But when you wanted to leave, you had to turn right out of the track and head for Latvia. This was fine if you lived in Riga but most people that go to Moscow Raceway, surprisingly perhaps, live in Moscow.

After about 5km you come to a big flyover and you then head back in the other direction and pass the race track again. Very, very slowly because there is a lot of traffic. Except, of course, most people just do a U-turn across the grass central reservation and save themselves 30 minutes.

But our driver had a shiny new Mercedes S-class and he wasn't going to do that, he had a better plan. When he got to the big roundabout, he headed to the right down a series of back roads which brought us out on the Baltic Highway about 10km the Moscow side of the race track which was a result. Except it was three hours later.

So we missed the plane, the visa ran out and I was detained by Svetlana, or whatever she was called. Maybe it was all part of President Putin's dastardly plan, but at least those macaroons were wonderful.

Chapter 32

CALIFORNIA DREAMIN' AND ADVERT CREAMIN'

I have always enjoyed America and made some something of a career working for various US TV channels.

When I was a teenager, one of the television programmes that fired my imagination was *77 Sunset Strip*, a tale of a Los Angeles-based private detectives who operated out of Hollywood's most famous street. It starred Efrem Zimbalist Jr and the super cool Edd Byrnes, who played the part of Gerald Kookson, known as Kookie. The show, produced by CBS, ran from 1958 to 1964 and in the UK on ITV. It was in black and white, of course.

Thus enthused, my teenage dream was to go to the States and Hollywood in particular. I knew there were a few decent tracks out there like Riverside, where the 1959 US Grand Prix was held, and the swooping Laguna Seca near Monterey with its famous Corkscrew Bend. I was also an avid reader of John Steinbeck so I knew all about Cannery Row, which was close to Laguna.

But my first trip to the States and California wasn't to either of these circuits. Riverside had already been razed to the ground when I jumped onto a Pan-Am 707 – I was heading to a brand new track called Ontario Motor Speedway, built just a few miles up the road from Riverside. The track was opened in 1970, an oval with a road section in the middle, grandstands that could hold 180,000 fans and built at a cost of $25million – the equivalent of $170million today.

The race I was to cover was the inaugural event to be held at the track, the Questor Grand Prix, which was open to both Formula 1 and Formula 5000 cars – a field of over thirty cars including all the big Formula 1 names. But there were also some of America's biggest stars in F5000 cars including AJ Foyt, both Al and Bobby Unser, George Follmer, Mark Donohue and Sam Posey. As the F5000 machinery had smaller fuel tanks, it was split into two heats with the result based on combined times.

In qualifying, Jackie Stewart in his Tyrrell was on pole with Chris Amon in the Matra alongside him. The best F5000 was Mark Donohue's Penske Lola in seventh spot. Right at the back was Foyt in the Agapiou Brothera McLaren M10B. Ol' AJ wasn't happy with the Chevrolet in the back of it, reckoning it was well down on power, but the team refused to change it. He had a solution and I heard him do this. Passing the pits he just pushed in the clutch, the motor revved to about 11,000rpm and promptly bits of piston, cylinder wall and valves shot out of the back and scattered, still smoking, on the track. He got a new engine for the race and finished 26th.

Welcome to Beverley Hills. ***Andrew Marriott***

On race morning, I grabbed a lift to the track with the great Mexican driver Pedro Rodriguez. I spent a fascinating half hour with him, just the pair of us. When we got to the gates he didn't bother to stop for anyone, despite some frantic waving from the gatemen.

Victory that day went to Mario Andretti in a Ferrari from Jackie Stewart, Denny Hulme and Chris Amon. The little known Ron Grable finished a remarkable seventh to take the F5000 class, ahead of two of three BRMs and several other F1 cars.

But the race turned out to be a one-off and the experiment was never repeated. Rather like Britain's Rockingham oval, the first event was its biggest, everything went downhill from there, although I returned to the track a couple of years later for a motorcycle race won by Barry Sheene's brother-in-law Paul Smart. It was his biggest ever pay day.

A great promotional photo for the 2022 Rolex 24 at Daytona. It is probably one of the last major sports car races I'll work at and I managed to interview most of the top names for IMSA Radio. ***Daytona Speedway***

After the race, I was able to check out the sights and I am pleased to tell you there really is a 77 Sunset Boulevard, right under the shadow of the Hollywood Freeway. But it is just a parking lot opposite a Denny's family restaurant. And there was no signs of Kookie.

Not ten years later the Ontario Motor Speedway was bulldozed to the ground after various financial problems and it made way for commercial and residential development. It was gone but, to this day, I still have the pair of cuff links and the T-shirt we were given by the organisers. Fifteen years later, exactly 14.5 miles further down Interstate 10, they built a brand new speedway at Fontana called the California Speedway. This one cost $100million back then and has seats for 122,000 fans. It has been rather more successful and is a regular NASCAR Cup venue. But the whole deal still seems pretty crazy to me.

Another memorable US trip came in 1971. One day I was sitting at what was the desk of the assistant editor of *Motor Sport* magazine – for this was now my exalted position – and the switchboard buzzed through. "American gentleman on the line, wants to speak to Mr Boddy." Mr Boddy was, of course, the esteemed editor of *Motor Sport* from 1936 to 1991. One thing 'the Bod' didn't do on a regular basis was actually come to Standard House, London EC2, preferring to work from his home in Wales. This proved a good thing for me – on several levels.

The gentleman who came on the line explained that he worked for one of the big Madison Avenue advertising agencies in New York and that their client was the US tyre giant BF Goodrich. They were going to be making a series of four TV commercials about their latest radial tyre and they would very much like one of them to feature the esteemed British journalist.

Do you know what I did? I told the ad exec that Mr Boddy didn't like flying (true) and almost certainly wouldn't endorse a product he wasn't familiar with (also true), but I knew a chap who might – guess who? I never did ask the Bod if he would have gone, but I doubt he would.

The next thing I know, for the first time in my life I was on a Pan-Am 747 jumbo jet – right at the front. I then spent the best part of a week filming at Road Atlanta driving a Chevrolet station wagon on the very latest rubber BFG could muster and eating Colonel Sanders Fried Chicken. Not only did I work on 'my' commercial, but I also did the driving for the other three. I followed cameramen hanging off the back of motorbikes and drove inches from cameramen laying on the side of the track. The only thing we didn't have was a helicopter – or beer. Back then, the only place in Georgia where you could buy alcohol was at a State-run liquor store – all something to do with the Twenty-first Amendment of the Constitution. Anyway, there didn't seem to be a government liquor store in Braselton.

Mario Andretti's Ferrari on the grid for the Questor Grand Prix at Ontario Motor Speedway. ***Andrew Marriott***

At the end of the filming, they handed me a cheque – or was that check? – for an amount which was equivalent of over six months of my *Motor Sport* magazine salary. Subsequently, they sent me a copy of all four TV commercials. I managed to transfer the film and played it at my 75th birthday party to much hilarity. I am still not sure why I wore a crash helmet throughout – this was a road car. I had always remembered the car as a Camaro – turned out it was something completely different.

So those were two very memorable trips to the States. I subsequently much enjoyed visits to report on Grands Prix at Watkins Glen, Long Beach, Las Vegas, Detroit, Dallas, and Phoenix. Add to that the Indianapolis 500, Daytona 500, Petit Le Mans, Daytona 24, Sebring 12 Hours, Petit Le Mans and countless other events the length and breadth of the county. I have seen American flat track motorcycle racing, drag events, and even karting.

Long Beach was a particular favourite and made all the more pleasant because I had made friends with a guy called Charles Curtis Jones, usually known as Chuck, whose father had been something of a pioneer by flattening the odd orange grove and building a shopping centre or two on the land. Chuck lived in a wonderful house in Tustin, south of Long Beach.

In the garden was a massive satellite dish and in his garage was a genuine Eagle Grand Prix car, an early Lamborghini and a brace of Ferraris including a 1954 750 Monza. He sported a fine moustache, and he was a talented cartoonist and illustrator. He had also built a very successful drag racer called the Sidewinder.

Chuck also ran a Formula 5000 team and his drivers included Al Unser and Clay Regazzoni. Later, he invested in the Ensign Grand prix team together with Rod Campbell. For each LGP we stayed with him and, if we were lucky, we got the bedroom with the water bed. Chuck's son Sean raced as a teenager in British Formula Ford and is now a partner in Bryan Herta's racing operation.

As well as reporting the Long Beach race, I also worked as part of the media team. I remember taking James Hunt on a promotional tour to San Diego. It was here I realised television was changing forever. We had arranged for James to be interviewed by KFMB, Channel 8, the CBS affiliate. The reporter turned up with a cameraman and nobody else. I enquired when the rest of the crew would arrive and was surprised to hear that was it – one guy. In Europe, we would still expect a cameraman, a cameraman's assistant, a sound guy and his assistant which was a completely redundant job. Quite often there would also be an electrician and a PA to keep a record of everything.

On another occasion, I ran a press conference for sponsor Unipart on the Queen Mary, the 1936 ocean liner

Art being created in the Road Atlanta Media Center. ***Andrew Marriott***

These screen grabs were taken from my TV commercial for BFG Tires. It was a very profitable trip to Road Atlanta. ***Marriott Archive***

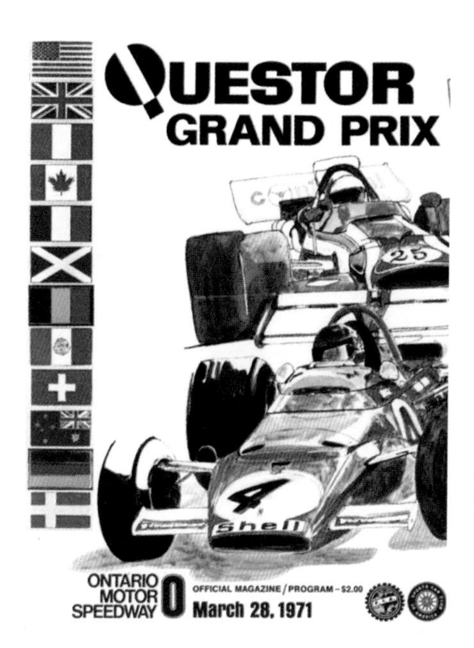

The poster for the one-off Formula 1 and Formula 5000 Questor Grand Prix. ***Marriott Archive***

which had been turned into a Hyatt Hotel. Among the guests was Rob Walker, then the *Road & Track* magazine Formula 1 reporter but before that a successful team owner. Rob was staying on the Queen Mary "in my usual cabin". It turned out this scion of the Johnny Walker whisky company had crossed the channel many times on the Cunard liner and had a favourite cabin. When he first checked in there was some confusion because the hotel room numbers did not equate to the old cabin numbers. But Rob and his wonderful wife Betty soon sorted it out.

So Long Beach and indeed America has been the focus of a sizeable part of my career and I was lucky to own a home in Naples, Florida, close to that swamp buggy track. I once turned down a possible major career move to Detroit and only personal family reasons held me back. By now I could have been a fully paid-up Yank. Love them or loathe them, the Americans know how to put on the big sporting event – from the marching bands to some minor celeb warbling The Star-Spangled Banner to kick off the proceedings. I can't wait to head back Stateside.

US drivers tend to be media savvy and seven-time NASCAR Champion Jimmie Johnson was a great interview during the 2022 Rolex 24. ***Ally***

Steve McQueen's hand prints are there in the sidewalk of Hollywood Boulevard, outside the Dolby Theatre which hosts the Oscars. ***Caroline Marriott***

Chapter 33

SILVERSTONE STORIES – STOLEN STEAK AND SUPERSTARS

Britain's top circuit has been a big part of my life providing many memories along the way.

I have worked at British Grand Prix at Silverstone in many different capacities and guises over the years – support race team manager, journalist, commentator, pits reporter, media director, sponsor PR and, most recently, even as a hospitality guest host. To be frank, I have lost count of how many times I have witnessed the race first-hand, but it must be well over 40. "Which was your favourite race, then?" they enquire.

Where do you start? It has to be based in what is now the Heritage Paddock. Goodness, at my first British Grand Prix in 1963, the brick toilet block in the paddock had red roses growing up its walls and I parked my Mini without one single person in a fluorescent jacket waving at me.

That year my all-time hero Jim Clark and Team Lotus was dominant and the Scotsman was on a streak of four consecutive British Grand Prix wins. On that summer's day, July 20 to be precise, we were certainly proud to be British because Jim headed up an all-British podium with John Surtees second in a Ferrari and Graham Hill third in a BRM.

Except, of course, there was no podium – I don't remember clearly, but I suspect they stood on what was little more than a farm trailer which was towed into position in front of the main Woodcote Grandstand by a tractor. I also have a feeling that he was probably joined by a famous character called Harry Marks.

Never heard of him? Well, Marks was a huge racing enthusiast who worked in the stores for top Birmingham tuning shop Broadspeed. With his wrinkled face, stopwatch around his neck, rakish moustache and tweed jacket, he looked as if he was some kind of senior official – except he had no role and was simply a fan. He never bothered with a pass – but he got everywhere with a Brummie gift of the gab and a casual wave of the hand. He was what they sometimes call a 'me too'.

At the end of many an important race, there would be the winner and alongside him with an arm around the shoulder of Clark, or whoever, would be Harry. Quite how he got away with it for so long I will never know. One commission we had at our sports marketing company CSS Promotions was to produce a brochure for Hesketh Racing. We wanted to make it a bit different so I asked the great cartoonist, satirist and comedian Willie Rushton to produce a special cartoon centre spread. He had completely free rein to do whatever he liked.

Rushton attended the British Grand Prix and produced a marvellous cartoon of the grid scene. I went to pick it up from a smart flat near the Thames in Chelsea. The first thing that hit me was not the great caricatures of James, Graham Hill or Alexander Hesketh but of the very man – Harry Marks. I hadn't told Rushton about him but somehow Harry even gatecrashed the cartoon!

It was similar deal a few years earlier on a chilly winter's day at Silverstone in early 1970 where I was masterminding the launch of the March Formula 1 team. Jackie Stewart was there; Mario Andretti had flown from the States as had STP boss Andy Granatelli. They all had invitations, of course.

Guess what – Harry Marks turned up as well to give the new team his personal endorsement. He definitely had not been invited to what was a private

At the British Grand Prix there is always an excellent display of previously successful cars at the BRDC's Farm hospitality area. I liked this tribute to Williams, I was running the Media Centre when Clay Regazzoni won in the FW07 on the right. ***Andrew Marriott***

sponsor and media event. As I said to Max Mosley afterwards, "You are really on the map now – Harry has given you his seal of approval."

They say that if you lived through the '60s you don't remember it but fortunately I stayed off the wacky backy and mind-altering substances – other than beer – so my recall is reasonable and I certainly remember the 1969 British Grand Prix. Anyway, I was reporting the race for *Motoring News* and can look up what I wrote at the time, if I could only get in the loft and find the appropriate yellowing and dusty report. Fortunately, in this instance that is not necessary.

The statistics say that Jackie Stewart in the Matra beat Jacky Ickx's Brabham by a complete lap. But the bald results don't always tell the full story. It was, in fact, a superb battle between Stewart and his firm friend Jochen Rindt in the Lotus. They constantly slip-streamed past each other, actually overtaking each other several times – and they didn't even have DRS!

Stewart even had time to signal to the Austrian that the left rear wing end plate of the Lotus had come loose and was fouling the tyre through Woodcote and Becketts. This was not gamesmanship but a genuine concern that his friend and rival might be flung into the barriers by a deflating tyre. Rindt then picked up the problem in his mirrors and made a pit stop – leaving Jackie to take the victory for Ken Tyrrell. I think Harry Marks was on that winner's rostrum too!

Particularly memorable was the 1973 race. Several chapters ago, I recounted how I had met with a very young emerging Formula Ford racer called Jody Scheckter in South Africa and had given him my business card. As I recalled earlier, Jody slept on our Baker Street flat floor for a while and we remained mates as he climbed the motor racing ladder. At one stage, I recommended him as a coming talent to McLaren's then Commercial Director, Phil Kerr, who promptly signed him.

But on that fateful 1973 British Grand Prix day, Phil probably wished he hadn't listened to me. Remember, Jody lined up in a third McLaren for that race alongside Denny Hulme and Peter Revson. It was only his third Grand Prix, having made his debut in his native South Africa a few months earlier and then retired in the French Grand Prix a couple of weeks before the Silverstone event.

He wanted to make his mark and sixth place in qualifying was a very

I interviewed Bernie Ecclestone several times at the British Grand Prix for Silverstone TV. ***Marriott Archive***

strong result. When the flag dropped, he made a great start in the M23. Up in the old Dunlop Tower, we strained to see as the cars came into view. Jackie Stewart had made a brilliant getaway from fourth on the grid and was in the lead ahead of Ronnie Peterson and there was 'my' protégé in fourth place. But as they came roaring through Woodcote. Jody lost it on the exit, spun wildly across the track and caused a chain reaction which eliminated all three works Surtees, left Andrea de Adamich with a broken ankle and brought out the red flag.

My late business partner Barrie Gill was working the pits for the BBC and got in among all the wreckage, bringing us a graphic description of the carnage caused by the young man from South Africa. Barrie got some criticism that day from some quarters for being too intrusive but for me it was a brilliant piece of reporting.

Eventually the race restarted and ultimately it wasn't such a bad day for McLaren because Peter Revson – perhaps the best looking Grand Prix driver ever – won from Peterson and McLaren team-mate Hulme.

Meanwhile, I had a bit of a problem on my hands. I had a lucrative contract to ghost write the Jody Scheckter column for one of South Africa's main daily newspapers, *The Star*. I needed to find Jody and get his side of the story. I finally tracked him down to the back of the McLaren truck – there were no vast hospitality units back then, of course.

He looked at me. "*The Star*," I said. "What are we going to say?" He thought for a moment. "I really don't know, but what I do know is however you write it, it is going to come out a lot better than if I actually say it – so just write something!"

Spectators always get a great view at the Silverstone track. ***Red River Sports***

I have no idea how I explained away the incident and I suppose if I went to *The Star*'s archives in Johannesburg I would find a work of considerable fiction.

Jody went on to win the British Grand Prix in 1974, but he wasn't the only Marriott flatmate to do so – John Watson added to the list in 1981 with his fabulous victory in the McLaren MP4, famously the first carbonfibre car to win in Formula 1. That was a very special day.

The 1979 race is another very special memory for, at the time, CSS Promotions was not only handling promotional and PR affairs for the race sponsor, but also running the Media Centre and handling PR for the Williams team. The Media Centre was actually in a marquee and back then was the responsibility of the circuit rather than the FIA, and we weren't governed by the various strict and sterile rules that exist today.

Victory that day was a landmark first win for Williams Grand Prix Engineering, as they were known back then. Alan Jones was hugely unlucky not to give Frank his first Formula 1 victory. Instead, Clay Regazzoni took the honours and I was able to interview him afterwards in the marquee, which was pretty emotional. Strangely, the other day, and by pure chance, I was listening to the horse racing from Ascot and there was this filly running actually called Clay Regazzoni. Had I known this earlier, I probably would have rushed down to the local Paddy Power and splashed out £100 on the nag. I am glad I didn't because it finished fifth.

In fact, we ran the British Grand Prix Media Centre for a number of years, first for John Player and later for Marlboro at both Silverstone and Brands Hatch. Thanks to a great team, I was proud to receive the award for the best press operation in 1983, for some reason that I have forgotten it was presented by the Zandvoort circuit. By the way – great to see the track back in the World Championship.

To help run the media operation, not only did I have the services of two of the best PR ladies in the business, Ann Bradshaw and Fiona Miller, but also a group of runners I called the 'Teenies'. This was because they were recruited from friends of the Tee family (who owned *Motor Sport* and *Motoring News* back then), and because they were teenagers. One of them, if I recall, was later to be Indy car racer Davey Jones and I think he managed to crash a car we lent him. Another was twice Champcar Champion and Indy 500 winner Gil de Feran. Gil met his wife-to-be Angela, while cleaning the Media Centre floor with me probably shouting at him to get a move on.

At CSS, when our sports marketing company was at its height, we had a hospitality division run by a redoubtable lady called Linda Patterson. Our biggest weekend was, of course, the British Grand Prix and this was in the days when each sponsor could pretty well do its own thing – and before the Paddock Club had become the only place to be.

One year in the 1980s, I think we had about five different hospitality

CSS Hospitality's boss Linda Patterson gets down on her hands and knees to do some weeding outside a hospitality marquee. There was no free lunch when she was around. ***Marriott Archive***

clients scattered all over the Silverstone site with Linda keeping an eagle-eyed overview on the whole thing. With such a big operation, she decided that once it was all over, all the CSS staff would have their own evening barbeque to wind down. This included everyone from the directors to various freelancers we had brought in for the day, plus a few mates.

With the race well over and most of the crowds heading home up, we started to settle into the beers and the steaks were sizzling nicely. Chef Jonathan Graham Brown started to serve the 50 or so people gathered around the tables under the awning of what had been a London bus. But Linda wasn't happy.

She sidled over to me and asked who a particular bloke was. "Is he one of your dodgy mates?" she asked. " No," I replied. "I thought he was one of your hospitality helpers."

She strode straight over to this fellow who, by now, had not only bagged the largest and juiciest piece of cow, but had taken a slice which was now dangling on the end of his fork about an inch from his mouth.

"Hey you, who are you, what are you doing here, which group are you with?" she demanded, just a little worried he was an important hospitality guest who had hung on for what, these days, seems to be known as the after party. "I, I , I am a food and safety officer," he stuttered. "I have to try the food to make sure these units are cooking everything properly." It was a brave but fruitless attempt by this arch blagger to save his free dinner. "Ooooout," said Linda and the poor hungry interloper had the fork wrenched from his hand, still with the steak dangling from it and was escorted out of the marquee. Laugh, we nearly cried, yet in a way I still feel a little sorry for him.

Other great races and happenings that I remember at Silverstone? Again, they tend to revolve around Williams. There was the wonderful Rosberg 160mph lap qualifying in 1985 with that Honda RA163 engine boosted up to 1000bhp. That stood as the fastest Formula 1 lap at 160.924mph until it was finally bettered by another Williams driver Juan-Pablo Montoya at Monza in 2002.

One man who so often sent the British Grand Prix crowd home with a smile was 'Our Nige'. But for me, his finest race was the 1987 event when he caught and passed team mate Nelson Piquet

At sports marketing agency CSS Promotions we brokered many different sponsorship deals for Silverstone including both the car and bike Grands Prix and everything from truck to grass track racing. ***CSS Archive***

Johnny Mowlem in the Red River Sports Ferrari GTE car navigates the complex with the BRDC Clubhouse in the background and a cloudy sky above. ***Red River Sports***

in the closing stages after he took the gamble of stopping for new tyres. To crown it all, he got out of the car and kissed the Silverstone tarmac. It must have tasted so sweet, if a little gritty. Always one for the grand gesture was Nigel, and actually I love him for it. My old flat mate MGD is the biggest Piquet fan and claims there were some peculiar circumstances and Nige really should have run out of fuel.

For about 20 years until the mid-2010s I was delighted to be part of Silverstone Television, the dedicated British Grand Prix channel run by Richard Hay of Hay Fisher Productions. We developed some pretty sophisticated programming for the big screens and closed circuit hospitality monitors, filling in when Bernie's TV people weren't giving us pictures – which was quite a lot of the time.

Until the final year – when I moved to the studio – my main role was as one of the two paddock reporters which embraced everything from fighting all the regulars like Ted Kravitz in the post-qualification and race bullpen scrum to interviewing the various personalities who turned up in the paddock.

Richard and Producer Ken Pollock did a fantastic job of also lining up one to one interviews with all the big names. Thus I got extended interviews with most of the F1 grid with Michael Schumacher and Lewis Hamilton (before he had all the tats) staying in my mind as two of the best interviewees.

Here we were on home territory but, as I mentioned in Chapter 10, it was those assorted film stars, politicians, comedians, athletes and boy band members who gave us the most trouble. Maybe it is age thing, but I really didn't know what was the latest hit from Kasabian was or the name of their drummer. I did know who the drummer was in the Rolling Stones, but Charlie Watts wasn't interested in motor racing unfortunately. Leo Sayer made up for

The late Willie Rushton's marvellous cartoon of the grid at Silverstone produced for the Hesketh Racing book. Someone borrowed the original for a TV documentary and it disappeared. ***Marriott Archive***

that and is always a great interviewee.

In the latter years, we were joined by Alan Hyde and he all too readily wanted to stick his microphone in front of the latest rap artist although, having said that, these stars were often surrounded by minders, no more so than David and Victoria Beckham when they turned up one year as a guest of McLaren. They escaped my interrogation.

But strangely the biggest scrum of all was in 2002 when it looked as if the Arrows team would miss the race because Tom Walkinshaw was having problems settling the Cosworth engine bill. Tom was finally forced into a corner by the Arrows motorhome and I can't previously remember being in the middle of such pushing, shoving and swearing in about ten different languages. But I got a decent interview. Maybe it helped that when he drove for the March F3 team I ran in 1970 and we never sent him the bill for various damage he inflicted.

Another aspect of this Silverstone TV gig was interviewing the drivers as they arrived on Sunday morning and chasing them to their motorhome with mic at the ready while the cameraman furiously had to walk backwards, which is never easy. The results ranged from a grunt to a good morning to the occasional full-blown interview from the more garrulous.

Bernie and his TV henchman loved to play games with Silverstone TV, making it increasingly difficult to operate, mainly by restricting access. So once an important interview was done, the cameraman had to hand it to producer Dave Smith, who then had to rush to a gate to give the tape to a runner – who wasn't allowed in the paddock, who then had to rush it the editing suite etc. The interviews could easily have been done live on a microwave link – but that would have been too easy.

Sadly, that era came to an end and now my British Grand Prix days are confined to the BRDC Suite or the Farm talking about great days long ago with old mates. Is that Harry Marks over the corner? How did he get in? Sadly, not so. He is long gone like so many of the famous names who have made Silverstone one of the greatest Formula 1 venues of all time. Long may it continue.

Chapter 34

AN ELEVATING MOGGIE AS THE POLISH COMES OUT

The Amelia Island Concours was on my bucket list for years but when I finally made it, the event produced a surprise or two.

I might have been hallucinating. I had spent ten hours on one of BA's finest 777s in Premium Economy cabins. Then I had driven a brand spanking new Avis Toyota Corolla for the four hours it takes from Tampa to reach Amelia Island, home of the fabulous annual Concours d'Elegance, second only to Pebble Beach extravaganza in California. It was here at the Ritz Carlton Hotel, Amelia Island, that my friend of 50 years standing, David Hobbs was launching the book *Hobbo – Motor Racer Motor Mouth*. In fact, I had co-authored this book with David, having rescued the project which had finally taken about seven years to come to fruition. So there was plenty to celebrate.

Together with Mrs Marriott, I checked in to the slightly down at heel three-star Residence by Marriott at Fernandina Beach rather than the plush Ritz-Carlton three miles down the road. Despite my name and my exclusive Marriott Rewards card, I had already stumped out the best part of £900 for a three-night stay. I just checked on Hotels.com and the rooms normally go for about £120 a night. The law of supply and demand, I guess.

On display at Amelia Island I spotted this 1967 Hurst Dune Baja Buggy raced by Steve McQueen.
Andrew Marriott

Anyway, I clutched my room card which said I was an Elite guest, and pushed the button for the elevator (lift to you and me), and the doors opened. You do not normally see a cat in a lift – a particularly furry cat, which was probably a cross between a Siamese and a Persian. You do not normally see a cat in what the Americans call a baby stroller wearing a coat and a bow and tended to by a woman in her 40s. I can't tell you much about the lady in question – or whether the cat in the stroller was part of some bizarre Amelia Island Concours event – because I was trying to work out why this upmarket moggie wasn't about to leap for freedom. That was until I noticed the poor thing was firmly strapped into the stroller.

I don't know why Americans call their baby push chairs strollers; whenever I pushed my kids around it was hardly a stroll. It was more like a desperate dash to get them home because they were screaming their heads off or, worse still, throwing up. Once, I remember pushing my eldest daughter endlessly round the corridors of some vast Las Vegas Hotel having inadvisedly taken the family to the Caesars Palace Grand Prix. Hardly a stroll.

Signing autographs at Amelia island on launch of Hobbo. It was a pleasure to collaborate with David and the book has sold well. ***Caroline Marriott***

Anyway, the following morning we headed for breakfast. The £300-a-night Residence did not have a proper dining room but it did have a breakfast area and, especially laid on for the big weekend, an omelette station. I didn't want an omelette, just a fried egg – easy over, of course – so I asked the somewhat bored looking chef for just that. "We don't have eggs," he responded. Some sage once said you can't make an omelette without breaking an egg – but this guy could because he had a bucket of some yellow liquid. Anyway, I had to make to do with some toast which took three passes through the toasting device before it took on a brown hue.

That done – and with no more cat sightings – we headed for the media car park. As I turned into what was, literally, a hole in a hedge, I was stopped by a woman who said I had to have a bright red car pass label. "But," I told her, "I have a letter here which clearly says that on entering for the first time, park up, go to the media centre and get your car parking sticker and come back and put in on your car." She took the instruction, read it, shook her head and squawked into a walkie talky. Someone squawked back and she reluctantly waved me on. It doesn't say a great deal for the local education system.

The Amelia Island Concours d'Elegance is a wonderful event in a magnificent setting. Created by former top motor racing photographer Bill Warner, his staff of eight plus an amazing 700 volunteers run the event as a charitable trust. It has raised over $3.2million for some very worthy causes. Bill recently sold the event to insurance company Hagerty.

As well as the main Concours, which is spread out over the final hole of the Golf Club of Amelia, you can test drive a number of supercars, attend lectures, dinners and at least four different auctions near by. I picked up a little magazine called *Auction Skinny* and discovered I could bid for anything from a Ferrari 365 GTS/4 to a Morris Minor Traveller – the latter at an estimated hammer price of $25,000. More in my price range was a glassfibre Cosworth DFV engine at $1000. An ex-Michael Andretti helmet was expected to fetch $6500 and a Ferrari Enzo $2.7million.

That year's Honoree was Emerson Fittipaldi, and director of operations Tim Prendegast had assembled a fabulous collection of Emmo's cars going right back to the Renault Gordini he raced in his early days in Brazil. Of course, there were his World Championship-winning Lotus and McLaren Grand Prix machines as well as his Indy 500 winners. Sadly no 1.0-litre Formula 3 car though.

Inside the Ritz Carlton were various booths selling all manner of memorabilia and other services including an outfit offering to rent you a business jet. They had a few caps with their name on scattered over the desk so I asked if I could have one as I had left my BRDC headgear in the car.

Three great German sports cars of different eras were on display at Amelia Island the year I visited. On the left a road version of 1998 CLK GTR – just 28 were produced years ago, I was driven down the Dubai Corniche in the example owned by FIA President Mohammed ben Sulayem. Top right is Martini liveried 1971 Porsche 917 and below the current Mercedes-AMG Project 1 hypercar. ***Andrew Marriott***

Reluctantly the sales guy let me take one but only after I lied that I did indeed travel in executive jets. Well I did, at least, go to Cannes for the Premiere of our film *Steve McQueen – The Man & Le Mans* in one.

Then, of course, there were the various drivers selling their books. Not only was *Hobbo* on sale for the first time but so too was the new autobiography from Hurley Hayward, very much a hero in these parts. John Fitzpatrick was selling his book, so too was Burt Levy with his terrific fictional motor racing series *The Last Open Road*. And there were a couple of others too. Indeed, if you popped round to British book seller Ben Horton's stand, you could pretty much fill a library.

I am very pleased to tell you that the queue to David's table was far the longest and I don't really think it is because, if you bought his book, you not only had it autographed by David but also by yours truly. David has a huge following in the States; he is something of a cult hero. Of course he raced in Formula 1, Indycars, Sportscars, NASCAR, Can-Am and won both the Trans-Am and Formula 5000 Championships. He drove for the likes of Penske, McLaren, Honda, briefly Team Lotus and BMW among others. He set up a successful motor dealership but also became a hugely popular and charismatic TV presenter and commentator for Formula 1, most recently on NBC, alongside Leigh Diffey and Steve Matchett.

I am not sure I really like this 1972 Ferrari 365 GTB/4 shooting brake but perhaps it is the World's fastest hearse. It is about enter the main Amelia arena. ***Andrew Marriott***

But for 2018, NBC lost the Grand Prix contract to ESPN who, to save dollars, decided to take the Sky F1 commentary team rather than a bespoke US orientated group. So for the first time in many US fans' memory they were denied David's pearls of wisdom and words like 'clag'. Almost everyone who bought a book wanted to talk to David about the situation and if it could be reversed.

Meanwhile, I was happily scribbling my moniker under David's until one bloke said very pointedly "I don't need yours". Evro Publishing had sent an allocation for Amelia with some more

The Amelia Island Concours, which was built into such a hugely successful event by US racing photographer Bill Warner and is now owned by the specialist insurance company Hagerty. There are always some rare, exciting and historic cars on view as well as the associated auctions. ***Andrew Marriott***

to follow for Sebring. In the event, every book that had arrived in the US sold and hundreds of people were turned away and had to resort to Amazon, I suppose.

So with the books all but sold out on the first day, David invited Caroline and me to a celebratory dinner at the afore mentioned $750-a-night Ritz-Carlton in their signature restaurant called Salt. Even better news was that the redoubtably Bill Warner was picking up the tab – and it wasn't going to be cheap. We were joined by Bob Varsha and his wife, David's older son Greg and his wife, and Indy 500 winner Johnny 'Lone Star' Rutherford, a one-time team mate of Hobbo.

You know some American waiters at the swankier places put on a show which wouldn't be amiss on a Broadway stage. Well, he flounced to the table. "Hello," he announced. "I'm Bradley and I'm going to serve you tonight and I want to get to know you all real well. Firstly, I am going to present you with our specialty salts." I wanted to say, Bradley, I don't really want to be your friend, I just want you to take my order and bring it without tipping it down my collar. But instead I shut up and listened to his flowery description of the various salt offerings. "This one is very special, we only have it this week and I – yes, he actually said that – have had it flown in from the Caspian sea." And this he said proudly, is all is all the way from the salt flats of Peru and so it went on. Where is the good old Saxa, I wondered.

Anyway, we had a very nice meal and I was very pleased that I didn't see the final reckoning because it was probably more than the GDP of Zaire. Greg Hobbs picked up the wine bill, which appeared to have three noughts on the end of it when I sneaked a furtive look, as well as the tip. He must be selling a lot of Hondas in Milwaukee. Bradley was certainly very pleased with the gratuity because he came round and shook all our hands at the end.

I missed out on the Big Banquet the following evening where Emerson was being interviewed, but if you think the *Autosport* Awards is expensive, it was at least twice the price and there was no guarantee Bradley would be your server. But it is all in a good cause. The Amelia Island Concours should definitely be on your bucket list.

One final thought. I was told about one particular autobiography written and self-published by a certain driver, who shall be nameless. He signed most of them. In fact, I heard that in the second-hand trade the ones that weren't signed were worth a lot more than the signed ones, because they were much rarer! I don't think David's book will be like that despite his autographing efforts. And I hope I can say the same.

Chapter 35

CROISSANTS AND CREVENTIC

It may not be the world's best known racing series but Creventic's relaxed and friendly manner reminded me of racing forty years ago.

Ring ring, ring ring. "Hello," said a voice I didn't expect to hear. "I don't suppose there is any chance you could do the pit lane for the Paul Ricard 24 Hours? We've been let down, you see." Hmph, I thought. Not sure I want to spend another night out of bed chatting about a series I know little about, plus I wasn't really sure I knew there was a 24-hour race at Ricard anyway. But it was the South of France in May, which certainly had an appeal and the race was on the same weekend that the French were electing a new president, so that might be fun.

But, the voice continued, "You won't have to stay up all night, we are off the air for eight hours, the series people are very friendly and they feed you a lot." So I said "OK," not realising that what the organisers actually fed us, at lunchtime anyway, was fish paste baguettes. Since that Ricard race I have enjoyed covering the 24-hour series on a number of occasions.

But this chapter is focussed on that first Creventic race and it turned out to be one of a number of firsts. Before I left, I thought I'd better do a bit of homework. First, I discovered that Creventic was short for Creative Events and was run a by a Dutch group whose main event each year is the Dubai 24 Hours. Its 24 Hour Series, supported by Korean tyre company Hankook, is actually an endurance race series and usually only four of them are held over 24 hours. The other three were run once round the clock and even a couple of those are split with six hours one day and six the next. Anyway, it didn't really matter as this Ricard race was a genuine full-blooded twice round-the-clock affair.

I quickly came to the conclusion that the class structure would take a bit of mastering. The top class was A6-Pro and there was A6-Am as well, both for GT3 cars. The Am cars could have a professional driver in them, but if he went faster than a certain lap time, then the car got bumped up into the Pro class, which seemed fair enough. But then they were also given a handful of 'joker' laps where they could go as fast as they liked. Somewhat fiendish, I reckoned, although this idea was subsequently scrapped.

There was another class for SP2 cars which was for machines like Porsche and Ferrari Cup cars, except that there was also a separate class called 991 which was also for Porsche 911 Cup cars, so take your choice. Add to that the fact that in this SP2 category you could also enter US V8-powered spaceframe silhouette saloons, and one of them had come all the way from Australia. Then there was a class for TCR touring cars which looked pretty competitive, and the Audi factory had even sent a man to look after a couple of Audi RS3s. Let's not forget the SP3-GT4 class, although there were only a handful of entries in that.

You know that on entry lists they like to put initials like FRA, ENG, or GER against the name of the driver to say where the person has come from, but the clever folk who produce the material for the series' website got clicking on some special resource which put the flags of the nation alongside the driver. It all looked very pretty.

A multi-egg boiler and the recycling of plastic bottle tops, just two of the many firsts I encountered when I started commentating on Creventic races. ***Andrew Marriott***

Joe Bradley with top cameraman Seb.
Andrew Marriott

The pits team. Joe, Diana Binks and me.
Radio Le Mans

Prior to the start of the Dubai 24 Hours, the local traffic police demonstrate some of their squad cars. Former police sergeant Joe was pretty jealous. ***Andrew Marriott***

I usually do quite well when it comes to flags and geography and stuff like that on BBC1's *University Challenge*. I took a look at the entry list and I am pleased to say I recognised the flag of Luxembourg but two others stumped me. One indicated there was a chap from Zimbabwe although it turned out he is based in the UAE. The last racing driver I met from Zim (before it was called that) was John Love and he very nearly won the South African Grand Prix a very long time ago.

I told the young driver, Axcil Jefferies, this and he had the good grace to act as if he was impressed. The other flag that caused me problems took more research and eventually I found out the driver came from Papua New Guinea. Sadly the chap was a non-starter having, I subsequently found out, been involved in a horrific and fiery testing accident in Australia.

I was pleased to see I was joining a happy Radio Le Mans group comprising Joe Bradley, Jonny Palmer, Paul Tarsey and Paul Truswell. I said at the beginning that this was a weekend of firsts, and it started when we went to the Europcar compound to pick up the rental car which fortunately turned out to be a Citroën people carrier. I have never heard such a long explanation of how we would be charged for any damage we caused. Maybe they could see we were frustrated racers. Anyway, the rental car bloke showed us some plastic device he had to measure how long and how big a mark you had made if you returned the car after an altercation with a 2CV or whatever. I asked the bloke if marks included seagull poo, but he didn't even smile.

Our next first was when we arrived at the hotel in Toulon. This was 9.30pm and next door was a restaurant in which they were stacking the chairs on the tables. Do you know what? They unstacked the chairs and the happy commentating quintet was served half-passable steak frites.

The next 'first' came the following morning in the breakfast room of this Holiday Inn Express motel. Maybe I have led a sheltered life, but I have never previously seen an eight-berth egg boiler, if you get my drift. You could do just one egg or as many as eight if you wanted – six minutes bubbling time and the breakfast egg was spot on. For 25 years I stayed at the same Le Mans digs and the lovely Madame Froget never mastered egg boiling, forever serving up *les oeufs* so runny that the white was still transparent.

So to the track and, although at this stage I didn't have a credential, we were cheerily waved though the entrance and all the way to the paddock. We arrived at the Creventic reception area in the impressive entrance to Ricard's pits block. On the desk they had a bowl of gummi-something sweets, a receptacle where you could recycle bottle tops (although there were a couple of half-sucked gummi-somethings in it as well) and a nice Dutch lady said she had prepared a season-long credential for me. She duly handed it to me and on it was the picture I always send to be used on such occasions. Except that I hadn't sent it to them: they saw I was the new boy on the team and had Googled the net, found the said photo of me looking a little racy complete with a TV headset on, peeled it from the internet and there it was. I knew this would be a good weekend.

A few weeks later I was at Le Mans for Fox Sports and my pass had me down as an uplink engineer and I wasn't allowed in the paddock but I could go in the grandstand. I have only been doing the same job for the same Americans for almost 20 years. While I am having a moan about Le Mans, I was also barred from the 8am photographer and TV briefing meeting because I turned up at 8.02am, having wasted 10 minutes arguing to get into the paddock because they had screwed up my pass.

Anyway, back to Ricard, where I was also handed my dinner tickets and told that on Saturday and Sunday the organisers would bring lunch parcels to the TV commentary box. By the way, you don't need to wear a fire suit or a silly French cycle helmet at Creventic races because all the fuelling is done round the back of the pits. Plus they don't expect you to get knocked on your head because they know you have been doing this a long time.

So I spent a happy Friday nosing round the paddock and filling up my notebook, preparing for Saturday's 2.30pm race start and watching qualifying. The race was going to be a good battle between the Herberth Motorsport Porsche 911 GT3 Cup car which had won the Dubai 24 with a driving team which included the Renauer twins, the Scuderia Praha Ferrari which had Eddie Cheever junior (or, strictly speaking, Eddie Cheever III) as the third of its the drivers, plus several strong Mercedes GT3s and Audi R8 LMS models including one with US ace Connor di Philippi in it. There were also two Renault RS01s from the UAE-based GP Extreme outfit which is owned by Roald Goethe's old business partner Jean-Pierre Valentini at the giant commodity trader Trafigura.

Jean-Pierre was racing one of the Renaults and looked pretty fit considering a few years ago he had spent several months incarcerated in an Ivory Coast prison while attempting to sort out some waste disposal problem he probably knew nothing about.

Come race day, it didn't feel like the South of France at all: it was cold and windy and rain threatened. It was so windy that the good folk from Creventic took down all their flags in case they finished up in tatters and we were left with just a single Luxembourg flag flying in the DUWO Racing pits – made of stern fabric those Luxembourg flags.

Don't touch anything, the audio control box in our commentary position overlooking the Barcelona 24 pits. *Andrew Marriott*

The Scuderia Praha Ferrari has been a regular winner in the Creventic series with an all-Czech driving crew. The series always has a very International line-up. *Andrew Marriott*

The rolling start was flagged away not with a French flag, a Dutch flag or even that Luxembourg flag from the pits, but with a purple flag with a large number 60 on it. This was another first for me, and I was baffled. I was advised that the race was starting under Code 60, a sort of self-policing virtual safety car deal with each driver setting a 60km/h pace, and remarkably it worked. Fortunately, the rain abated and we were soon racing at full speed.

I forgot to mention that the Creventic people, despite battling with the weather and flag situation had, as promised, brought to the distant commentary box some rations. There were crisps, an apple and, as mentioned before, a roll with what appeared to have fish paste in it. This was quite a picnic except it didn't include a hard boiled egg – perhaps Creventic doesn't have one of those multi-egg boilers that the hotel had discovered.

I quickly found out the pits were a joy to work in: everyone was very helpful and the back of the pit garages weren't divided into more rooms than a Towcester bungalow, as is now the case at Le Mans. My German cameraman Seb was one of the very best with whom I have had the pleasure of working.

There is always a huge entry for Creventic's premier race the Dubai 24 Hours. Here is a busy pit lane and note the baby on the wing end plate. ***Andrew Marriott***

But get this. I was missing out on the food and beverage situation in the commentary box. The organisers had shown up with a pot of coffee. Then one of the drivers, who was down on the entry list purely as JM Littman, and was racing one of those nice Audis, had arrived with ice creams for the commentators. Very definitely another first.

Later I found the said Littman and thrust a microphone towards him hoping I might be rewarded with an ice cream at the end. I discovered that he was actually Jean Marc and he had adopted the JM rather in the style of AJ Foyt. Also I discovered that he came from Muswell Hill, where I live. He also said he started racing husky dogs before he switched to cars which, frankly, was yet another first. It just so happened that I used to see a bloke walking husky dogs at the bottom of my street ten years earlier. Same bloke – small world! For the record, after a good battle he finished second in the TCR class, so he deserved his interview. But I never did get an ice cream from him.

We finished at midnight with a great battle going on between the Czech-run Ferrari, the Audi R8 with Connor de Phillipi in it and the Herberth Motorsport Porsche of the Renauer twins – Robert and Alfred – Daniel Allemann and Ralf Bohn. We headed for our Holiday Inn and were just about three miles down the road when we were confronted with a wild boar which we skilfully avoided but it was yet another first.

Creventic seems to have a trophy for everyone and proudly displayed the silverware before a rain-soaked 2021 Sebring 24 hours. ***Andrew Marriott***

We returned at 8am the next day to find we hadn't missed much but the Porsche was pulling away thanks to some slick pit work and strategy from the under-stated but very efficient Bavarian team. I was back on the pit lane and the next thing I know is that a kind marshal is offering me a breakfast croissant, which I passed on to Seb, the cameraman. You see, I had already tucked into one of the hotel's now famous eggs from that multi-cooker. But a marshal giving a pits reporter breakfast on the lane – yes, another première.

Later I missed another coffee run from the organisers but I did have the Sunday picnic lunch. Still no boiled egg but significantly the baguette was filled with what looked suspiciously like wild boar pate! Meanwhile, the stands weren't full; perhaps everyone was too busy voting.

Ultimately, the Bavarian Porsche came home the victor from the Audi driven by Connor, Adrian Amstutz, Martin Kodric and ex-GP3 ace Patrick Kujala. Third was the Ferrari with young Cheever, Matteo Malucelli and Josef Kral in it, while in fourth spot was the Renault RS01 driven and owned by the bloke who had been in jail in the Ivory Coast, Jean-Pierre Beltoise's son and the chap from Zimbabwe. On the podium there seemed to be a trophy for everyone.

The British Track Club Lotus Evora of Martin Jewell, Simon Atkinson, Adam Knight and Stuart Ratcliff won the SP3/GT4 category even though it had comprehensively blown up in the middle of the night, while the Ginetta crew of Adrian Barwick, Dan O'Brien, Julio Martin and Philippe Salini still finished second in class despite the Leeds device having gone up in flames.

It was a racing weekend to remember and certainly one full of new experiences. I can thoroughly recommend the Creventic 24 Hour Endurance Series. I immediately vowed to be back for more including the fish paste baguettes, pits croissants, gummi-wotsits and, perhaps next time, an ice cream from Mr Littman.

GETTING OLD

Professional racing drivers usually retire before they are 40 but there are some notable exceptions. Journalists go on a bit longer.

"What do you want for your birthday, dad?" asked daughter number one. "I don't know," I replied. "You'll have to think of something." I was rather hoping a decent bottle or even two of Sancerre might arrive. But the next thing I knew was that a magazine called *The Oldie* dropped through the letterbox. "Thanks a lot," I thought but subsequently found it a very good read, and much better value than an £11 *Autosport*. OK, I know the price went down again but I have to say I really enjoy *The Oldie*. That's probably because I've been around a while and there is some superb writing within its covers.

I've heard all the '75 is the new 57' type platitudes, the 'age is just a number' kind of thing and even the somewhat crass 'you are as old as the woman you feel!'. The other day I told someone I was 67 when it was the other way round – not because I was being untruthful but because I forgot I was that old. But then again, age affects your memory.

It was Oscar Wilde who wrote "The old believe everything, the middle-aged suspect everything and the young know everything." Henry Ford said "Anyone who stops learning is old, whether at twenty or eighty. Anyone who keeps learning stays young. The greatest thing in life is to keep your mind young."

I am not so sure I agree entirely with Oscar but I fully subscribe to the great car maker's view. Sorry to strike a sombre note in this penultimate chapter. Age is something I have been thinking about recently – actually ever since I interviewed Damon Hill's son Josh a few years ago when he was in Formula 3. I have reported on the exploits of Graham Hill, closely followed and worked with Damon and then, there I was, interviewing a third generation of racing Hills. At Daytona in 2022, I added a third generation of Andretti. So it made me feel positively vintage for just a moment, until I remembered good old Henry's quote.

After all, I reported my first Formula 1 race at Mallory Park for my local paper at the age of 18 back in 1962 and I covered what is probably my 51st Le Mans 24 Hours in 2019. I have to say I got as much thrill interviewing Fernando Alonso for Radio Le Mans that year as I did John Surtees when he won at the Leicestershire track all those years ago. However, experience pays, because in 2019 I got the first winner's interview with Fernando. Back in 1962, I was third in line to talk to Big John after his win. Some progress then.

So after fifty or so years in the paddock and the pitlane, I reckon I can still cut the mustard. Of course nobody is going to hire me these days to join the massed ranks of Formula 1 commentators and pundits, but I am happy that I can still work races like Sebring, Le Mans, the Barcelona 24 Hours or indeed at historic events like the Daytona 24 Classic. So I am not about to hang up the mic just yet.

But enough of me – you racing drivers out there, when should you retire, hang up your helmet and decide you have driven your last lap? Several things set me wondering about this – and there seems to be no one correct answer. Let's look at some facts.

Very few Grand Prix drivers have competed at the top level over the age of 50 – just ten of them, I believe. Luigi Fagioli won the 1951 French Grand Prix at the grand old age of 53, Juan Manuel Fangio was the oldest World Champion at 46 and until 2022 our oldest current

Three drivers who raced on into their seventies and who take part in Daytona 24 Classic event. Former Ferrari Formula 1 racer Arturo Merzario, European Touring Car Champion Dieter Quester and Derek Bell. ***Andrew Marriott***

Experience versus youth. Juan Manuel Fangio in the number 2 Mercedes Benz W196 takes the tight line at Monaco's Hairpin squeezing out younger team mate Stirling Moss in this Neil Collins painting. The six-time World Champion won his last title at the age of 46, by far the oldest Champion. ***Neil Collins***

Formula 1 racer was, of course, 41-year-old Kimi Raikkonen.

When they leave Formula 1, a few grand prix drivers switch to sports car racing and extend their careers. For instance, Giancarlo Fisichella is still earning good money as a pro driver in the World Endurance Championship at the age of 47 and former Lotus F1 racer Pedro Lamy is a year older than that. Obviously there are plenty of so called 'gentleman' drivers racing into their 50s and 60s – but I was thinking more of the professionals here.

Indeed, for most high profile professional sports, golf excluded, around 40 seems to be the limit. Few of the top 100 tennis players are over 37, although at 40 Roger Federer is still at the very top. The oldest footballer in the Premier League is 43. And remember those golfers, after all, do a lot of standing around. Talking of standing around – and indeed toeing the oche whatever that is – I have to tell you that recent PDC World Darts champion Michael van Gerwen is only 30.

For some reason, instead of saying average Americans say the median, which I though was what they call they central reservation. Yes, it is all a bit different in the States. For many years the NASCAR racers have been known as 'the good old boys'. The average age of a NASCAR Cup driver is 39 which compares with the Formula 1 average of 27 and Indycar at approximately 32, so I suppose you could call them old. But 2019 NASCAR Champion Kyle Busch clocked in at just 34, and is the same age as Lewis Hamilton.

As recently as 2019, a guy called Morgan Shepherd raced in the second-tier NASCAR XFinity series (formerly known as Busch and Nationwide) at the amazing age of 78. In 2017, he actually led one of the races. He raced in the series for 33 years – competed in 453 races, and won 15 of them. In the top league he has four wins, most recently at Atlanta in 1993.

Let's not forget the marvellously named Hershel McGriff, who won the competitive Winston West series in 1986, aged 59. He retired from that series at the age of 75 but in 2019 returned at the grand old age of 90 to race around the little 0.375-mile asphalt oval of Tucson Speedway. The newspaper *USA Today* ran a nice story complete with a shot of Hershal extracting himself from the cockpit of the Bill McAnally Racing Toyota completely unaided. He did finish last, but he finished.

So it all begs the question, can you still be quick at over 50? One of the drivers who still impresses me at events like the Silverstone Classic is long time BRDC member John Burton in his Chevron. I well remember the 2019 Classic races and the wet greasy Sunday morning track. John was in his Chevron B26 in a big field of cars which included several similar but later 2.0-litre sports cars.

In Saturday's race, Dean Forward had won well in the ex-Foulston McLaren M8F Can-Am beast and John, by his own admittance, had screwed up the settings on the B26, and came home a disappointed seventh. But Sunday was a very different story and the mighty Burton soon moved to second place after Forward's McLaren sprung a water leak and he was right on the tale of German industrialist Georg Hallau in the ex-David Hobbs Lola T310. Can-Am machine. At the end of the 17 laps John, who has raced the same car for twenty or so years, was just 2.7sec off the back of the thundering 7.0-litre monster.

Rather unkindly, I stuffed my microphone under the nose of winner Hallau and said something like "How did you beat a 77-year-old who had 6.0 litres less power than you?" Georg's English is not great but he got the irony of it and was visibly deflated. But the moral of the story is that you can still be quick even in your 70s – but even so John Burton is exceptional. Mind you, he did have to adjust his hearing aid a bit before he could hear me interviewing him! It wasn't just a one-off either – earlier that year John had scored a pair of wins at the HSCC's Legends of Brands Hatch Super Prix. I well remember reporting John's exploits for

Hershal McGriff raced at the age of 90 and was able to climb into his Toyota Camry NASCAR machine. ***Marriott Archive***

MN back in the days of his Worcester Racing Association Ginetta G12 back in 1967.

Silverstone was a happy stomping ground for Britain's oldest ever racer, the great Tom Delaney, whose father took part in 1903 Paris-Madrid road race. Tom started racing in 1930 with a Lea Francis and he continued to race the same car for the next 76 years. In fact, he did so until a few weeks before his death in April 2006 at the age of 95. A couple of years earlier he had crashed at Silverstone and was thrown out of the machine. Although he rolled clear, he was run over by the wayward Leaf as it bounced off the Armco. He was carted off to hospital but on closer inspection only had a sprained wrist. From his hospital bed, he called his mechanic to see if the car could be repaired for the following day's racing. Sadly I never met this remarkable man but I think his record of being the MSA's oldest licence holder will last for a good few years yet.

Another recent memory I treasure was at a Daytona 24 Hours Classic. In 2019 the star attraction was the Lowenbrau Porsche 962 HR1. This car is the most successful 962 to race in the IMSA series and it boasted a custom-made non-Porsche chassis built by Kevin Doran for team owner Al Holbert of Holbert Racing – hence the HR1 tag. Between 1985 and 1988, Holbert took the car to ten victories and won the IMSA GTP title in the machine. On occasion he was accompanied by our own Derek Bell including at the 1987 Rolex 24 at Daytona – one of Derek's three wins at the event.

The car quite recently changed hands for just under $1million and became the property of a young tech entrepreneur called Rodrigo Sales, who has made his fortune in the US in the price comparison website business. He entrusted the car to Floridian Porsche expert Kevin Jeanette and has been racing it in what the Americans call 'vintage' events.

Around Christmas 2018, Kevin threw a barbeque at his Florida home and Derek was in attendance. So was Rodrigo, together with Derek's son Justin and Kevin's son Gunnar, who has a lot of racing success both in historic and modern sports cars. That's when he is not sky diving, base

Derek and Justin Bell in the Daytona Victory Circle, Caroline and myself at 'Downton Abbey' and with Caroline and a Gulf Porsche 917at the première of Steve McQueen, The Man and Le Mans. ***Marriott Archive***

jumping and taking part in various other hazardous sports. I wouldn't like to be his insurance broker.

Talk turned to the recent Daytona 24 Classic and Kevin hatched a plan, after a beer or two, that at the 2019 event, they should run HR1 shared by the two Bells, Gunnar and the owner Rodrigo. Now we tend to forget, because he looks about 50, that Le Mans legend Derek was actually 78 years old at the time. The last time he won at Daytona was 30 years earlier and the Porsche will still do the best part of 200mph as it swoops off the tri-oval before braking for Turn One.

It seemed like a good idea at the time and Derek agreed, but really thinking it was merely the beer talking. But then a few weeks before Daytona, Derek got a call from Kevin confirming it was all going to happen. Also on hand would be Al Holbert's son Todd, who would race a Porsche 944, also in the beer brand's livery. The team would all have brand new Lowenbrau race suits although Derek proudly told me, he could still get into the old one.

The Daytona event is based on the Le Mans Classic with the entry split into six groups who all get to race four times over the period of 24 Hours. The Lowenbrau Porsche was in Group B for cars built between 1983 and 1993. Opposition to the Gunnar Racing entry included an ex-Kremer Leyton House 962, Greg Thornton's March 83G, a 1991 Nissan NPT90 and a couple of Porsche 935s including a K1 to be driven solo by Matteo Ferrar-Aza, then the reigning Masters Historic F1 Champ. It was easily fastest in qualifying.

Tom Delaney started racing back in 1930 and was still competing until a few weeks before his death at the age of 95. A phenomena. ***VSCC***

In a perfect world, of course, all this opposition would falter and the old champ himself, still fast at the grand old age of 78, would climb aboard for the final stint and take the chequered flag, some thirty years after his last Daytona win. In the pits would be his son, who had handed the car over to him while car owner Sales and Gunnar would cheer him on to what was probably the final victory in a star-studded career. But things like that only happen in the movies, don't they? Except that just once in a while they do, because that is exactly what happened.

I have to say it brought a tear in the eye to many hardened observers. It is something to contemplate when you get out of bed in the morning and wonder if it is time to hang up your helmet. Derek's success and that of the likes of John Burton and good ol' Hershal all go to prove that age is no barrier to racing, reporting or having fun as you head towards 80.

Fernando Alonso is the oldest Formula 1 driver racing in the 2022 season at the age of 40.
Toyota Gazoo Racing

Chapter 37

SOMETHING FOR THE WEEKEND?

I spent 30 years in the sports marketing business and mixed with World Champions, politicians and the occasional priest.

We were on the crest of a wave at CSS Promotions Ltd back in the '70s and '80s. A new form of marketing called sponsorship had really taken off and we were one of the top exponents of the art. Plus we were managing a raft of sports stars including recently crowned World Champions James Hunt and Barry Sheene, motorsport legends such as Mike Hailwood and Stirling Moss, cricketers David Gower and Bob Willis, boxer Alan Minter, snooker's Terry Griffiths, and both national cricket and football squads.

I almost forgot Mark Thatcher! I've just found our sales brochure from the period and, to quote: "Mark Thatcher, a young man on his way to the top. Determined to prove his motor racing talent and win his way into Grand Prix racing." Oh dear!

Throughout the book, I have made references to various incidents which occurred during the 30 years from starting the company to finally selling it just before the turn of the century. But this final chapter is really a bit of a catch-all to include a few of the other random nuggets that don't fit neatly into the other chapters. So I might as well start with our former prime minister's son and right now I want to say that, as a racing driver, he was a lot quicker than people gave him credit for – witness his results driving for the BMW team in the European Touring Car Championship. Arrogant and, at times, annoying, but not a bad racer at all.

But all everyone remembers about his motorsport career was that, in January 1982, he got lost for six days in the Sahara Desert with Anne-Charlotte Verney in a Peugeot 504 on the Paris-Dakar Rally, and that his distraught mother cried on television. Then an Algerian military helicopter finally spotted him, together with a few others who were stranded, and Mark was on his way home. All this was, of course, front page news in the UK.

Managing his return was where we came in. My chairman and business partner Barrie Gill had a call from old mate and fellow Yorkshireman Sir Bernard Ingram, who was Maggie's press secretary at the time. Barrie was summoned to 10 Downing Street to discuss how the return would be handled. By the way, Maggie wasn't the only one needing a hanky; Mark also had a weeping girlfriend.

Back at the office, Barrie and I sat in our boardroom and we went through all the difficult questions Mark might get asked and scripted all the best answers. Thus armed, we headed to Heathrow; me to jolly along the assembled media in the airport's special conference room and Barrie onto the private plane to coach Mark through what would be a tricky question-and-answer session.

By the time he was in front of the newshounds, he was well rehearsed and a quite difficult situation was largely defused. However, from there he headed straight to a London Hotel where the girlfriend was part of the organisational team actually running some Miss Great Britain contest or other – with plenty of paparazzi in attendance.

So far so good – except this wasn't the official weeping girlfriend who

At the Essex event at the Albert Hall we liaised with Mark Thatcher to get his mother to attend and we also managed the press conference after he returned from being lost on the Dakar. At the same venue we promoted the Grand Prix Night of the Stars. Barrie Gill on stage with Emerson Fittipaldi and Eric Morecambe. CSS

We handled the promotion, sponsorship and media for the Birmingham SuperPrix for all of its five years. We brought in Halfords to sponsor the event and many other partners. It remains the only genuine city street racing circuit in Britain. ***CSS Archive***

had been pictured in the papers but a completely different somewhat racier women. Our good work was unravelled as the headlines shouted "Love Rat Mark Returns".

Incidentally, I had been in that same Heathrow conference room a few years earlier when James Hunt had returned from winning the 1976 World Championship in Japan. We had arranged for him to meet the press on his triumphant return and, in retrospect, we would have been better to have left it another day. James had enjoyed himself on the plane in more ways than continuing his membership of the 'mile high club'. He had drunk a large amount of champagne and this was obvious as he stumbled into the conference room carrying – I kid you not – a mechanical toy monkey which held a pair of cymbals. I think some Japanese fan must have presented him with this gift at Tokyo Airport.

"James, congratulations on your triumph," trilled the lady from *The Guardian*. At this point, James flicked a little switch in the monkey's back and it started banging its little metal discs together in celebration of his success. Each time someone said well-done, the exercise was repeated to much hilarity.

The live television arrangements for that Japanese race were a little complicated. Both ITV and BBC showed it live. While Barrie Gill was commentating from the track itself for the Beeb, I was doing it solo for ITV but actually in the London studios of Independent Television News. This was not an ideal arrangement because I was sitting at a desk with only a little black and white monitor for company. There were some colour pictures coming in and they were in the control room the other side of the glass panel in front of me – and which I could just about see.

As you may remember, the race started late because of the appalling conditions. James's arch rival Niki Lauda pulled out and Mario Andretti won the race while James's third place in the McLaren was good enough to take the title. I am pleased to say that, despite the black and white monitor, I was able to call the race correctly at the end. Of course, this story has been dramatised in the film *Rush*. Indeed, I got a call from one of the producers saying they had the ITV footage with my commentary and wanted to use it but for technical reasons, could not. However could I come to this voiceover studio in Wardour Street and reproduce it.

So there I sat with a huge screen projecting the old footage and me trying to sound like I did forty-odd years earlier. It is one of the most difficult things I have ever had to do – but if you watch the end of the film you can just about hear me in there somewhere.

James was a hugely engaging character and we loved working with him and most of the time he was very professional – but you could never be quite sure if he would turn up on time or be dressed appropriately. One year, he won some forerunner to the *Autosport* Awards called the Tarmac Trophy. It was a Park Lane London black tie do – James arrived in scruffy jeans and a T-shirt, and I am not sure he actually had any shoes on. If he did, they were sandals. The Tarmac managing director handed over the trophy and the cheque but I don't think he was too impressed with Master Hunt. They never sponsored the award again.

Although from very different backgrounds, Barry Sheene and James were soul mates and their relationship is well documented in a film I made a few years ago with Gabriel Clarke and John McKenna called *When Playboys Ruled the World*. I think you can still find it on YouTube.

At CSS, while Barrie largely looked after James, I helped Sheene with all his various media and commercial contracts while Linda Patterson was also a strong member of the team. We got Barry quite a few lucrative editorial deals including one 'writing' road tests for *The Sun* newspaper. It worked like this: I had a road test car delivered from a manufacturer, drove it down to Barry's place near Gatwick Airport, The Manor House, Charlwood, Surrey. Barry then drove it around the local lanes dictating his thoughts about the machine into my tape reporter as we went. We then had a photoshoot with the car, usually with *The Sun*'s star snapper Peter Jay. I returned to London, bashed out 500 words whatever, loosely based on what Barry had said. A few days later, the test filled a page of Britain's best-selling newspaper.

One day I get a call from *The Sun*'s Frank Nicklin telling me the next test would be special and they were not only giving it a double page spread but the article would be linked to a competition in which a reader would become the proud owner of the actual test car. "Great," I said, "what's the car?" It turned out to be a device called a Morris Ital, which was a successor to the Morris Marina but with a new body that apparently had come from the Italian styling company Ital. In truth, they had assisted with the design of the actual tooling to make it and the box-like lines were the work of Leyland's in-house stylist Harris Mann. All this was in the dying days of British Leyland and the car had little to recommend it.

I parked in front of Barry's grand Manor House entrance and he stepped out. "Moriarty," he said, "if you think

Barry Sheene didn't think much of the Morris Ital but enjoyed this Porsche on a snowy day at Silverstone along with friends George Harrison ad Steve Parrish. ***CSS Archive***

I am going to drive a shitbox like that, you can think again. I don't even want to sit in it." At the time, his regular motor was a Rolls-Royce Shadow, so I suppose it was a bit of a come down. Anyway, he did pose in it for the photos and I drove it back to London. Obviously, I could not write that this was one of the worst cars ever produced by Leyland but somehow I cobbled together a gushing test report. It probably even had a sidebar stolen from Robert Glenton (see earlier chapter) Will it Fit Your Garage When you Have Won it? Some lucky person did exactly that.

Newspaper competitions were a big thing in the '80s. Another one we did with *The Sun* also involved Barry. This was in conjunction with the Co-operative Society Footwear division. Back then, the Co-Op actually made its own shoes and had shoe shops. The competition was to join your favourite sporting hero as he took part at a big event. I think we did four or five of them. Join David Gower at a Lords test, Terry Griffiths at some snooker tournament and Mark Thatcher in the desert. Actually, I made that one up. But I was directly involved with the join Barry Sheene at the British Motorcycle Grand Prix at Silverstone competition.

It was a nice prize; attend Silverstone as a VIP guest, have a night in a local hotel, dinner with Barry and bring along a friend. There were quite a few correct answers, so I just picked one at random. The winner turned out to be a girl of about 25 from Wolverhampton and it was a good job I was born there because when I phoned her up to give her the great news she answered in an almost unintelligible Wulfrunian accent. It also transpired she had never stayed in a hotel in her life and she wanted bring along a girl friend.

Somehow, we got the hapless pair from Wolverhampton to Northampton and into the Silverstone pits where, between practice laps, they were introduced to Barry. He signed their T-shirts across their busts. "You've got a lovely pair, Sylvia," he enthused. He'd be locked up these days.

That evening at the Moat House Hotel Northampton we had the dinner and the top bloke from the Co-op Footwear division – an old Etonian who had sold his family shoe-making business to them – actually quizzed Sylvia and her mate about why they shopped at the Co-op. It was excruciating. Barry left for his next sponsor engagement – or maybe to splash on some Brut – while the girls were now at the section in the itinerary which says 'at your leisure'. Otherwise translated into, we can't think of anything else for you to do.

Flushed with meeting their hero, staying in a swish hotel for the first time and probably a glass or two of champagne, this pair decided to head off and investigate the Northampton night life. They returned to the hotel with two rough blokes on their arms and headed to the bedroom. I am not sure what happened next but all I know is that a fight broke out and the

Our early clients included the London Rubber Company and Hesketh Racing for who we produced this magazine. We persuaded LRC brand Durex to sponsor the Surtees team which led to some great promotions even if it did upset the BBC. ***CSS Archive***

two Northamptonshire lads had to be forcibly removed. A bit of damage was done to the room but that's why you have a contingency budget.

So I got to know the Moat House management which proved helpful a few years later when we were running one of those Silverstone truck races. That year we hired a Finnish daredevil motorcycle stunt rider called Artu Nyqvist. His best trick was to hang off the back of his Kawasaki at about 60mph while it towed him along behind the beast, feet on the tarmac. For this trick he wore wooden clogs which smoked nicely as he performed the stunt. He then somehow levered himself back on the saddle – I can only presume he had some way of operating the throttle.

You know the Finns; quiet until they have had a few drinks. He had polished off the best part of a bottle of vodka in the bar – as his hotel bill later revealed – but when he got to his room he decided he wanted a few more. After he had emptied the mini-bar, he picked it up and threw it out of the still-closed hotel bedroom window. Fortunately, it landed in the car park without causing any further damage. As I said, you need some contingency in your budget.

One of our favourite clients was a company called Peter Pan Playthings of Peterborough. They had bought the rights to sell the Aurora AFX motor racing slot game in Britain as an upstart competitor to the hugely popular Scalextric. They had a decent budget to promote the product and also wanted the endorsement of a famous driver. Of course, we suggested James. However, this was when drivers were still being killed all too regularly and they said to us that if James dies they would have to scrap all the boxes, which would cost a fortune. So deal over.

Fortunately, we were able to demonstrate to them that there was a marvellous opportunity to sponsor the new British Formula 1 Championship – and subsequently the Aurora British Formula 1 series was popular for several years. Even Barry Sheene almost got in on the act. I arranged for him to test a Surtees with the possibility of taking part some of the races. I even had Aurora helmet stickers made for him. He tested the car in secrecy at Brands Hatch and George Harrison came along to cheer him on. But for a long forgotten reason, the deal didn't go ahead.

There is an ironic postscript to this story. PPPoP also had in their inventory a miniature snooker game and they had done a deal for the comedian Sid James, beloved of the *Carry On* films, to endorse it. His craggy face was all over the boxes. Irony of ironies, just three weeks after it was launched he had a heart attack and died and they had to repackage them all.

Our Chairman Barrie Gill was an inspirational and charismatic leader although, on occasions, he got carried away with implausible ideas. One of them that stuck in my mind was a blind cross-channel swimmer for whom who he thought we could easily snare a big sponsorship deal. Not surprisingly there were no takers. So whenever he came up with one of his madder ideas, in unison we chanted back "blind cross-channel swimmer".

One of our best-known clients was the London Rubber Company who, at the time, owned Durex, Britain's best-selling condom brand. They also made all kinds of other products, including baby powder and gripe water. They really were covering all the bases.

Over the years, we worked with them on the well-known Durex Surtees campaign, but also a several Speedway racing sponsorships. The general idea was to try to normalise the name and stop the smirk factor, and I believe it worked. At the meeting where they confirmed their sponsorship of Team

Two two-wheeled clients side by side. Barry Sheene and Steve Parrish both benefited from CSS sponsorship deals. ***CSS Archive***

Surtees, Barrie just could not stop himself. As they left the board room – and it was a Friday afternoon – he came out with the classic line "Anything else you require for the weekend, sir." The younger of you probably don't remember that condoms used to be sold by gentleman's hairdressers and, as you paid for you latest short back and sides, they often posed this question.

Durex was at the centre of a row over the televising of the 1976 British Grand Prix and we were right at the centre of it. The Beeb announced they would not televise the race because viewing the Durex logo on the side of Alan Jones's car might upset some viewers. There was no question that back then the governors were a prudish group. But Durex was something of a useful smokescreen. There was a code of practice about the sponsorship of cars taking part in televised events, right down to the size of the lettering and the Elf logos on the Tyrrells definitely contravened the rules. But the Beeb didn't want to be seen to be causing trouble and had suffered some budget cuts, too. So they had a useful get-out while Durex got plenty of positive publicity.

At the time, we were not only looking after the PR and promotion of the Durex Surtees but also the much larger John Player account and had, indeed, brokered the deal for Imperial Tobacco to sponsor the actual race as well as handling the PR and running the press office. Imperial's sponsorship manager Peter Dyke was far from happy that his valuable television exposure was being compromised thanks to one of his agency's other clients. In fact, we had a series of very difficult phone calls which indicated we might not be working for them for much longer!

Fortunately, we had a very good relationship with John Bromley, the legendary head of ITV Sport. Over an expensive lunch, which was how you did business back then, we agreed that through our sister company Formula 1 Films, we would cover the race. Bromley couldn't change the schedule for live coverage but he would show the highlights in the following Saturday's World of Sport. This was a great solution because, while the coverage would be shorter (you can find it on YouTube) the audience would be larger than the BBC would provide. Of course, it turned out to be a cracking and controversial race with our client James Hunt taking the victory. We had wriggled out of a tricky situation but it gives an indication on the influence of CSS back some forty years or so ago. Barrie and I did the voice-over, which was a nice bonus.

At the time, we were in swish Mayfair offices at 35 Bruton Street, W1. Also in the same building was a legend of the high-risk insurance industry called Willie Robertson and he mainly insured rock and roll tours and that kind of thing. But he came up with a couple of sporting ideas for us which worked really well.

The plan was to insure against some very unusual sporting event like a golf hole in one which, if it actually happened, it carried a large reward. Thus you could shout about this in the media and obtain headline-making publicity. You had to pay the underwriters the premium but as the risk was low so the premium was affordable.

The first time we tried it was when we were running the Sun Marlboro Darts Tournament at the Wembley Arena. We insured against something called a nine-dart 501. The minimum number of dart throws you need to get

The 1980 CSS sales brochure shows the extent of the events and sponsors we were promoting. ***CSS***

from the starting point of 501 to zero is nine. Someone does it about once every ten years. This gave *The Sun*'s darts (and speedway correspondent) Dave Lanning plenty to write about – could the cheeky cockney Eric Bristow win £50,000? What Dave didn't write about was the actual Tournament Final on the Sunday. The problem was he was pulling double duty as the on-stage master of ceremonies and the whole thing was running late as the boys weren't hitting the double tops. Actually, there had been a fight on stage in the morning between two arrows chucking brothers and it held everything up.

Whatever, as *The Sun* deadline got closer, Dave beckoned me to the edge of the stage. The gist of it was that he wanted me to write his story which is exactly what I did. I got the back page lead in *The Sun* but under his byline and he never did buy me that beer he promised.

Flushed with success, we decided to set up a big £50,000 prize for another *Sun*-backed Marlboro sporting contest- the Transatlantic Trophy motorcycle match races. This was a contest of six races over Easter with the opening two at Brands Hatch on Good Friday, the second pair at Mallory Park on the Easter Sunday and moving on to the final two races at Oulton Park on Easter Monday. The eight-man teams came from the United Kingdom, including captain Barry Sheene and the US squad included 'Fast' Freddie Spencer. The champion nation was based on a points system and both teams were full of top riders. The bikes were actually Formula 750 machines like Yamaha's famous TZ750 but Barry was on a stretched version of his Suzuki RG500 World Championship bike.

We insured against a rider winning all six races, something that had never been done, but wasn't impossible. Barry's Suzuki was pretty strong that year and with his track knowledge he reckoned he

The CSS Christmas card one year featured a cartoon showing the sports personalities that we represented. They are World Middleweight boxing Champion Alan Minter, World Champion motorbike racer Barry Sheene, England cricket captain David Gower, Stirling Moss, Celtic ad Liverpool footballer Kenny Dalglish and snooker World Champion Terry Griffith. They were all big names in the 1980s. ***CSS Archive***

It's war on the creepy-crawly hairy horrors

Lord M ill on holiday

THE SHEENE MACHINE

Speed ace Barry joins The Sun

I put these two at the top of their class

Catarrh and You!

WIN A £10,700 JEEP FOR JANUARY

YOU CAN WIN A FABULOUS FORD IN FEBRUARY!

I had a lot of fun with Barry Sheene including ghosting his Sun road tests. Judging by the dedication on this photo he had a high regard for me too. ***Peter Gilbert***

would have a shot at winning all six and the big prize. Needless to say, *The Sun* cranked up the headlines such as "Bazza can grab fifty grand".

So to Brands Hatch, and the two races were both won by the Suzuki No 7. Up to Mallory Park, and Sheene stormed to victory in race one. Race two and he was out front but then he caught his knee on the apex of the tight Hairpin and slipped off, finishing fourth. To rub salt in the wound, he won the final two races. Five out of six didn't count and Willie's underwriters kept their money. The fact that BS had led Britain to victory wasn't of much consolation to him, to be honest.

Insurance companies have a way of keeping their hands in their pockets. One year, after looking at the long-term weather forecast, we took out weather insurance for a Spring truck race at Brands Hatch. You can insure against bad weather either causing a meeting to be cancelled in the event of snow or simply the crowd being reduced due to the poor conditions. That particular day, it never stopped raining and the crowd was well down. But I hadn't read the small print – the rainfall was actually measured somewhere else at the nearest weather station and strangely it was one of the few places that day which avoided the constant downpour – lesson learned.

But back to the hugely popular Transatlantic series and yet another story involving B Sheene. Together with Brands Hatch's motorcycle impresario Chris Lowe, we had visited the Daytona 200 motorbike race to pick the US team which also involved negotiating their start money. This particular year, the race was won by a guy called Dale Singleton who was allegedly a pig farmer from Georgia. He was a big publicist and so he brought to the track a lucky piglet called Elmer as his mascot. Actually, I think his brother was the farmer but it was a good story. Anyway, he did a deal for him to come over and captain the US squad.

Prior to the series, a few days before Easter and once the American team had arrived and settled in, we organised a big press conference at a major London hotel by Tower Bridge. I had the somewhat inspired idea of hiring a piglet, so that Dale felt at home. It is probably easy to do that now with a few clicks on Google, but back then hiring a small porker took all day. It would, I reasoned, make a great story for *The Sun* and the TV cameras – and then we could have bacon sarnies for lunch. Actually, that last bit is not true. Elmer, despite disgracing himself, was safely returned to his farm.

So how did the piglet disgrace himself? Unfortunately, our man Singleton missed his plane and failed to make the conference so Elmer 2 remained unwanted in a crate. Then I had another flash of inspiration – why not get Barry Sheene to hold the pig for the photoshoot. I could see the headlines: "Barry gets the Bacon". So the minder extracted the piglet and handed it to BS who smiled for the camera, until suddenly the porker emptied its breakfast all down his front. "Moriarty, you are going to pay for this!" he shouted.

Barry might not have had much of an education but he was super bright. He was fluent in Spanish, spoke reasonable French and Italian and was able to make himself understood in mechanic's Japanese. He was brilliant with the fans and I remember him organising his autograph sessions at race tracks. He would take over a programme seller's booth and then have everyone line up in an orderly way as he signed away, always with words of encouragement.

He had a phenomenal memory for names, including some of the fans, but if he forgot a name he would call the person 'ace' and they went away delighted the world champion had called them an ace. He always gave his sponsors good value. I remember him going on a Michael Parkinson BBC TV chat show in a crisp white shirt having been told he couldn't wear Marlboro logoed race attire. The shirt had a top pocket into which he inserted 20 Marlboro (inside the cigarettes were actually his favourite French Gitanes). The bright TV lights came on and through the thin shirt pocket you could just make out the red and white Marlboro logo.

Over the years at CSS, we organised everything from the *Grand Prix Night of the Stars* – where James Hunt famously played the trumpet with surprising skill – to the Avis Formula One tennis Trophy hosted by World famous comedian, Bob Hope. We became a major force in football, managing the

Elio de Angelis, seen here racing in the JPS Lotus 93T in the 1985 Canadian Grand Prix, was one of the many Formula 1 drivers I worked with but was a particular favourite. ***CSS Archive***

England squad and putting together numerous sponsorship packages from the Barclays League to the Milk Cup. We also managed the England cricket team, placed the non-alcoholic beer brand Arctic Lite as the sponsor of the British Gliding Championship, and got Wrights Coal Tar Soap to sponsor a Find a Fast Bowler for Britain.

I shouldn't forget the unlikely deal we did for Barry's sidekick Steve 'Stavros' Parrish. We got Makaha Skateboard to back his Grand Prix motorcycle effort one year. To add to the fun, we twisted Beatle George Harrison's arm to add to the budget through his Harisongs company. George is the most famous person I ever met – a wonderful, sincere and brilliant guy with absolutely no side, who loved his motorsport. I was at a Donington Park British Motorcycle Grand Prix a month or so after my first wife had died and George came up to me to say how sorry he was. I have no idea how he knew but it was a wonderful gesture I will never forget.

We expanded the business to include an outside signage outfit called Aerosigns (later re-named Icon Displays), which we purchased for peanuts from the owners of Brands Hatch. It became a superb business under a chap called John Francis, while Neil Collins led our Design company which had Coca Cola as its biggest client. By then, we also owned our own office building next to Leicester Square tube station.

But after the best part of 30 years Barrie, myself and the rest of the board decided it was time to cash in our chips and at first the US ad agency Bozell took a stake in the company. With them, we ran some great campaigns for the Bahamas Tourist Board, including a revival of the Bahamas Speed Weeks and some spectacular Powerboat races around Paradise Island.

Then we got close to a deal where we were to be purchased by the people who owned Madison Square Garden. The plan was to merge us with one of our rivals run by the Olympic hurdler Alan Pascoe in a bid to produce a super agency to take on Mark McCormack's IMG. That fell at the final hurdle and, on the rebound, we did a deal which saw us effectively taken over by the Stellar Management Group. Run by an IMG breakaway outfit led by Julian Jakobi (best known as the Manager of both Prost and Senna) and John Webber. They managed a raft of show business and sports stars including various Formula 1 drivers. So we became CSS-Stellar and initially had great success when the company floated on the Alternative Investments Market.

In retrospect, the deal didn't work out as we had hoped and the dynamics changed as our sales director Steve Herrick had died from an unexpected heart attack and Barrie succumbed to lymphoma. Meanwhile, our brilliant financial director Julian Hill was pushed to one side and he left as did another director Graham Bridgwater. A year or so later, I departed to form Pit Lane Productions. Subsequently the CSS-Stellar share price collapsed, hence my classic car is a Turner rather than a Ferrari Dino. The business was finally sold as a tax loss to an outfit attempting to mine gold in Wales. But, as George Harrison sang, 'All things must pass'.

The first sports personality we represented was James Hunt who signed up in 1975 although I had known him from Formula Ford days. ***CSS Archive***

It had been a wonderful period of my life starting, of course, with that *Marlboro Sports Special* idea on that South African Airways flight and subsequently setting up our first offices in London's Shepard Street which had previously been a high class brothel – oh, I forget to tell you that story.

Somewhere in the middle of this, I managed to bring up four daughters – Helen, Lydia, and twins Emma and Verity – despite the loss of my wife Beth from cancer in July 1994. One of my best friends kept me positive and told me there would be light at the end the tunnel – and there was. I got married to Caroline nine years later and Sophia and Edmund joined the crew.

I suppose I could have remained in Derby designing hospital incinerators and hopper-fed under-feed stokers. By now I would be retired, been frustrated with the performance of Derby County and the highlight of the month would have been attending the local Rotary Club lunch. It probably would have been a lot less stressful but I doubt if I would have met so many wonderful people, visited so many parts of the world and had so many experiences and stories to laugh about. I don't think it would have made much of a book.

Index

Index